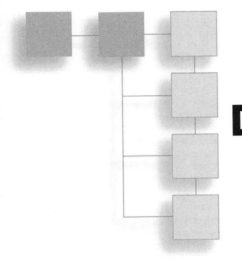

GAME
DEVELOPMENT
PRINCIPLES

ALAN THORN

Cengage Learning PTR

CENGAGE
Learning®

Professional • Technical • Reference

Australia • Brazil • Japan • Korea • Mexico • Singapore • Spain • United Kingdom • United States

CENGAGE Learning

Professional • Technical • Reference

Game Development Principles
Alan Thorn

Publisher and General Manager,
Cengage Learning PTR:
Stacy L. Hiquet

Associate Director of Marketing:
Sarah Panella

Manager of Editorial Services:
Heather Talbot

Senior Marketing Manager:
Mark Hughes

Senior Acquisitions Editor: Emi Smith

Project Editor: Kate Shoup

Technical Reviewer: Joshua Smith

Copy Editor: Kate Shoup

Interior Layout Tech: MPS Limited

Cover Designer: Luke Fletcher

Proofreader & Indexer:
Kelly Talbot Editing Services

For product information and technology assistance, contact us at
Cengage Learning Customer & Sales Support, 1-800-354-9706

For permission to use material from this text or product, submit all requests online at **cengage.com/permissions**

Further permissions questions can be emailed to
permissionrequest@cengage.com

All trademarks are the property of their respective owners.

All images © Cengage Learning unless otherwise noted.

Library of Congress Control Number: 2013937128

ISBN-13: 978-1-285-42705-8

ISBN-10: 1-285-42705-X

Cengage Learning PTR

20 Channel Center Street

Boston, MA 02210

USA

Cengage Learning is a leading provider of customized learning solutions with office locations around the globe, including Singapore, the United Kingdom, Australia, Mexico, Brazil, and Japan. Locate your local office at: **international.cengage.com/region**

Cengage Learning products are represented in Canada by Nelson Education, Ltd.

For your lifelong learning solutions, visit **cengageptr.com**

Visit our corporate website at **cengage.com**

Printed in the United States of America
1 2 3 4 5 6 7 15 14 13

ACKNOWLEDGMENTS

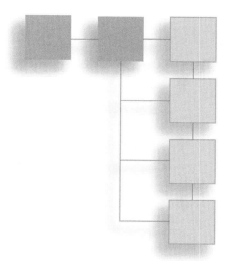

The acknowledgments section is a place where I, the author, give thanks and acknowledge all those people and things that have helped make this book what it is and have ensured its quality. For this, I give special mention to Emi Smith, for arranging and managing the work; to Kate Shoup, for her splendid editing skills that continue to teach me a lot about shortening the length of sentences; and to the technical editor, Joshua Smith, for ensuring the accuracy of what I said. I would also like to thank you, the reader, for taking an interest in game development and for wishing to learn new things about how to make games.

—Alan Thorn, London, 2013

About the Author

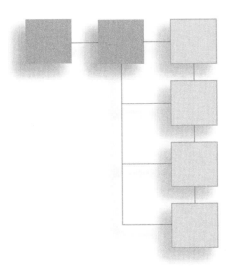

Alan Thorn is an author, mathematician, and independent video game developer based in London, UK. He is the founder of game development studio Wax Lyrical Games and the creator of the award-winning PC adventure game *Baron Wittard: Nemesis of Ragnarok*. He works freelance for some of the world's largest entertainment corporations and has lectured on game development at some of the most prestigious institutions in Europe. He has written seven books on games programming, including *Teach Yourself Games Programming, Game Engine: Design and Implementation*, and *UDK Game Development*.

CONTENTS

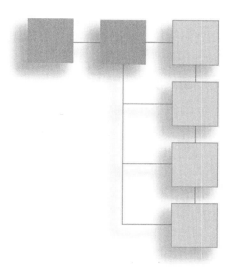

Introduction

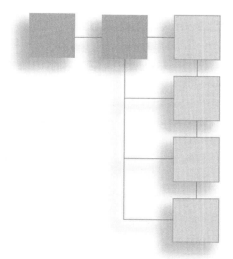

"In theory there is no difference between theory and practice. In practice there is."

—Jan L.A. van de Snepscheut (attributed)

The word "theory" can be a dirty or unpleasant word in an industry, such as the video games industry, that is concerned largely with the practical and with results. "Dry," "boring," "dull," "irrelevant," and "needlessly complex" are all things that have been said by detractors of theory and everything it commonly denotes.

It can often be difficult to persuade students, professionals, and even book publishers that theory in the field of game development holds a special and significant enough place in its own right to warrant its own book or course. It is, however, an understandable skepticism and especially so in game development. Those who are bold enough to pursue game development as a career or pastime are typically motivated to do so because they have previously been gamers themselves and have enjoyed a very real and hands-on experience of playing games. As a result, one of the last things on their mind is abstraction and theory. Newcomers to game development (stereotypical newcomers, that is) want to escape the humdrum, to sit down at their keyboard and mouse, and to bring life to their masterpiece game ideas and worlds. They want to make a real game that can be played by real gamers. They want to get their hands dirty, producing games that make gamers feel the excitement and emotion they themselves felt when playing games by others. They want instant gratification—or as close to it as they can get it. They do not, however, want to sit down with a book and read about physics, formulas, art, photometry, numbers, charts, and bell-shaped curves. This is not necessarily because they have no interest in these things, but more because they want to simply get on with it and complete a fun and playable game.

Stereotypical newcomers often see theory as more of an obstacle or a hindrance than an aid or a tool. It looks like something that is not especially important and that, if studied seriously, could genuinely threaten to destroy the fun factor that drew them to games in the first place. For these kinds of newcomers, games are a black box in the sense that their innards and workings are close to a complete mystery. As such, it is difficult for them to understand exactly how or why any but the simplest of theory could be relevant to game development. Some even go further and persuade themselves that theory could not possibly be as important today as it was in the past. This is because newer and cleverer software must surely always be taking the sting out of development, making the work easier and more accessible than it ever has been.

However, those who have earnestly tried making a game on their own, without a firm grasp of the theory, quickly encounter a set of common but very serious technical problems to which they have no satisfactory solution. In response to these problems, some developers persevere; others just lose interest and give up, moving on to different careers or pastimes. But almost all of these developers will have experienced a common set of unpleasant symptoms during development. They include a feeling of powerlessness and inadequacy; a feeling of struggling uphill and of fighting against the software and tools rather than of working with them. They feel as though they are the pawn and not its mover. They are frequently frustrated and angered that their hard work is not turning out with the high quality they intended, despite their vision and very best efforts. In the end, they decide to cut features from the game, scaling back and abandoning specific ideas and plans. This is not because the ideas were bad or foolish, nor is it because they themselves are untalented or unskilled. Rather, it is because they simply lack the ability to see how they could ever go about implementing those ideas with the tools and knowledge they have available. The result is that their game either never gets completed, or *does* get completed but is decidedly underwhelming when compared to the original plan.

These unpleasant symptoms and their results are all too common among many a newcomer. This modern form of a trial by fire has put a premature end to the studies and potential careers of many people who might otherwise have gone on to produce hugely successful games. The cause of these symptoms is almost always a lack of, or a gap in, the understanding of a basic core of general theory, which underpins game development as a discipline. This is a core that I shall hereon call "game development principles," and these principles form the subject matter of this book.

WHAT IS THIS BOOK ABOUT?

The title of this book is *Game Development Principles*, and it is book about theory, at least insofar as it is possible for any book on game development to be about theory. By "theory," I mean that this book is about the interdisciplinary sets of ideas, concepts, workflow practices, tips and tricks, and general details of an extensive body of knowledge as it applies to making computer games. This book will consider topics from a range of disciplines, such as vectors and matrices from the world of mathematics, planning elements and storyboarding from the world of design, and vertices, meshes, and illumination from the world of graphics and rendering, plus much more besides. In short, this book attempts to detail succinctly and comprehensively a core of critically important theoretical knowledge that is shared by most competent game developers. This knowledge underpins almost all the work a developer does when making games, and applies across the board regardless of the specific tools that developer might use, be they 3DS Max, C++, UDK, Unity, Photoshop, and others. This body of knowledge (the game development principles) consists of all the foundational and abstract stuff that almost all game developers need to know to get started making games like a "professional." Ultimately, it represents everything I wish someone had told me when I was starting out so I wouldn't have had to learn it all the hard way.

In thinking generally about what this book is, it is also worth discussing what it most certainly is not. This is not an all-in-one book that demonstrates how to use a specific tool or software program for quickly creating video games. This book does not read as a hands-on tutorial, explaining step by step how to use specific programs, such as the UDK. It does not include active instructions that are to be followed or memorized, such as "Click this button to do X" or "Click that button to do Y." Software and their features come and go and change from version to version. Instead, this book focuses on the more abstract ideas and the more permanent principles that have remained in many ways unchanged throughout the past decade. These are the ideas that developers take with them everywhere in their minds, and which they apply every day in every tool they use.

Of course, the theory and ideas are not considered dryly and in isolation, as though practice and theory were entirely disconnected. The ideas are frequently complemented by concrete examples using specific tools current in the games industry. The tools I use here are by no means the only tools available; the use of these tools is only to illustrate the core theory being discussed. Thus, the examples should not be read as a complete guide or even a beginner's guide to the tools themselves. The key to learning from the practical examples is to consider how the abstract ideas discussed there apply more generally elsewhere and everywhere.

WHOM IS THIS BOOK FOR?

Most books are written for an intended audience or readership, and this book is no different. The intended audience represents a complete range of character profiles (imaginary people) for whom I am writing. In effect, it refers to the general and educated assumptions that I, the author, must make about you, the reader, so that when writing this book I include only the material and information you expected and wanted, and also so that I present it in terms that are both approachable and meaningful.

Making assumptions about people—any people—is not something that I like doing. This is because assumptions can turn out so terribly mistaken. But the assumptions here are *general* and are not *personal*, and they are necessary to make this book useful to the greatest number of readers. To illustrate my intended audience, I include the following four character profiles that I have in mind. These profiles should be taken with a pinch of salt—that is, only as a rough and general guideline to the intended audience rather hard and fast specification sheets. In no way do I wish to suggest that anybody who differs from these profiles will not benefit from the book or does not make the grade. They should not be read as character sheets defining those who have natural talent or those who have it in them to learn game development. Nobody yet who has been born was ever born a game developer or any other profession, as far as I am aware. Thus, I wish to encourage anybody who is keen to learn and willing to succeed.

Malcolm

Malcolm is still in high school and soon to go to university. He loves playing video games in his spare time, and sometimes even when he should be doing other things. He has a collection of consoles and mobile devices, and has also tried making his own games on his home PC. He has tried a range of game-making programs and has asked a lot of questions on Internet forums, to which he has received answers of varying quality. But despite all this, and without being able to explain exactly how or why, he feels stuck and unable to proceed further.

Jessica

Jessica is at university and is bored with her studies. She is thinking about dropping out and trying a different course in game development with the hope of being an artist at a game studio. She likes video games and almost everything creative: art, music, writing, and movies. She has never tried making a game before, and really does not love the idea of having to learn a lot of theory. However, she is prepared to do so provided someone can show her the relevant theory to learn so that she does not waste time.

Ahmed and Ezra

Ahmed is 45 years old and has left his job as a landscape gardener to start his own small game-development company. He and his wife (Ezra, who is 47) plan to run the business themselves from an office room at their home, performing all the game-development work without hiring any contractors or third parties. They are prepared to do almost anything it takes (within the law!) to make their business a success. Neither Ahmed nor his wife has experience at making games, but they are now keen to get started on their new career path.

Jeff

Jeff has made a lot of games for mobile and PC platforms. His knowledge of theory is very limited; as a result, he can only make games as long as he does not leave his comfort zone. He sticks to specific tools and is careful not to include any ambitious features in his games. But, he would like to improve himself and his skills so that he can take on new projects and reach new markets.

WHY IS THIS BOOK NECESSARY?

Those who read the opening paragraphs of the introduction might still be skeptical about the relevance or importance of a book on theory for game development. This skepticism typically takes one of two forms.

The first form runs something like this: "Theory is important for game development, certainly. But it does not need so strong a focus or isolation, and definitely not a whole book like this one. The best way to learn the theory is to start out using a game-development tool, such as Unity, and picking up the theory as you go along, piece by piece. You'll soon get the hang of it." There is much to be said for this approach. It does in many respects represent the dominant method for learning theory in the games industry today, since almost all game-development books and tutorials focus on specific tools rather than on theory. They introduce and discuss the tools, and then discuss theory as a complement to them. This traditional method of learning game development, however, typically involves our making many false starts, hitting many dead ends, and making many gargantuan mistakes before finally coming across the "right way" of doing things. It often forces us to learn how to do something by first making us see how *not* to do it. This book, however, aims to smooth out the learning path of the traditional method—a path that normally makes us take several steps forward and then several steps back before changing direction. This book allows us to travel in more of a continuous line from A to B. It does not protect us against making mistakes completely, but it offers the means of making fewer of them, and of learning more from them when they do happen. By learning a core of fundamental theory as distilled and concentrated in this book, and by reading and learning that as a foundation prior to developing a game, you can gain a head start in your development work. That is, you can anticipate possible mistakes on the horizon and can take actions ahead of time to avoid making them—thus saving yourself time, effort, and frustration.

The second criticism concerning this book's importance is one that might be leveled against almost all game-development books generally. It runs something like this: "The information contained in this book might be both valuable and important, but there is nothing here that cannot also be found elsewhere in other books, or in videos or other tutorials on the Internet. In fact, not only can the same information be found elsewhere, but more of it can be found, too. A single book like this, written by one author, cannot possibly hope to compete against the masses of information available online produced for free by the collective efforts of thousands of people." In response to this objection, I should first admit that *all* of the information contained in this book can probably be found elsewhere online. But this should not entirely surprise you because the games industry, like most technical and scientific industries, relies not on arcane or secret knowledge divined from a closed group of Illuminati, but on infinitely knowable and systematic knowledge. Further, this is knowledge that has been developed and well-documented by a generally open and public community of academics and professionals. Second, I should also admit that the Internet features more information on the subject than this book could ever hope to contain. This book does not pretend to be the last word on the matter, nor does it claim to tell you everything there possibly is to know on the subject. No book could ever achieve that. It is possible a student could spend days, weeks, or months searching the Net and piecing together all the information contained in this book. But none of this can reasonably be seen as a criticism of the book. The main purpose of this book is to act as a guide for the student or developer who is bemused by the information overload—who does not know where to begin or what to learn first or last among the masses of things there are to know. In this book, I have applied my years of knowledge and experience to assemble this fundamental core of information and to present it as a digestible introduction to game development. I have put in the time and the hard work of creating a starting point or a springboard so that you do not have to. This book will guide you by the hand and provide you with an empowering foundation of knowledge. This is a foundation that should help you to identify the next steps your learning should take and the next tools you should use, and to be able to use those tools with a greater confidence and skill.

Is This Book Out of Date Already?

The "lifetime" of a book refers to the amount of time in terms of years or decades in which a book remains relevant and useful to its readers, all of whom exist in a constantly changing world. It is the time in which a technical book, such as this one, still has something significantly valuable and worthwhile to say about its field. The question as to whether a book is out of date is a question about whether its industry or field has changed enough as to make the contents of the book lose their significance for its readers. Some books, like books on arithmetic and the basics of mathematics, seem to be immortal in that they will never grow out of date. Other books, such as tourism and sport books, always seem to be temporary and valid until further notice.

Issues about book lifetime are especially important to readers in the computing industries because they are industries that change so quickly and dramatically. They are industries in which both the rate of change and the extent of change are typically very high. Thus, readers often want to know that the book they are about to read will not only be current and valuable at the time of reading, but stands a good chance of remaining so for some time to come—certainly for long enough to allow them to absorb and apply the information contained within. So what can be said about the lifetime of this book?

This book has a unique place among game-development books with regard to its lifetime. Its lifetime, if it could be estimated in years and plotted on a scale, would be somewhere to the left of mathematics books (which are almost immortal) and to the right of practical books on specific game-development tools such as Unity or the UDK (which typically have lifetimes of less than five years). This makes it difficult to put an exact figure on the lifetime of this book. But it is not an exaggeration to say that the core game development principles it discusses have remained intact throughout at least the past decade, despite the dramatic changes in tools, software, technologies, and standards. These specifics can all be said to have changed around that pivotal core of ideas and abstractions, which has remained more or less constant and looks to remain constant for the foreseeable future. For this reason, the game development principles discussed in this book can be thought of as being here to stay for some time to come, at least for all that can be known at the time of writing. Thus, the reader can approach this book with some confidence and comfort that the knowledge contained within has a lasting relevance and importance to the contemporary games industry.

BOOK STRUCTURE: HOW SHOULD THIS BOOK BE READ?

This book and its chapters have been tailored to act as a both a reference and a guide. It is a reference for those readers who are already developers and who wish simply to flick through the chapters, finding relevant sections for refreshers or reminders or to fill gaps in their existing knowledge. It is also a guide for students and those new to game development who wish to read the book sequentially from beginning to end as a complete foundation course. The chapters have been written and arranged to be amenable to both types of readers. Chapters are self-contained in the sense that each focuses on a narrow field of game development and, generally speaking, does not require the reader to have knowledge of other chapters. Frequent chapter headings and summaries should make it easy for both the reference and guide readers to orientate themselves within the text and to find specific areas of interest.

To get the most from this book, however, it is recommended that it be read as a guide. The guide reader should find that on completing the course, he or she will be equipped with the knowledge and know-how to approach game development with a newfound confidence. The process of learning to make games is primarily about developing a new way of seeing. The artist learns to sketch by seeing the world in terms of shapes that can be charted on a blank page, and the pool or snooker player develops his or her skills by seeing the balls and the table as a problem of angles. Similarly, developing knowledge of game development principles is about coming to see video games differently from the gamer—not as a complete entity or body of work but as a set of technical and artistic components that are working together as a machine. Each chapter of this book is devoted to the game development principles as they apply to a specific field of game development, from programming and graphics to music and publishing. One by one, each chapter introduces how to see those aspects as a developer and not a gamer by using only a single pattern. Each chapter starts out from the perspective of the stereotypical newbie, a complete beginner who has no knowledge of the game development principles but who has chosen to make a game on his or her own regardless, relying on common sense and intuition to get him or her through. It then proceeds to consider the technical problems and hurdles that quickly present themselves, many of which at first sight appear to be intractable and insurmountable. Afterward, it introduces the game development principles as proposed solutions to those problems. In this way, the practical and hands-on relevance of the game development principles will become more apparent.

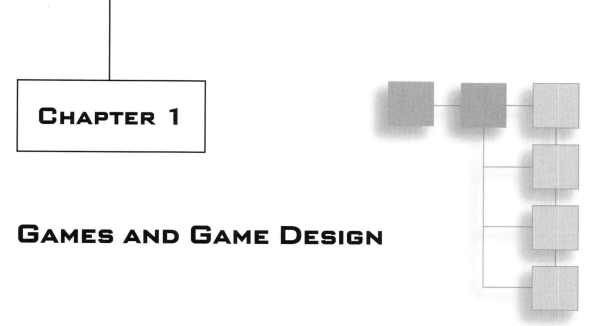

CHAPTER 1

GAMES AND GAME DESIGN

"Whenever a theory appears to you as the only possible one, take this as a sign that you have neither understood the theory nor the problem which it was intended to solve."

—Karl Popper

By the end of this chapter you should:

- Understand game genres, platforms and perspectives.
- Have a general idea about the game-development process.
- Understand the stages and aspects of game development.
- Understand the importance of game design and the designer.
- Appreciate the role of the game design document (GDD).

In 2007, a sociological study by Harris Interactive concluded that 94% of all males in the United States between 13 and 18 years old play video games, and that those surveyed spent in excess of 14 hours per week engaged in that activity. Of those surveyed, 23% claimed to have felt "addicted" to games, and 44% claimed to have friends who were addicted. This increasing cultural influence of video games is also evident in the economy where, in 2009, video games in the UK outsold movies by £1.8 billion GBP ($2.8 billion USD) to £1.1 billion GBP ($1.93 billion USD). In that same year, the video game *Call of Duty: Modern Warfare 2* ranked as the #1 best-selling DVD product according to Amazon, outselling the *Twilight* and *Harry Potter* series.

This book is not the place to engage in the controversial debate about the social and cultural benefits and dangers of video games. These statistics are provided here to give you only some of the many uncontested insights as to the extent of the influence of video games on contemporary culture. Video games, in short, are a cultural phenomenon whose growth as a form of entertainment and recreation in just the span of a few decades is unprecedented in the history of human civilization. It is for many people an exciting and extraordinary movement to be a part of, whether as a gamer, a developer, or both. As such, there has been a steady and decided rise in the number of people annually entering the games industry, either by finding employment at an existing game studio or through entrepreneurism by founding their own independent startups. Universities across the world are also offering degree courses and other workshops devoted entirely to game development.

With all this talk of games, there has become a pressing need and desire among journalists, gamers, and developers to introduce a more refined language and terminology to discuss them. It is a language that enables one in some senses to categorize games, to refer to them, to measure them, and to compare them. It is with this language that you will begin your study of games and game-development principles in order to understand games further. Later sections of this chapter will address the issues of game design and game development in a general sense.

GAME TALK: GENRES, PLATFORMS, AND MORE

A formal study of video games should begin, perhaps, with a clear definition of the term "game" or "video game." Here, however, these terms shall be left undefined intentionally for two reasons:

■ There is no clear consensus about what a game *is*—about all the things that a game must have in order to be a game.

■ A definition of the term "game" is largely an academic and philosophical matter that has little bearing on game development. After all, most people who play games and who go on to become game developers do not need to be told what a game is. They play and enjoy games, and they design and make them, even if they cannot state what a game is in any precise or formal way. They know enough about what is popularly called a "video game" to get an idea of what it means and what they like—and this idea has proved adequate for gamers and game developers.

One thing that can, however, be said about video games from the perspective of the gamer is that they are diverse. Games are about many things, they can be played in many ways, and they appeal to different people at different times. Some games have the player assume the role of a world-saving protagonist, seeing the world through that protagonist's eyes, and shooting and dispatching enemies with devastating fire power. These kinds of games include *Duke Nukem, Rise of the Triad, Quake,* and *Elder Scrolls.* Other games show the player a more aerial or remote view of the world, putting him or her in the position of a general or commander who coordinates the strategies of vast armies and hordes of creatures. Such games include *Starcraft, Heroes of Might and Magic,* and *Starpoint Gemini.* Others still have the player control no character at all and see the world from no particular perspective, requiring simply that the player position and move abstract shapes and objects. Games belonging to this group include *Tetris, Columns,* and *Solitaire.*

Behind all of this superficial and transient diversity between specific games, however, a number of abstract and constant dimensions of the video game have become generally well-known and established, and are referred to by a jargon—that is, by a specific and tacitly agreed-upon set of terms and titles. This vocabulary is to some extent borrowed from the movie industry and is used for labeling games, putting them in category boxes, comparing them, and trying to understand the kind of game being discussed. These terms form part of a common game-speak language that is shared by gamers, game critics, and game developers alike.

According to this vocabulary, the most common dimensions identified in a video game are as follows:

- Genre and sub-genre
- Production type
- Platform
- Graphical style
- Delivery method
- Perspective

The exact names of these categories, as I have given them here, are not well-established and do vary from source to source, but these are the terms I prefer. That being said, whatever someone might choose to name them, the *categories themselves* are a persistent feature of the gaming literature.

Genre and Sub-Genre

"Genre" is a French word with Latin roots that has entered the English language to mean "type" or "kind." It refers to the *type* of any work of entertainment, including video games. Thus, the expression "video-game genre" is equivalent to "video-game type" or "video-game kind."

When a person asks, "What kind of game is this?" they are essentially asking a question about its genre. Video-game genres include the following:

- Shooters
- Role-playing games (RPGs)
- Real-time strategy games (RTSes)
- Puzzle
- Simulation
- Adventure games

Note

This is but a small sampling; there are many more than can possibly be listed here.

Shooters are among the most popular. They typically require the gamer to take on the role of a gun-wielding hero who must shoot and eliminate opponents. RPGs, another popular genre, often enable gamers to construct their own characters and then to play out that character's life in a fantasy world, completing all kinds of tasks and quests and solving all manner of mysteries.

"Sub-genre" refers to a category *within* a genre. It is used to further refine and specify the genre of game under discussion. A game might be defined as a strategy game, but even within the strategy genre there exist many dimensions of difference that meaningfully separate some strategy games from others. Real-time strategy and turn-based strategy are examples of a genre and sub-genre being used together in discussion. Real-time strategy (such as *Starcraft*) is used to designate strategy games where armies move, compete, and operate simultaneously; turn-based strategy is used to designate strategy games where players take turns to control their armies—one player makes a move, and then another player makes his or hers in turn. Other examples of sub-genres include first-person shooter and third-person shooter (more on this shortly), 2D adventure games and 3D adventure games, single-player RPGs, and MMORPGs (massively multiplayer role-playing games).

See Table 1.1 for a list of games, game genres, and game sub-genres.

Table 1.1   Game Genres

Genre	Sub-Genre	Examples of Games
Shooter	First person (FP)	*Duke Nukem Forever, Doom, Call of Duty*
Shooter	Third person	*Dead Space, Max Payne, Resident Evil*
RPG	Single player	*Skyrim, Legend of Grimrock, Fallout*
RPG	MMORPG	*World of Warcraft, Star Wars: The Old Republic*
Adventure	Point and click	*Myst, Alter Ego, Moment of Silence*
Simulation	City building	*Sim City, City Life, Cities XL 2011*
Strategy	Real-time	*Starcraft, ARMADA 2526, Anno 2070*

Production Type

A game's production type is less something about the game or in the game and more the type of developer that made the game. For this reason, this category is frequently politically charged and controversial, with many developers claiming one label or rejecting another.

A game's production type is usually one of two mutually exclusive types:

- **AAA.** AAA (pronounced "triple A") is surprisingly not an acronym, but is meant to conjure up ideas of "premium quality" and "A-grade excellence." It is typically used by the gaming press to refer to blockbuster and smash-hit games—games that have been created by studios working with very large budgets and whose games are supported by expensive advertising campaigns. AAA, in short, refers to the Hollywood of video games. Companies frequently associated with this label (AAA studios) include Electronic Arts, Ubisoft, Blizzard, Bethesda, Microsoft Game Studios, and Bioware. Their games (AAA games) include *Mass Effect, Elder Scrolls Series, Starcraft*, and *Bioshock*, among others.

- **Indie**. Indie (which is an abbreviation of "independent") is frequently understood to signify any developer (whether a team or an individual) who creates a game without the financial support of an AAA publisher—that is, developers who make a self-funded game and sell and distribute it themselves in the marketplace or through a small publisher (whatever "small" is supposed to mean). Unfortunately, this definition soon becomes hazier and more non-descript because it describes the overwhelming majority of video games created today, including almost all the thousands of games released monthly for mobile platforms such as Android, iOS, and Windows Phone. It also includes almost all home-made and student-made projects as well as almost all of the freeware and commercial Web games available.

In conclusion, the terms AAA and indie are loose and political, and nobody really seems able to pin down their meanings more than I have done here. Those entering the games industry seeking full-time or contract-based employment as an artist, designer, or programmer at a large studio will typically be classified by the gaming press as "working in AAA games." Conversely, start-ups looking to found their own companies and make their own games will typically be classified as "indie." It is a practice that is controversial but common in the games industry, and all attempts to refine the meaning of these terms have met with no less controversy.

Platform

The terms "platform" and "target hardware" are frequently used interchangeably to refer to the system or type of computer and operating system on which the game is intended to run successfully. Platforms include gaming consoles (such as Xbox and PlayStation), computers (such as PC and Mac), and mobile platforms. "Mobile platforms" is an umbrella term for systems such as iPad, iPhone, Android systems, Windows Phone, and Microsoft Surface. Sometimes, a game will support only one of these platforms either for performance or technical reasons, but it is presently more common for developers to produce games that are cross-platform—that is, games that support two or more of the aforementioned platforms. This is because the range of systems on which a game can run places dramatic and significant limitations on the size of audience and market that a developer can reach. The more platforms that are supported by a game, the larger the potential audience.

It remains very unclear at present as to what the future holds for game development with regard to platforms and platform support. The dominant paradigm for development at present is to create a game for as many platforms as is technically feasible and as the budget allows. However, HTML5 games and, even more, so-called "cloud computing" offer a Utopian promise of a platform-independent future—a future in which games are stored and executed not locally on the user's system as they are today but on remote servers that simply stream the results across the Internet via a single protocol to lightweight clients of all kinds and specifications, such as PCs and smartphones. In short, it describes a future, whether to be realized or not, in which games are played via an interactive streaming service. In principle, such a service would be accessible to almost all platforms that had Internet access of a sufficient bandwidth and that supported the specified protocol.

Graphical Style

The term "graphics" refers to the visual aspect or component of a game. It encompasses everything about a game that can be seen—everything that appeals to the sense of sight. Games differ from each other not only in the superficial or obvious sense that each game has its own set of unique graphics, but also in the sense that each game features graphics that may belong to one of several more abstract and general styles. These styles impart a visual feel or character to a game, and they can be thought to exist along an imaginary line or a continuum based on the level of realism and believability they achieve. At one extreme of the continuum is the notable style of photo-realism—a style through which developers seek to make their game appear as realistic as technology allows. The chief aim of photo-realism is to make a game as indistinguishable from video or photographs as possible. When playing a photo-realistic game, the gamer should not be aware that the graphics are synthetic; they should not know that the graphics have been produced by artists or computers. Photo-realism is a style that as yet has not been achieved by most games in real-time 3D, given the current limitations of most consumer hardware. See Figure 1.1 for an example of photo-realism in contemporary gaming.

Figure 1.1
Photo-realism used in *Baron Wittard* by Wax Lyrical Games.
Source: *Wax Lyrical Games*

In contrast to the style of photo-realism is that of illustrated realism, to which many games belong. Here, the intention of the developer is to produce graphics that *resemble* the real world, either closely or loosely, but to do so with a specific artistic style applied. Just as a life drawing sketch depicts the real world as observed by the artist through pencil strokes and shading techniques, a game using illustrated realism shows the real world through a stylistic lens. This style is featured in many games, including: *Call of Duty, Scorpion Disfigured*, and *Cities in Motion*, to name but a few. See Figure 1.2 for an example of illustrated realism.

Figure 1.2
Illustrated realism as featured in adventure game *Baron Wittard: Nemesis of Ragnarok* by Wax Lyrical Games.
Source: *Wax Lyrical Games*

Toward the other end of the continuum of styles lays that of implied realism, a term that defines a group of related styles including cartoon style and pixel art. All these styles produce graphics that essentially simplify and deviate from the real world, but that nonetheless capture something of the real as to make it *implied*. A cartoon house, for example, may differ in many respects from any real-world house that you might have seen, but still enough of the real exists in that house to enable you to recognize it as a house as opposed to, say, a car, a T-shirt, or an armadillo. Implied realism can be found in many games including *Sam and Max, Wallace & Gromit*, and the *Legend of Zelda*. See Figure 1.3 for an example of implied realism.

Figure 1.3
Implied realism used in *Bounders and Cads* by Wax Lyrical Games.
Source: *Wax Lyrical Games*

Delivery Method

The delivery method specifies the way in which the game will be delivered or put into the hands of the gamer after purchase (assuming the game is commercial rather than freeware or "freemium"—more on these models later). Essentially, it defines the physical or digital mechanism that enables the gamer to get access to the product after purchase.

Before the advent of the Internet, there were generally only two ways in which gamers could access their games:

- By visiting a high-street store and purchasing the game from a box on the shelf
- By ordering the game from a catalogue and having it delivered to his or her home through the postal service

Both of these methods continue to exist today and are together referred to as "retail." However, the Internet now makes a range of additional delivery methods possible and easier, of which I shall name two here:

- **Digital download.** With this method, gamers purchase a game and then download it instantly via the Internet either directly from a developer or publisher or through an application store or gaming portal. Once downloaded, the game can be installed and executed on the local computer.

■ **Browser-based or browser-embedded.** With this method, a game is streamed and played within a webpage viewed through a Web browser such as Internet Explorer, Firefox, or Google Chrome. The gamer does not explicitly download a copy of the game and execute it locally through his or her operating system, but rather plays the game directly inside the webpage. This includes most Adobe Flash games as well as almost all HTML5 games.

Perspective

First person, third person, aerial view, and view from nowhere are examples of what is generally termed the perspective or camera view of a game. To participate and act in a game and to be an active force in what happens in the game environment, a gamer must be able to see that environment. They must be able to observe what is going on in the game world so as to respond and act appropriately. That game world is typically seen by the gamer through the lens of a virtual camera, which is located at a specified position and orientation within the environment. This view or window is referred to as the perspective of the game because it refers to the perspective or eye location of the viewer or gamer in relation to everything else. There are a number of common view configurations that have over the decades earned themselves the names given at the start of this paragraph.

First person or first-person perspective (FPP) is a view configuration in which the virtual camera is attached and synchronized to the eyes of the main player-controlled character. This camera is arranged to move wherever and whenever the main character moves during the game, and it moves so as always to be positioned and aligned to his or her eyes. The result of this configuration for a game is that the gamer is always presented with a view of the world as seen through the eyes of the main character. This type of view is common among games of the shooter genre—in fact, so much so that shooters with this kind of view are given the hybrid-title of "first-person shooter" (FPS). FPS games include *Duke Nukem Forever*, *Rise of the Triad*, and *Call of Duty: Modern Warfare*.

The label "third person" is generally given to the perspective of a game in which the gamer controls a character but does *not* see the world from that character's eyes—that is, does not see the world in first-person perspective. Modern third-person games often (but do not always) show a view of the world from a chase-view camera, which is a third-person camera that follows the main character and is positioned slightly behind, above, or to one side of that character. Games featuring third-person cameras generally include *Sonic*, *Mario*, *Tomb Raider*, *Dead Space*, *Mass Effect*, *Black Mirror*, and *The Legend of Zelda*.

The first-person and third-person cameras both depend for their existence on a player character and are defined in *relation to* that character. First-person cameras show the world from the eyes of a character, and third-person cameras show the world at an offset from a character. From this it follows that the terms "first person" and "third person" are both inappropriate for talking about the perspective of games that do not feature player-controllable characters, such as card games, strategy games, puzzle games, or simulation games. In such games, there is no character to be first person *to* or third person *from*. In these cases, the perspective of the game is either not explicitly given or is listed as being one of several other kinds, two of which are as follows:

- **Aerial view.** Aerial view identifies the perspective used frequently in god games or strategy games. These are games in which gamers construct cities and civilizations or armies and empires. Here, the view of the game and game world is presented in a top-down or overhead style from a camera floating or suspended in air looking downward at events as they transpire. Games featuring this perspective include *Civilization*, *StarCraft*, and *Heroes of Might and Magic*.

- **View from nowhere.** This view is used generally to identify the perspective of many puzzle games or card games that do not feature characters, worlds, or spaces in the conventional sense. These are games in which the player neither controls a character nor acts as a commander of other characters. Instead, it refers to abstract games where gamers almost never have control over the perspective of the game and must move blocks, rotate shapes, play cards, or manipulate on-screen elements. Games of this kind include *Tetris*, *Solitaire*, *Hearts*, *Chess*, *Scrabble*, *Crayon Physics*, and more.

THE ANATOMY OF A VIDEO GAME

The previous section detailed a critical set of terms and nomenclature that are part of a wider language for talking about and referencing games. This language is shared by most gamers, game journalists, and game developers. The game developer, however, must go beyond this general language, which describes the video game primarily from the point of view of a gamer—that is, from the outside as a "black box." Instead, the developer must begin to see the game from the inside, as being a whole composed from discrete and important ingredients—a functional conglomeration of constituent and interacting pieces. In short, the developer must anatomize the game and see the stuff from which it is made, piece by piece.

As with most technical disciplines, there are many levels and degrees at which this kind of analysis can be performed. This section shall perform only the most summary and general analysis by examining the main technical and abstract pieces that compose a video game. If a video game could be cracked open, you would find that it was made from three main pieces:

- The engine
- The assets
- The rules

These can be visualized in Figure 1.4.

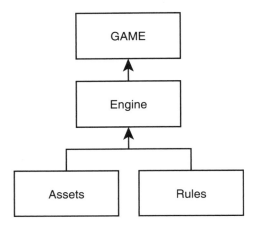

Figure 1.4
Anatomy of a video game.
Source: *Alan Thorn*

The Engine

The engine is the remit of the programmers and is the life force of a game—the thing that makes a game come alive or do things. It is a part of the video game in the same way that the heart is a part of the body. And like the heart, the engine is not just any dispensable or throwaway part, but is an essential or integral part. The engine is not equivalent to the video game itself; they are not one and the same thing, just as a heart is not a body. By creating an engine and only an engine, a developer does not thereby create a complete game. The heart and the engine are both a part of a larger whole, and the whole is greater than any of its individual parts. Nor is the engine equivalent to any of the specific graphics, sounds, design, story, or characters that might be included in the game. These are the assets, which are discussed in the next section. Rather, the engine is more general and abstract than these.

Beyond stating this, however, there exists no uncontroversial or unchallenged industry-standard meaning for the term "game engine." It is not a term with a precise and agreed-upon meaning, like graphics or sound, or a mathematical definition. Rather, the term "game engine" is deployed loosely in many contexts to convey a general sense or idea rather than a precise meaning about which there can be no negotiation. But nor is it an *entirely* subjective term, either, such as the term "beauty" or "good," because most developers would not be willing to recognize almost anything as a game engine. Consequently, rather than stating all the things that an engine *is*, or rather than stating all the properties an engine *has*, it will be more profitable to explain what an engine is supposed to *achieve* and how it is supposed to solve a problem that developers encounter when they go about making games—in particular, when they go about trying to make more than one game.

To illustrate the problem and how an engine can help solve it, consider a scenario with two rival game-development studios, Studio X and Studio Y. Imagine that Studio X, a new indie developer, opened its door for business and began work developing a retro-style platform game in the vein of *Sonic* or *Mario*. Games in the platform genre feature a character that must progress through levels, running and jumping across platforms, defeating enemies, and finding the exit point toward the next level. When development was complete, Studio X released its platform game, *Super Jumper*, to the delight and applause of many a satisfied gamer. Its game proved a stellar economic success, out-selling a competing platform game, *Platform Panther*, produced by its lesser-known rival, Studio Y. *Super Jumper* was so successful, in fact, that a sequel was both demanded and expected by its adoring fans. Studio X began work immediately on this sequel so as not to disappoint.

It was Studio X's intention from the outset to release the sequel as soon as possible to capitalize on the success of the first game while the hype and buzz were still active. But no sooner than work had started, Studio X ran into developmental troubles that threatened delays and disappointment. These troubles did not arise because of specific challenges posed to the studio by the sequel in hand, but because of the way in which the studio made the first game. Back then, the studio had not considered the possibility that its work might have helped it in the future with work on sequels. Back then, it had considered each game as a self-contained entity and their development as separate and distinct processes. Back then, each game was to be built from the ground up. No work from the former game could possibly be of use for the latter because each of them were to be released and sold as separate games. The result: Studio X produced and released its uninspiring sequel in no less time and with no less effort than it took to make the first. And this release was accompanied by much disappointment for fans of the original game, and by much loss of sales for Studio X.

Worse, Studio X was upstaged by a smarter Studio Y, which released its sequel in half the time it took them to make their first game. This was not because Studio Y cut corners or rushed development. Each member of the team worked just as hard as they did on their original game. Nor was it because Studio Y reduced the content or length of the game. In fact, its sequel was bigger and better than the first. Studio Y's success was due first and foremost to their foresight.

Studio Y realized while developing the first game that many of the properties and features common to all games and to all platform games could be extracted from their particular contexts and given an abstract or general form. The developers realized, for example, that *all* platform games feature a player character subject to the laws of physics—who, after jumping in the air, must eventually fall to the ground by gravity. This rule would apply just as much to the sequel as to the first game, no matter what the character was named or how the character looked or sounded. Similarly, both games would need to play sound and music in connection with events in the game. Although the sounds themselves might vary between games (whether gunshot sounds or thunder claps), the technical mechanisms by which the sounds are played to the speakers need not change because they do not depend on the content of the sounds.

Thinking in this way, Studio Y could recognize not only some but almost all the generalizable components of a game and integrate them into a single system that could be reused or recycled to produce many different games. Certainly, there would be many features—such as graphics, sounds, and story—that would be specific to each game and would therefore have to be created on a game-by-game basis. But despite these differences and specifics, Studio Y had the cleverness to identify the underlying commonalities of all games and to package these into a core or framework that they could use and reuse as the template or foundation for building and powering many different games. This template or foundation, so to speak, is what developers call an "engine" or "game engine."

Third-Party Engines

It should be mentioned that in the contemporary games industry it is not common for developers to create their own engines, as Studio Y did in the example. Instead, they create games using ready-made engines purchased from other companies. These engines are known more formally as "third-party engines" or "third-party tools" (because they have been created by outside third parties) but are more commonly referred to just as "game engines" or "engines."

For many developers, especially smaller developers, there are good reasons—both economic and technical—to use engines developed by others. First, doing so saves a developer from having to spend time reinventing the wheel—that is, developing a general engine framework themselves—enabling them to concentrate instead on developing the content of their game. Second, many third-party engines are now well-established, already bug-tested, and supported by a large community of developers, saving a developer both time and resources in testing and quality assurance. There are, however, also reasons (as you shall see later) for developers to develop their own engine.

Chapter 10, "Distribution, Publishing, and Marketing," lists some of the most common engines available. The first steps on the road to learning game development often take the form of learning one of these engines.

The Assets

The engine is distinguished from most other parts of a game by its general and ultimately abstract nature. Generalness and abstractness are the characteristic and essential features of an engine. They are primarily what make it recyclable and powerful and allow it to apply to almost all games. The term "assets," in contrast, refers to the specific and the contingent. It refers generally to all the things a developer must make on a per-game basis. The engine is the infrastructure and the assets are the superstructure; assets rest on or are built above the engine. Assets include the following:

- Graphics
- Sound
- Story
- Design
- Animations
- Scripting
- Videos
- Cut scenes
- Interface components
- Musical scores
- Voiceover tracks

In addition, assets include all other parts that are specific and contingent to the game—the things that are said to compose the content of the game.

Given the specificity of assets and the generalness of the engine, it might be argued here that some assets are general and not specific to games in the sense that they can be reused across multiple games. A graphic of Sonic the Hedgehog, for example, can be used in many *Sonic*-themed games, not only in one of them. This is both true and important. But this kind of generalizability is distinct from the generalizability found in an engine. The Sonic graphic is limited in its usability because it carries within itself a context. Thus, it can be used and reused meaningfully only within *Sonic*-themed games. This is because its very nature (being a *Sonic* graphic and not a

Mario or a *Zelda* graphic) is intimately tied up with the content and specificity of games. The engine by contrast is general in the wider and more fundamental sense expected from infrastructure in that it can be reused across almost all games that you can imagine because it does not by its very nature depend on game content at all.

There is another and further characteristic shared by all assets that again differentiate them from the engine. Specifically, assets are static and lifeless. That is, assets just *are*. They do not *do* anything of their own accord. They are what they are, and have neither intelligence nor initiative. Graphics are digital images, sounds are digital noise, and movies are digital animations. None of these components individually has the ability to act for itself in the game. That is, graphics cannot animate of their own accord, and sounds cannot decide when they should or should not play. Something in addition to these lifeless assets is needed to bring them to life—namely, the engine. It is one of the roles of the engine to intelligently coordinate and harmonize the assets together into a complex ensemble that we call a game. It is ultimately the engine that works on the assets, behind the scenes, to ensure that game events occur at appropriate times and that these events are presented to the gamer meaningfully and as intended. It is the engine that ensures game characters run, jump, and attack only when they should, and that the appropriate run, jump, and attack animations and sounds are played accordingly. In short, assets without an engine to guide them would be little more than a collection of images and sounds sitting in a folder on the hard drive, and an engine without assets would be like a life force searching for potential in a world that is forlorn and vacuous.

The Rules

The term *rules* is synonymous in game development with phrases such as "game logic" or "core design," and it is the video-game equivalent of the rules of a board game. Rules exist as an independent and abstract ingredient of a game and are neither a part of the engine nor a part of the assets. Rather, the rules act as intermediary between the two components, telling the engine how it should govern the assets during gameplay for a specific game.

The rules may detail many properties of the game, depending on the kind of game. They may consist of very specific statements, such as "When X occurs, then do Y," or "When gamer falls into lava pit, lose 100% of health." However, most games have a rule set that defines at least the following:

- The number of players
- The win condition
- The loss condition
- The acceptable ways for achieving either the win or loss condition

In some games, the win condition might simply be reaching the exit point of a level, where each level of the game is classified as a mini-game. For others, such as an RPG game like *Skyrim* or *Fallout*, there will likely be a more complex hierarchy or structure of win conditions. There will be at least one win condition for each and every quest accepted by the player specifying what he or she must do to complete the quest, and then finally an overarching or ultimate win condition specifying all the quests that must be completed for the entire game to be won.

The Stages of Game Development

The video game, then, can be seen generally to consist of three main parts:

- The engine
- Assets
- The rule set

For this reason, the process of developing a game is the process of developing these three parts. There are, of course, exceptions to this rule. For example, a developer could and often does take a shortcut by a number of means, such as by using a third-party engine or by contracting out work to other parties on any one of these parts. This section, however, does not concern itself with such scenarios and specifics as these, and instead assumes that no such shortcuts to development will be taken at all.

To the developer who has accepted the responsibility for developing the entirety of a game, including its engine, the question arises as to how that development should begin and be organized. The problem that presents itself to the developer at the outset of development is one of time and project management. (These are issues to which I will return in Chapter 2, "Game Software Development.") The problem in short is, there are many ways one could make a game, but which way is optimal? What is the easiest, quickest, and smoothest route to making a game, given that its development consists of making an engine, assets, and a rule set?

Unfortunately, there is no obviously right or wrong answer for all games and all developers at all times, but some general approaches do recommend themselves more than others. Generally speaking, the development process can be broken down into a set of phases or blocks of time. These phases are not industry standards as such or codes of conduct agreed upon by any institution or body, but are simply general phases that a developer can identify in the working practices used by many game developers when they make games. Specifically, the development work can be seen to span over eight distinct phases, where each phase is to be completed one at a time and in sequence. This process, which I refer to as stages of game development, looks something like Figure 1.5. Here, each phase or module can be seen as a processor unit: It accepts an input, processes that input, and then produces an output. Further, each module in the sequence takes as its input the culminative outputs from all previous modules, meaning that the final module produces the final output—that being the completed video game.

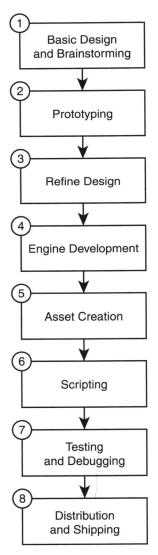

Figure 1.5
Stages of game development.
Source: *Alan Thorn*

Basic Design and Brainstorming

Most projects begin with or are born from an idea, and game development is no different. The idea is the spark of inspiration recognized by many as the starting point for human creativity. Perhaps this idea dawns on you while playing games made by others or perhaps it enters your mind in quite different and/or mundane circumstances, such as during a visit to the dentist or in the waiting room of a train station. It matters not so much, if at all, when or where the idea strikes so long as it strikes at some point and in some way. The purpose of the basic design and brainstorming phase of development is to take a raw idea with potential as an input and transform and refine it into a more structured and comprehensive plan for a game as an output. The point of this stage is to create a design for a game—to answer the question "What is this game about?" and to give that answer using game speak (that is, in terms of genre and sub-genre, perspective, target audience, platform, graphical style, and others).

There are many methods and steps developers can use to transform an idea into a design. One of the earliest and most notable methods in the design phase is brainstorming, the process of raising, exploring, and listing connected ideas and trying to see where those ideas, when so connected, might lead. Developers often record the results of brainstorming using a spider diagram or a mind map—a type of chart in which ideas and their interrelations are represented graphically on the basis of the old maxim that a picture is worth a thousand words. (See Figure 1.6.)

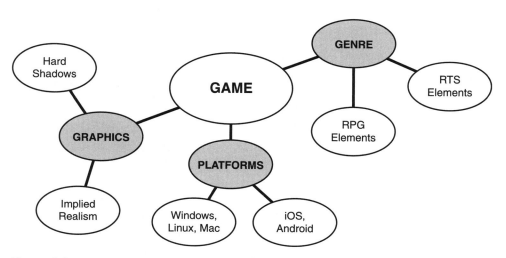

Figure 1.6
Spider diagram.
Source: *Alan Thorn*

In combination with the practice of brainstorming, developers also use the existing game-speak categories (genre, platform, style, etc.) as a means to structure and direct their thinking, seeing the categories as posing specific questions that the design must answer comprehensively. Questions include "What is the *genre* of this game?" "Which *platforms* are to be supported by this game?" and so on.

You'll learn more about game design and its specifics later in this chapter; for this reason, I shall consider design only briefly here. For now, it is enough to say that the aim of the design phase is to create a design document—a reference document detailing everything a developer needs to know about the game to create it successfully. The document should comprehensively encode the imaginative vision for the game such that any technically capable developer who reads it will be able to comprehend the game as much as the designer.

It is, however, critical for developers not to underestimate the importance of design in securing success in game development. Surprisingly, many claim vehemently not to underestimate its importance, but often their practice and behavior are at odds with their claims. There is a sense among some newcomers (particularly among those making games on their own) that anything but the most basic design is a trivial and time-wasting activity—something that can be and should be minimized. The idea that seems to underpin this sense is that if the design of a game is already in someone's mind, and if that person can see it already with their mind's eye, then it can do nothing for them but waste their time to put those ideas on paper. This is because all they can really be doing during design is spending time writing down what they already know. The traditional response to this attitude often highlights the benefits that documenting design has for other members of the team:

- It communicates to them the creative vision of the designer.
- It enables them to share his or her vision and to understand what is to be created.
- It gives other team members the comfort of knowing that if the designer were to be struck down dead on the following day, his or her design would not be destroyed as well.

This response, however—while true and important—both misses a critical point and is unlikely to sound persuasive to those not working in a team. The point is this: Writing down ideas can help you understand them better than you thought you knew them yourself. It can alert you to mistakes—perhaps even mammoth-sized mistakes—that seem obvious to you after your ideas are committed to paper, but that did not strike you at all when your ideas existed only in your head. The process of planning and creating the design document can be an alarming reminder that we frequently do not know our own mind with the laser-sharp precision that you like to think you do.

Prototyping

The prototyping phase is in many respects an extension of the previous design phase in that it gives developers a chance to test their ideas—to push and pull them to see where, if anywhere, they break. When a property developer is planning a new housing estate or entertainment complex, or when a car manufacturer sets about creating a new sort of car, they all initially build a scale model of their design—either a real-world model or a virtual model on the computer. The purpose of this model is twofold:

- It acts as a feasibility study, enabling the developer to foresee whether the implementation of the design is technically possible and economically worthwhile.

- It acts as a troubleshooter or diagnostic because developers and engineers have a hands-on opportunity to foresee problems that the design did not and to propose solutions or workarounds to those problems.

Game development has its equivalent of this modeling or visualization phase in the form of the prototyping phase, and this phase exists for the same reasons and justifications. On the basis of the design document, created in the previous phase, programmers and artists work together to assemble a miniature and draft version of the game that is nonetheless playable—although far from production quality and far from how the final version will look. But this version enables the developers, the techies of the team, to troubleshoot all potential problems that could have an impact on the design of the game. The output of this phase is not only a working prototype, but a list of the issues identified from the creation and testing of that prototype. This list has significance for how the game is designed, and for this reason the next phase of development is once again the remit of the designer.

Refining Design

The previous phase involved accepting a design document as the basis for creating a miniature version of the game. The purpose of this was to enable the programmers and artists to identify potential technical issues that have a bearing on the design of the game. The point of the refining-design phase is for the game designer to amend the design to address and resolve all the identified issues. The output of this phase should be an edited and final version of the design document, although in some cases this phase and the previous will repeat on a cycle as further amendments are tested and prototyped. The aim is for this phase to be considered complete only when the design is complete; thus, this phase results in a final design document that is used for development of the final version of the game.

Engine Development

The engine-development phase is the first of several implementation phases, all of which assume that a final design has been made. The objective of these nuts-and-bolts phases is to make that design—to turn those words on a word-processed sheet of paper into a final and fully playable game. The engine-development phase is the first implementation phase, and for good reason. The engine has been identified as the abstract foundation or infrastructure of a game—the framework on which a game rests. Just as the development of a building begins with its foundations, so the development of a game begins with its infrastructure.

The work of engine development is performed largely by programmers and, in larger game studios, by specialist and dedicated programmers commonly referred to as "engine developers." These developers use a range of technologies, tools, and algorithms to assemble the engine according to a different and engine-specific design document. This phase of development typically occurs alongside others in the implementation phase, each feeding the other, including the asset-creation phase as well as the scripting phase. Chapter 10 book includes a list of many of the tools and technologies used by engine developers, as well as references to further information about this field of development.

Asset Creation

As mentioned, assets are the contents of a game: graphics, sound, videos, scripting, music, and everything else that a gamer experiences during gameplay. Therefore, the asset-creation phase is the process of creating content. It is a process performed by artists, programmers, musicians, directors, voice actors, photographers, and more besides. Indie developers, smaller teams, and even one- or two-person teams will typically have members skilled to some degree in all of these areas as well as in the software and tools needed to produce such assets. The asset-creation phase is typically the longest in duration of all the game-development phases for any team, mainly because a game has many assets and assets are costly to produce in terms of time. This phase works alongside the engine-development and scripting phases. Its final output is the complete collection of final and production-quality assets contained within a game—that is, all of its graphics, sound, music, and video.

Scripting

The scripting phase is distinct and separate from the engine-development phase, even though engine development requires scripting and coding. It is still a separate phase even if it is performed by the same group of programmers. Programmers who create an engine are said to have coded an engine because the instructions they use to build an engine are collectively termed "source code."

Regardless of the terms, programmers creating an engine are building an abstract infrastructure that is generally game-independent. Engine code is not game specific as an asset is game specific. The scripting phase in contrast is where programmers write all the game-specific instructions—the game-specific code. It is where they codify the specific game rules using a programming language. These are rules that are fed into a pre-existing engine, where they are processed and used to govern the interactions and use of game assets during gameplay. These are the instructions that make a game work or hang together—the instructions that bring the assets to life along with the engine. This kind of higher-level code is referred to generally as "script," and the activity of creating it is referred to as "scripting." The output of this phase in combination with the engine-development and asset-creation phases is a playable and potentially complete video game. It is "potentially complete" because the software, at this stage, is subject to the play-testing and debugging of the subsequent phase.

Testing and Debugging

The debugging and testing phase is a skeptical phase performed by programmers and game testers. It accepts a potentially completed game as input and subjects that game to skeptical enquiry—a series of predefined tests—to see how it reacts and performs. These tests are typically designed to pull no punches and to check that the game is working not only as specified in the game-design document, but is working generally in the spirit of good craftsmanship.

The point of the testing phase is to break the game wherever possible—to push it and play it in all kinds of possibly unforeseen ways with the express and unreserved purpose of trying to cause an error or glitch. This is not because the tester is malicious or gains sadistic pleasure in picking holes in the work of diligent programmers, but simply to identify as many ways as humanly possible in which the game can be made to fail. Having generated such a list as this, the aim is then to identify which of the failures are not reasonable failures, or are unacceptable failures. Certain kinds of failures, for example, are not thought problematic, such as when the game terminates as the user switches off the computer. But other kinds of failures are not deemed acceptable, such as when a game crashes every time a user tries to clicks a button to save his or her progress.

These kinds of failures, along with many others (known as "bugs") are deemed to be in need of a fix, or a patch. The job of creating these fixes is within the remit of the programmer during the debugging stage. The process of debugging is an exercise in tracing software bugs, identifying their cause, and then repairing them in such a way as to not cause further problems. The result of the testing and debugging phase is a completed game, ready for distributing and marketing to the end user, or gamer.

Distribution and Marketing

The final phase of development is typically performed by a different group of people, and it requires a completed game as input. The aim of this phase is to both make gamers hungry for the game and to make the game available to them to satisfy their hunger. The work of the marketing and advertising professional is occupied with the former, and the work of the distributors is the work of the latter. Chapter 10 details more on marketing games and on their distribution, primarily for the benefit of those looking to make a living by developing games on their own or through their own company. However, the primary focus of the rest of this title is on the construction of a game, and thus on the development phases one through seven.

GAME DESIGN

The five Ps—prior planning prevents poor performance—serve as a maxim that is frequently repeated, and it is one to which there is some truth in the field of game development. The section "Basic Design and Brainstorming" earlier in this chapter listed the rationale and some of the justifications for a comprehensive design, although these are not the only justifications that can be made. A creative, clear, and comprehensive vision of what the game is to be about and how it is supposed to work acts as a guide or source of orientation for a project. It helps steer the project toward a path to success because members of the team have a common goal or target in mind about how the game is supposed to be or feel. It helps those same members steer away from the obstacles, the metaphorical rocks, and the time-wasting deviations, simply because such dangers are made identifiable by what they are not: That is, they are not listed among the aims of the project in the design document. The design document is, as you have seen, an important component created at the beginning of the game-development process, and that is thus a part of the input for every subsequent stage. This document is created by the game designers, and it is their role to invent fun, interesting, and good games. This section considers design and the role of the designer in more detail.

The Aim of Game Design

Most game designers would reckon among their list of responsibilities or obligations a duty to create good games as opposed to trashy games or bad games. But these terms—"good" and "bad"—are problematic and raise philosophical conundrums that are not entirely without practical influence in the field of game development and in any field of art more generally. For this reason, I shall consider this influence and its implications briefly here.

Most passionate gamers and game developers have a real yearning to make aesthetic judgments about the games they play. They say things like, "This is a fantastic game!" or "This game is terrible!" When they say these things, they generally intend them to be understood as descriptions of an objective truth—to be taken as matters of fact about which it is possible to be right or wrong. However, the question arises as to what can be said, if anything, to the objector who says that such claims are not really matters of fact but are only expressions of personal opinion that have no authority beyond the people who express them. To this objector, a game designer, whatever he or she does, can never actually design a good game because there is no matter of fact that any game is good or bad. This ultimately philosophical objection—and the very serious problems it raises for whether artistic judgments are matters of fact or opinion—has divided many developers, with some taking one side and some taking the other about what the aim of game design is (if it has an aim in this sense at all). For my part, I can see no satisfactory way of overcoming the skeptical objection, despite a number of proposed solutions.

For this reason, many have taken the more moderate view about the aim of the game designer. They see their aim as less about creating good games and more about creating games that in their *opinion* are good, games that statistics suggest many are likely to enjoy, or games that have a likelihood of appealing to many gamers or to a specific niche in line with the developer's target market. All these aims (and more) are entirely possible and feasible even if it turned out that all judgments about games were opinions and not matters of fact. For this reason, I take this more moderate aim as the aim of the game developer. But opinions do differ widely on this issue and some are resolutely not prepared to see the issue and aims in the more moderate terms I have given here.

The Game-Design Document (GDD)

Perhaps the most fundamental role of the game designer, whatever his or her motivations for creating a game, is to produce the game-design document—a document that ranges in length from half a page to a book-sized volume, depending on the game and circumstances. It is, as you have seen, typically started in the earliest phases of development and is completed or finalized after the prototyping phase, where it can account for and accommodate many of the practical suggestions from most other members of the team.

The central aim of the GDD is to articulate the creative vision of the game in a clear, concise, comprehensive, and technologically independent way to a readership of game developers—usually the other developers on the team. It is worth reiterating here that the content of the GDD is targeted at developers, not gamers. For this reason, the GDD will not read like a sales pitch or an advertisement for the game whose chief purpose is to win a sale and gain notoriety. Its aim is not to convince gamers of the game's worthiness of their time and attention. Nor will it read like a game review or be self-consciously evaluative of its own features compared to those of the competition. Rather, its content will be tailored more academically to an audience of experienced developers contracted to work on the game project and whose responsibility is to ensure that the design is realized as closely as possible. For the GDD to be clear, concise, and comprehensive to this audience, it must contain a set of explicit details about the game, usually including its title, platform, target audience, and supported platforms, as well as others that shall be discussed in more detail shortly.

Further, it was said that the GDD is typically written to be technologically independent, meaning that it will not make directly prescriptive statements or concrete demands about how the game is to be implemented. The document states what the game is, but not how the game is to be made. For example, it can and will state the genre of the game, such as RPG, platform, shooter, but it will not state whether the game will be developed using the C++ or Java language. It can and will list the characters, the story, the setting, the synopsis, and a corpus of other details, but it will not detail whether the game will be made using the Unity or the UDK engine, or whether the artwork will be created in tools such as Photoshop, Maya, or Blender. These implementation details are typically specified by producers and team managers after the GDD has been created or during the prototyping phase. The work of these people will be detailed further in Chapter 2, which focuses on the software-development process.

So what exactly will the GDD contain if it is not targeted toward gamers and it is not to make concrete demands about the implementation of a game? The contents of the GDD will inevitably vary from game to game because games differ, but generally speaking it will use a combination of text, diagrams, illustrations, and pictures to paint as complete an image as possible of the game to be created. To illustrate in more detail, subsequent sections of this chapter consider some of the most common details and specifics included in a typical design document.

Title, Platform, and Audience

The GDD typically begins with a title—either the final game title or, at least, a working or provisional title used for referring to the game during development. Mention of the title is usually followed by a statement about the platforms to be supported by the game and the audience to be targeted. The term "platform" is, as you have seen, part of a general game-speak language and refers to a category specifying the type of computer on which the game can execute successfully. Such systems might include PC, Mac, Xbox, PlayStation, mobile, and others. The target audience is the demographic, or type of gamer, to which the game is aimed, much like this book is aimed at a specific type of reader—namely, a reader interested in making games. The worldwide population of gamers, varied though it is, is frequently divided up conceptually on the basis of statistics into various groups or types by developers and advertisers, mainly for the purpose of developing and marketing games successfully.

Note

Some of the more sizeable target audience groups include teenage male, teenage female, elderly female, and children. One of the most sizeable groups is 35–45 year old males according to an ESA 2011 report. That same report concluded that 58% of the gaming population was male, and further that 55% of the gaming population played games on mobile devices, such as phones and tablets like the iPhone, iPad, and Android devices.

Summary and Story

Many games feature a story and are in some way story-driven or story-centric, meaning that they include characters and environments and that the game charts the unraveling of events involving those characters and environments. For the game to be an interactive experience, the gamer must take a participatory role in that story in the sense that the gamer's actions will influence how the story unfolds. But typically, their influence here is only to choose which way the story should move from among a set of predetermined paths. The gamer's role only affects which path the story actually takes from among a range of possible paths. The GDD, however, must detail the story and *all* its possible permutations. It typically does this by stating the story in stages or through revisions to make it more easily digestible for the developer as a reader.

The first stage of detailed discussion in the document is the summary, synopsis, or abstract. Here, the designer states the story and the general concept of the game in overview, making explicit mention of the basic premise (what the game is about, in one or two sentences), the setting, the role of the gamer, and the gamer's objective in the game. The summary will typically not be longer than 500 words, and will include details about what the gamer does in the game, when and where the gamer does it, and what the gamer's aim is in order to complete the game.

After the summary has been given, the story and details of the game rules can then be provided in a more complete and formal way—in a manner that sensibly extends upon what was said already in the summary. If the story has branching elements or branching paths that enable the gamer to pick and choose how events unravel, then all the branches and permutations must be given here. Diagrams and charts are often used to complete the explanation and to help the reader visualize the directions the story can take. The aim of the more complete discussion is to firmly orientate the reader in the document—to convey a full understanding of the story, the objective, and the rules of the game to the reader. By "full understanding," I mean the kind of understanding that leaves the reader only with questions about the finer points of the story and parochial questions about the rules, and not questions about whether the story might really be wholly different from the one he or she has actually imagined or about whether the rules in the text might be entirely different from those he or she has actually understood. The aim of the design document from that point forward, having oriented the reader, should be simply to add flesh to the established framework—to elaborate on and fill in gaps for the basic game premise that has been outlined already.

Characters, Equipment, and Locations

The collective aim of both the synopsis and the detailed synopsis of the GDD is to provide a clear picture of the essence of the game using text, images, and diagrams as appropriate. This overall description of the game will include its premise, story, main characters, theme, and rules.

To consider the example of an RPG game, such as *Oblivion*, *Skyrim*, or *Avernum*, the GDD will likely include detailed statements about the game's fantasy setting (being set in a world of dragons, goblins, orcs, etc.), the main antagonist and protagonist characters, the overarching story, and the background to the world in which the game takes place. However, neither the synopsis nor the detailed synopsis will list or detail all the cities and towns or places that can be visited in the game. Nor will it list all the characters that can be met or all the weapons that can be collected and used. The job of the GDD is indeed to list and detail these features, too, but these are detailed as elaborations of the main concept. They are specified in the document in sections subsequent to both the synopsis and detailed synopsis.

The specifics of these later, elaborative sections will vary enormously from game to game, but they might include detailed lists of characters, weapons, spells, armor, equipment, cities, towns, dungeons, space stations, and political organizations. Typically, these elements will be accompanied with color or black-and-white conceptual sketches and drawings, referred to as "concept art," packaged as a part of the GDD and intended to help readers—especially artists—better visualize the details being discussed.

CONCLUSION

The primary aim of this chapter has been to begin a process of transformation: transforming how a person might see video games and the general process of game development from the eyes of a gamer to those of a developer. This transformation is from the perspective of someone who sees a game from the outside as the end result of a development process to the perspective of someone from the inside who sees the game largely as a machine that works because of the interaction between its constituent pieces. The transformation thus far has involved examining some general language used for talking about games, an exploration of the game-design process, as well as the anatomizing of a game to see its largest and most noticeable parts, including the engine, assets, and rules. The next chapter considers the technical and logistical problems that face developers when they set about making a game on the basis of the completed design document.

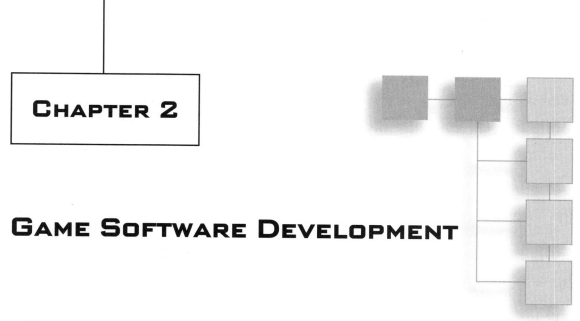

CHAPTER 2

GAME SOFTWARE DEVELOPMENT

"Running a project without a work breakdown structure is like going to a strange land without a roadmap."

—J. Phillips (attributed)

By the end of this chapter you should:

- Understand the importance of project management for game development.
- Have understood the general principles of RAMS.
- Appreciate the benefits and risks of the waterfall model.
- Appreciate the benefits and risks of the agile model.
- Understand the software release cycle.

Chapter 1, "Games and Game Design," discussed at some length the game-design process and saw as its aim the creation of a game-design document, or GDD. The purpose of that document, once refined and amended by the prototyping phase of development, is to detail comprehensively and concisely what game is to be made in such a way as to be both technically independent and accessible to a general readership of game developers. The GDD tells readers through words, diagrams, and pictures the kind of game to be created; it enables the developers on the team to re-create in their own minds and imaginations the vision of the game designer. In short, it enables them to know, in the abstract, the final goal or vision that is to be reached.

The GDD does not, however, stipulate in practical terms how that goal is to be created; it does not detail all the practical steps of coding, asset creation, and testing that must be completed in order to translate the design into a fully working game. Decisions about how the game is to be made, who is to do it, and the tools these people are to use, as well as how their work is to be scheduled and arranged, are made typically by the producers and project managers of the team working in consultation with other developers, such as programmers, artists, and musicians. The work of these producers and project managers—and thus the work of how game development should be structured, managed, and arranged—forms the primary subject matter of this chapter.

PROJECT MANAGEMENT AND ITS JUSTIFICATIONS

Before considering the reasons and justifications for project management, it is necessary to consider more precisely what project management is. To do that, it is necessary to consider the narrower concept of a project. The development of a game is considered to be a project—in particular, a software development project. A project in this sense consists of a number of abstract elements (see Figure 2.1):

- **Professionals.** The professionals are those people skilled in the work of game development who are contracted to work on the project throughout all or some of its duration. These include programmers, artists, designers, audio engineers, voice actors, and others.

- **Tools.** The tools are the software and hardware components that the professionals use to make games. They include programming languages (such as C++ or Java) and asset-creation software (such as Photoshop, Illustrator, Maya, 3DS Max, Blender, and others).

- **Concepts and ideas.** The concepts and ideas encompass both the game design and the general creative vision of the game. These guide and focus the professionals in their use of the tools, telling them what exactly the tools will be used to create.

- **Time.** Time refers to the amount of time in terms of days, weeks, or months that developers on the project have been allocated for using the tools to develop the creative vision. In other words, it's the time allowed to do their work.

- **Finance.** Finance describes the total budget allocated to the project—the total amount of money that may be spent to support all the professionals on the project to use all the specified tools to create the design and ideas within the stipulated time.

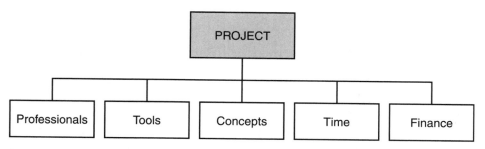

Figure 2.1
Anatomy of a game project.
Source: *Alan Thorn*

All these listed elements of the project may be considered, somewhat controversially, as resources. It is controversial because some object ethically to people being thought of simply as resources, even if it is for the benefit of the project or for visualizing ideas. But, putting these ethical concerns aside here for the sake of brevity and clarity (not because they are unfounded), the process of project management can thus be seen as a process of managing resources. Specifically, the central aim of the project manager is to ensure that the game design is realized as faithfully as possible while spending resources optimally. "Optimally" means not only not exhausting the resources, but spending as few of them as possible without compromising the vision of the game. This, in essence, represents the aim of project management: the question of how to economically and practically turn an idea into a fully working game.

Some people doubt the importance of project management, just as some doubt the importance of game design. As in the case of game design, these doubts are of varying degrees. The most radical of them typically comes from newcomers to game development or from those who are so discomforted and bored by design and planning work that they would rather be doing anything else. There are also more moderate and stronger objections to certain kinds of planning and project management, which are considered later in this chapter when I address the agile model of software development. The objections considered here are the more radical kind, which seek to eschew almost all project management. These are the kind of doubts that aim to dismiss project management from the development landscape completely as a waste of time, irrelevant, or the kind of thing about which only large companies need concern themselves.

These doubts, on closer inspection, are usually held by lone developers and small teams. They are targeted not so much at any and all project management; after all, there is a sense in which everyone involuntarily engages in project management as soon as they begin to think about and reflect on the work they are going to pursue, even if those thoughts are not committed to paper. Rather, their doubts are targeted specifically toward the more precise and formal project-management processes detailed here—that is, to those processes that see the project as a collection of resources that need managing, that require a much more systematic and concrete plan of action, and require much more foresight and documentation. Their objections see planning as bureaucracy; they run in parallel and are similar to the objections that may be raised against game design generally, as you saw them in Chapter 1. They rest on the idea that knowing how to make a game—being able to use the tools—is enough in itself; therefore, nothing else is necessary. Everything else must be a superfluity. They reason that being able to program in a programming language, being able to make graphics and music, and being able to assemble these together into a complete game is all that is needed from the team. They know themselves the work that needs to be done and they have the ability to do it, so they see no compelling reason why they should wait around or hesitate in getting started by drawing charts, planning timesheets, or breaking down the workload into steps and stages. All that might be useful for large teams where the work of hundreds of people must be coordinated across time and locations around the world, but it can have no relevance or bearing for the smaller teams that work closely and alongside each other. For people who think this way, project management is little more than an excuse for not getting on with things.

This line of reasoning against is fundamentally flawed, however—and you can make that flaw more apparent by considering a pertinent analogy—one that is hinted at by the quotation at the beginning of this chapter: "Running a project without a work breakdown structure is like going to a strange land without a roadmap." Travelers who visit a strange city without a map can probably find their way to destinations within the city on their own, assuming they can move and see and comprehend. Certainly, they have within themselves both the potential and ability to travel from their current location to their destination, wherever that might be. But without the map, their travel in the city will always be encumbered and problematic. Without the map, they will hit dead ends, take wrong turns, trace and retrace their footsteps, and take longer than they might have done if they had brought a map until eventually, after much trial and error and deduction, they arrive where they wanted to be, exhausted and late and feeling rather silly. They could, of course, get lucky; luck could deliver them to their destination just as the winds land a stranded boat safely on the shore. But luck is a notoriously unreliable friend. It cannot figure prominently in the plans of those desiring consistent success.

The process of project management and the schedule of work that it can produce might be likened to the map for a game-development project. Those who must take the journey of game development, can use that map as a tool for identifying all the work ahead and foreseeing problems that might arise. With the benefit of this vision and foresight, developers can make their lives easier. They can take the shortest and most problem-free route to their destination and in doing so will spend the fewest resources on the project.

CREATING A PLAN WITH RAMS

One of the chief aims of project managers on game-development projects is to produce a plan or a schedule that defines explicitly how a game design on paper is to be transformed into a playable game—a final product. This plan of action typically includes the game-design document as well as details about who is to work on the project, the tools they are to use, and the time and budget they have available. Further, the plan specifies the schedule that work is to take. ("Work" here is being used to refer to the totality of programming, graphics, audio, sound, and other developmental tasks for the game.)

It is the role of the schedule to state the order in which work must be performed and the times at which that work is to begin and to be completed. Usually, this schedule or timetable is created by breaking down the total work of the project into smaller, constituent modules (sometimes referred to as tickets or chunks); the final game is seen as being the sum total of the modules. Each module is assigned to a specific member of the team, who is expected to complete it by a specific and pre-arranged time or deadline. Thus, artist members will not be assigned general and non-descript tasks such as creating the graphics for the game, but more specific roles, such as creating character X or texturing a treasure chest. Likewise, programmers will not be assigned general roles such as coding the game, but more specific and concrete modules such as creating the physics framework and scripting artificial intelligence.

Specific decisions about how the work is to be divided into modules, the order in which the modules are to be completed, and the extent to which modules should be planned in advance vary from developer to developer and project to project. However, the strategy that a developer does decide upon—which helps him or her make these kinds of decisions—is known as a "development methodology." The two most popular and general methodologies in the software industry for games are the waterfall model and the agile model. As you shall see, some see these as competing methodologies and others see them as complementary; indeed, there is a whole culture war surrounding them, which will not concern you here. Here, the focus will be on the methodologies themselves, both of which are considered later in this chapter.

For now, it is sufficient to begin by considering four general and abstract principles that typically guide a project manager or producer when anatomizing the development work of a video game, regardless of the development methodology chosen. These four general principles guide people in deciding where and how to break down the work of a game optimally and into modules that can be assigned to specific members of the team. These guiding principles are not industry-standard or agreed-principles, but are rather principles that I have identified based on game-development work in the field both as a developer and as a project manager. These principles can be summarized with the acronym RAMS, which stands for recyclability, abstractness, modularity, and simplicity (see Figure 2.2).

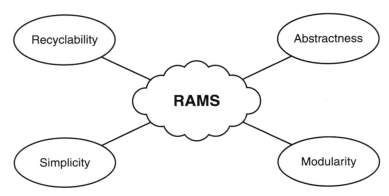

Figure 2.2
Four design principles: RAMS.
Source: *Alan Thorn*

Recyclability

One of the chief aims of the project manager is to maximize productivity: to manage project resources—people, tools, time, and budget—in an optimal rather than a wasteful way. The project manager's aim is to realize the design into a fully working and playable game; productivity is increased during development whenever the project manager finds an opportunity to achieve his or her goal by spending fewer resources than he or she would do so otherwise.

One way of increasing productivity is through recycling. Materials and process (and modules!) that can be reused multiple times in the same project are considered recyclable. The more frequently and widely they can be reused, the more recyclable they are. One project that consumes half the resources of another project to produce exactly the same result with equal or greater quality and efficacy is generally considered to be the more efficiently organized project of the two. Recyclability therefore is a criterion—a principle that guides you in arranging your work optimally. It is a matter of not only dividing the development work into amenable modules, but of dividing them along the lines of reusability. It involves identifying in the work all the areas at which duplication of work can be avoided. In short, recycling helps you search through the game content for assets and elements that are repeated again and again, and to recognize them as tasks worthy of a separate and self-contained module in the development plan.

To illustrate recycling at work in game development, consider the case of a Formula 1 car-racing game, in which the player takes on the role of a driver who must complete his career by finishing first consecutively at each and every race circuit. Such a game as this involves a lot of work: At the coding level alone, programmers must code the car physics, the menu systems, the tournament fixtures, and the intelligence of competing drivers. Nevertheless, this work (and the rest of it) can and will be broken down by project managers into a set of manageable and narrow modules to be completed in sequence, and these modules will all be assigned to specific members of the team.

Managers who have divided the work according to the principle of recyclability will have identified the audience graphics as a potential area of recycling, among other areas. "Audience graphics" refers to those images and models of people in the audience who are located in the seating area of the race circuit environment, and they are typically included in the game to increase the environment's believability—to make it appear as though there really are interested human spectators at the circuit. There are at least two ways in which a manager could integrate this audience work into the plan. The first, which does not adhere to the principle of recyclability, is to identify not one, but several modules of work for creating the audience. Together, these would require the artists to produce a unique but similar group of audience members for each and every race circuit in the game. This strategy means that several artists must use time, effort, and tools to create different audience members for every circuit. In contrast, the second, and recyclable, method is to identify a single audience module in the work plan. This module would require only one artist to create a small and single block of audience members that can be repeated many times not only throughout each and every circuit in the game, but throughout the seating area of the same circuit in order to fill the seats completely. In this way, a single graphical element—the audience—can be tiled and repeated in the game to create the illusion of greater detail with no extra work at all. When the principle of recyclability is applied consistently across all the work of a game, including all work of graphics, sound, and code, it can lead to an accumulative saving of time equating to days, weeks, months, and perhaps even years.

Abstractness

Identifying the abstractness, or abstract qualities, in a module of work (such as a graphical task or coding task) can help a project manager see its potential for recyclability. Abstractness is essentially about producing generalizations from particular instances, and it is a matter of degree. A complete abstractness can be identified by its entirely general nature, for it makes no reference to particular cases. The idea of a chair, for example, is an abstractness because it refers to chairs in general (the chair, as in the concept of the chair) and not to any particular, real chair, such as *this* or *that* chair, which might happen to exist with you here and now.

It was demonstrated in the previous section that in a Formula 1 game, it was possible to identify a range of race circuits as well as an audience for each circuit. From these instances, you could go on to derive the more general idea or abstractness of an audience; doing this helped you to see that the audience could be recycled. From those details, a general and non-particular idea was constructed—an idea that did not depend on any particular instances, but applied to all race circuits as such. The principle of abstractness is useful for game developers because by seeing the modules of a game as abstract rather than particular, the developer comes to see their versatility and recyclable potential. Their versatility is proportional to their degree of abstractness, and thus is directly related to recyclability. The more the project manager sees the game and its work in the abstract, the more he or she can appreciate its potential for recycling, and thus increase productivity.

Modularity

Identifying development work as both abstract and recyclable can be only a formative step in clearly listing and stating all the work that must be completed for a game. Even after the project manager has accepted the raw intuition that an element of work is abstract and recyclable, that person must still express that intuition in a form that is understandable to other team members and that enables them to carry out their work in a target-oriented way. The principle of modularity is what enables project managers to do this—to express their development plan in an understandable and accessible form to those who must execute the work.

The principle of modularity is fundamental to almost all forms of problem solving. It begins by considering an entity as a working whole (such as a game) and then proceeds to subdivide that entity into constituent and discrete pieces or modules, each according to their purpose or function and to their abstractness and recyclability. It leads you to see the completed game as being the end result or function of a process and sequence of mini-tasks—to see the game as the sum total of its design, graphical, programming, and audio work.

By the principle of modularity, each module of work is seen as both independent and exchangeable—independent in the sense that it is distinguished from other modules by its function (for no two modules belonging to the same whole should share the same function), and exchangeable in the sense that it could be replaced without damage to the whole only by another module that serves exactly the same function. For example, a cog in a machine is both independent and exchangeable. It is independent in that no other cog in the machine can be in the same place or do the same thing at the same time. It is exchangeable because it can be removed and replaced only by another cog of equivalent size and shape. Thus, a game can be conceived as a jigsaw puzzle pieced together from independent and exchangeable modules of work. None of these modules can be removed without reducing the whole, and no module can be replaced safely except by another that performs the same function.

Two modules that perform the same function need not have the same innards or implementation, however. Their function and output might be identical, but their working methods might differ for there may be many roads to the same destination. For example, a generic module that requires an artist to create a cartoon character for a game might remain silent on the issue of implementation. It might not in itself stipulate whether the character is to be created in Photoshop or Paint Shop Pro, nor might it indicate whether the character be male or female. In these cases, the aim of the module is only to produce a character (any character); the details of how it is produced are left here to the artist's discretion. Such a module as this would in principle be substitutable for any other module whose aim or goal was to produce a character in this sense, regardless of how that character came about.

In this way, modularity enables a game to be divided into modules, and further enables each module to hide the details and specifics of its implementation while maintaining its relationship to the whole. The module does this by focusing on achieving a single purpose. In short, the principle of modularity recommends that an entity is subdivided into smaller functional units. Doing this offers the developer two design and logistical benefits:

- It enables them to translate complex entities into a collection of simpler ones according to the contribution each makes to the whole.

- It enables them to make changes to the implementation of specific modules without affecting the implementation of other modules or the working of the whole.

Simplicity

The 13th century Franciscan Friar William of Occam stated a controversial principle that "entities should not be multiplied unnecessarily," now known as Occam's Razor. Although its usefulness is hotly contested in the fields of science and philosophy, it does nonetheless have importance in the field of video games.

Applied to video games it might be translated into the mantra: "Keep things simple." In this case, keeping things simple refers to a process of reductionism, or the process of reducing the complex into the simple. This works side by side with modularity. The principle of modularity recommends that the work of a game be subdivided into a range of modules, each according to its unique function; the principle of simplicity is there to remind you that the process of modularity must be performed with simplicity in mind—that is, with the aim of reductionism. Modularity combined with simplicity suggests that the work of a game should not only be subdivided into modules, but should be subdivided into the fewest number of modules possible.

Simplicity, however, should not be mistaken here for the ideas of simple or crude in their derogatory senses. Its relevance and application to games as a principle should not be thought of as being limited or restricted to only simple games, or to games that are short, small, or lightweight. Planning the work for a game according to the principle of simplicity does not entail that the final game cannot be complex or intricate to the gamer. It entails only that, when applied appropriately, the work for the developer will be as simple as can reasonably be made possible—that developers will not waste time duplicating work or taking the longest route to every destination.

It is also worth clarifying here two other possible misunderstandings that might arise from the principle of simplicity. First, the principle is resolutely not equivalent to a recommendation of laziness, cutting corners, or avoiding all developmental challenges for the sake of comfort and ease. The principle of simplicity is to be seen first and foremost as a rational recommendation not to complicate work that is already complicated enough even in its simplest form; and further as a principle that applies only as long as it is consistent with achieving the game at the intended quality. Second, the principle is not to be understood as a form of cowardice or professional cheating, or as a device for working around rather than solving difficult problems. There can be little to recommend the complex solution over the simpler when both lead to exactly the same destination and when both are within the reach of members of the project. There are indeed many technical challenges and problems that pose themselves to the game developer, as you shall see throughout this book, but the principle of simplicity in no way discourages the developer from tackling those problems. It requires only that problems, when encountered, are solved or worked around as simply as possible with an eye to achieving the goal of the project (the game)—and *not* for the sake of an academic or personal interest in the problems themselves (fascinating and stimulating as they may be).

This process of simplicity might proceed as follows in a practical case: A developer identifies each and every module or item of work belonging to a game, and then for each module he or she pauses to ascertain its function. If any two or more modules share the same function or very similar functions, then these modules are candidates for amalgamation. That is, these modules should then be merged together into one larger module unless there are other compelling and overriding reasons against doing so. Having performed this process once for each module of the project, the developer should repeat the procedure for all newly formed and larger modules, and then repeat it indefinitely on each level upward until the process yields no more amalgamations. In this way, the developer can know that the simplest arrangement of modules has been found.

DEVELOPMENT METHODOLOGIES

The four development principles summarized by the acronym RAMS are foundational insofar as they can be recognized as underpinning the project-management work for almost all games, even in cases in which the principles are not expressly stated. From this starting point, however, project management can take many different directions because developers differ about the best way to realize these principles in a practical scenario.

Specifically, opinions differ about exactly how much work, if any, should be planned in advance and about how much work, if any, should be left unplanned and completed at a later stage. Opinions differ also about how modules of work should be structured; the order in which work should be completed; and how the development process overall should be understood and imagined. For example, should all modules be planned in advance and then completed in sequence one at a time along a linear road to completion? Or should only some modules be planned from the outset, and should developers be permitted to jump back and forth from module to module, working on one and then another without anyone of them being completed in a specific order?

Answers to these questions have been proposed and refined over the course of several decades into software-development methodologies, with differing answers leading to different methodologies. The two most notable and contrasting methodologies used in contemporary game development, and in software development more generally, are the waterfall and the agile models. A game developer will typically adopt only one of these models and apply it to his or her work throughout the entirety of development. These models are now considered in more detail.

The Waterfall Model: Linear Development

Until relatively recently, the waterfall model was the dominant design methodology used in most mainstream game development. This model takes its name from the image of a stereotypical waterfall, an image that is supposed to convey an idea about the linear, sequential, and step-by-step way in which work in this model progresses. (See Figure 2.3.)

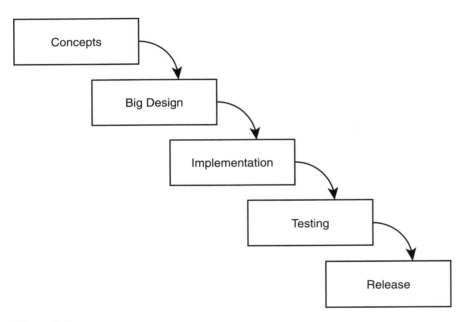

Figure 2.3
The waterfall development method.
Source: *Alan Thorn*

Although variations of this model do exist, the standard and typical version recommends that development starts from a comprehensive and complete design. Before implementation work on a game can even begin, the developer is required to have produced a big design up front—an immutable and uncompromising document that comprehensively describes the details of everything that must be created for the game. This will include target audience, summaries, detailed plots, character profiles, level designs, and enemies and weapons lists among other details as applicable. The best-case scenario document is one that leaves out nothing of importance about the game. The document is one that can be read from beginning to end by a developer on the team to gain a complete understanding and vision of what the end product will be and thus the target or destination that is being aimed for.

After the big design is completed, after perhaps weeks or even months of planning and discussion by way of brainstorming and prototyping, work on the project is ready to be planned and executed. The waterfall model recommends that, because the design is to be considered final and unchangeable, development should be broken down into a finite number of modules in general according to the principle of RAMS. Each module is to be specified and declared in advance; each is to have its own assignee and deadline; and each is to build upon the previous one in a logical and linear sequence.

According to this model, a game is the sum total of its modules, and all modules are to be completed in a linear sequence by their respective assignees on the stipulated deadline, just as water cascades predictably and mechanically from top to bottom, step by step down the decline of a waterfall. The completion of each module represents another cog or component that can be attached to the larger whole gradually being assembled piece by piece, but it is only at the end of development that the whole finally materializes and the developers can stand back and see their work in action.

Note the main features of the waterfall model:

- Big design up front
- Static and unchangeable design
- Mechanical
- Predictable
- Linear
- Sequential

The traditional waterfall model is in many respects the epitome of structure, hierarchy, order, and systemization. It names the key phases of development as follows:

- Conception
- Initiation
- Analysis
- Design
- Construction

- Testing
- Production/implementation
- Maintenance

The Waterfall Model: Pros and Cons

The waterfall model offers both benefits and drawbacks to software development and to game development more specifically. Some think the pros to outweigh the cons, and some believe the reverse. However, almost all but the staunchest of advocates on one side are agreed that there are both pros and cons.

First, the pros. The waterfall model offers many advantages to the developer:

- It allows them the comfort and security of being able to know in advance the software to be created, provided development proceeds according to plan.
- It enables developers to quantify the amount of work involved as well as to estimate the deadline for the final completion date of the project and all the intervening modules.
- It envisages and structures the development work in a modular, sequential, and intuitive way—one that enables developers to foresee and appreciate the importance of their individual work as it contributes to the whole.
- It enables developers at the design stage to anticipate and prepare solutions to difficult problems that might arise farther along in the development process.

In short, the waterfall model is aimed at expanding the horizon of knowledge about the software to be created. Its aim is to provide the developer with a comprehensive knowledge of the work that is ahead by always looking back at the immutable big design.

However, despite the benefits offered to developers by the waterfall model, a significant and important problem arises from a tension between the immutable nature of the model and the changeable nature of software and technology markets. Specifically, in the volatile and liquid conditions prevalent in the video game market, developers are always striving to offer newer and better features and content for their games. They aim to introduce content that makes use of recent innovations in technology or that in some direct way responds to the features being offered by competitors. Gamers, too, expect developers to "strive for better" in games—to include new features or extensions or to change existing features of their software to satisfy demands that have been made known.

Consider the case of two imaginary but competing online RPG games set in a fantasy world of goblins, dragons, and elves: Game X and Game Y. Game X is released shortly before Game Y and includes a range of character-customization features—features such as being able to change the facial structure of characters, and setting their height, gender, hair, and eye color, as well as voice tone—that prove popular with gamers but that are not currently present in the upcoming Game Y. The developers of Game Y have a desire to upstage Game X in every respect possible that is within their means, and their intention is specifically to add bigger and better character customization features than those featured in Game X. This scenario—along with all similar scenarios—has a feature that threatens all games developed using the waterfall model: It requires changes to be made to the design after implementation work has begun. This kind of change is costly in the waterfall model.

The waterfall model, as you have seen, conceives of the development work as a chain of modules. The first link of this chain is the immutable and decidedly non-negotiable design, from which all of the other modules inevitably follow as sequential links. Invalidating, changing, or undermining that first link of the waterfall model could have potentially catastrophic implications for all work that follows.

In some best-case scenarios, small or minor changes could be inexpensively made to the design of the game and the modules could be adjusted to account for the changes, especially if those modules have not yet been started by their assignees on the development team. In some slightly worse-case scenarios, more time and resources must be invested into changing the design, some work will be wasted as a result, some modules will be adjusted, and overall the project will be completed later than originally anticipated. In the worst-case scenario, the design might need to be entirely overhauled; all or almost all of the work will be wasted, scrapped, or abandoned; and the project might begin again or might be cancelled entirely.

The result of all these scenarios is a net increase in resource expenditure. Sometimes the increase will be minor and sometimes major, depending on the extent of change. Nevertheless, these examples serve to highlight a serious problem with waterfall development when applied to some contexts and markets. This has led some to abandon the waterfall model entirely and others to modify or adjust it accordingly.

The Agile Model: Iterative Development

The agile software methodology is fashionable among many in the contemporary games industry. Its name, "agile," is supposed to highlight the way in which the model enables developers to respond, adjust, and adapt with agility to changing markets, demands, and technologies. The agile model in its current and most stated form is frequently seen as a solution to the problems associated with the waterfall model—the problems of immutable design and a rigid development structure. In contrast to the waterfall model, which is seen as sequential and linear, the agile model is considered to be incremental, iterative, or cyclical. (See Figure 2.4.)

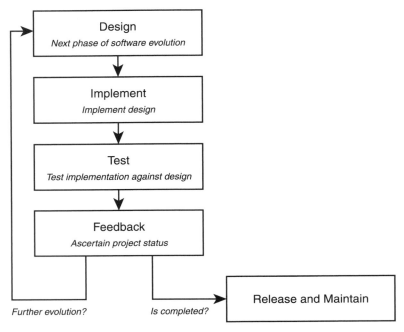

Figure 2.4
The agile development method.
Source: *Alan Thorn*

The waterfall model saw game development as something that could be plotted diagrammatically along a line from left to right, with a complete big design on the left moving toward a completed game on the right and discrete and predetermined modules of work between. The agile model sees software development primarily as a process of evolution—one in which the game (as a whole) is treated as a work in progress that is regularly refined in increments. Agile takes a forward-looking rather than a backward-looking approach in that the game is seen as something that must continually (or cyclically) be tweaked and extended to meet a changing design, just as a homing missile constantly adapts toward a shifting target. The idea of each cycle of development is to produce a new version of the game that is a closer approximation of the design than the result of the previous increment.

Not unlike the waterfall model, the agile model begins with a basic idea for a game. But agile does not insist that the game be designed comprehensively in a big design up front. Rather, it enables room for change and scope. It insists only that enough of the game be designed to create something workable for the first increment of development—that is, after a period of, perhaps, five to six weeks. Something "workable" means something playable or something testable. Agile does not see the game as some large entity that comes together only at the finish line of development when all the pieces are finally in place, but as a something that should come together at the earliest opportunity—even if that something is basic or prototypical in nature. The output of each stage or increment (or cycle) of development for agile is not simply a small piece of a larger puzzle, it is the whole puzzle itself—just further refined and extended, and it will continue to be refined and extended by later increments. In this narrow and specific sense, software is seen to evolve through the development cycle.

As stated, development begins at the first increment for five to six weeks, and the work of that increment often proceeds in a modular fashion—the waterfall model in miniature. Eventually, a workable framework is produced according to the design. This initial game or prototype will likely be far removed from the final product intended, as games typically take longer than five to six weeks to develop and typically are developed across many increments and not just one. But, that is not a problem for agile, because the process repeats again and continues cyclically. The next time around, more design refines the existing model and adds new features if appropriate. Development then proceeds for another few weeks to produce something workable according to the refined design, and the process repeats yet again: another cycle of design that builds on the previous stage, more development, further refinements, and then repeat. In fact, this cycle of iterative development continues, with each cycle producing a new and refined increment or "species" of the software, until finally, after closer and closer approximations, the destination is reached and the project is completed. This, in essence, represents the idea at the heart of agile.

The Agile Model: Pros and Cons

Like the waterfall method, agile offers developers many benefits—but they come with drawbacks. Regarding the benefits: The incremental and iterative nature of agile empowers developers and the development process with a certain kind of agility or capacity for change that is not achievable with the waterfall model. Its eschewing of a large and rigid design up front means that developers can evolve and adapt their software to a design that changes in response to fleeting market conditions, such as changes in technology or the activity of competing game studios. Further, the evolutionary nature of agile can offer members of the team a range of important motivations, morale-boosters, and inspirations from the earliest stages of development. Each member can be a witness to the project as it evolves through its increments. Members see the game not just as something that exists in their imagination or on a sheet of paper, which will come together at some point in the distant future, but as something that can be experienced now (albeit not in its final form). They see it as something that works now and evolves quickly in response to their contributions. In addition, this evolutionary work-in-progress style encourages earlier playtesting and debugging of the game. It constructs the activity of debugging and testing as something that occurs alongside development rather than something that happens only at the end, when there is a final game to test.

Agile is not a panacea for all kinds of games and software projects, however. It carries with it a range of risks, dangers, and problems, which developers should not underestimate. Some of these negatives arise directly from the nature of agile itself; others arise more indirectly—because of the way agile can lead some developers to think about or to understand the development process. The main disadvantages to agile itself trace their root directly to its shortsightedness or openness—the fact that design is reduced to a minimum to enable developers to change the software at short notice should they need or want to. These disadvantages take various forms, with some being more general than others.

First, developing with an eye on the present rather than the future can cause developers to lose sight of their longer-term goals, causing them and their projects to be victims of the moment, reactionary, and never progressive. That is, developers are always responding to market conditions or competitor decisions but never actually leading the way in any notable respect.

Second, without a clear plan of action and sense of direction such as that given by a comprehensive design up front, it is easy for the project to drift by ceaselessly or prematurely evolving, and it is difficult to estimate the cost for such an unknown quantity. With no clear finish line established, development can drift through cycle after cycle, adding new features, refining existing features, and responding to competitive products but never actually coming to a clearly identifiable end. Alternatively, it could stop short of some ideal or optimal point. Budgeting for such projects is an exercise in budgeting for unknowns and the unknowable. It is problematic primarily because upcoming expenses cannot be clearly known or estimated in advance, and thus contractors and tools cannot be acquired at fixed, known, and concrete prices.

Note

The gradual "sneaking" of additional features and ideas into the project, extending its length, is commonly known as "scope creep," or sometimes "feature creep" when referring specifically to application features.

In addition to these concerns are other indirect issues that can arise more because of misunderstandings that some people can form after thinking of development in terms of the agile methodology. Specifically, some people can reason to themselves and to others that agile is first and foremost an anarchic development process requiring practically no design; it is simply about beginning with a small project and gradually strapping onto that project extras and bonuses as the mood or idea arises. The path to this kind of conclusion can be seen as following from the way in which agile expects a minimalist design and sees software as evolving cyclically across discrete increments. Although this understanding can and sometimes does arise, it is important to recognize that this is not the traditional understanding of the agile model. Agile does expect design. It does expect in sum total no less design than that required by the waterfall model. The difference lies crucially in where in the development process that design occurs. For waterfall, the design is up-front; for agile, the design is staggered in bite-size forms across increments.

Agile Versus Waterfall: How to Proceed?

The software-development methodology is, as you have seen, a package or toolbox of ideas, concepts, tips, and workflows that can be deployed by project managers to coordinate the development work for a game project. Two of the main methodologies are waterfall and agile. Previous sections surveyed both these models, explaining what they are and some of their key advantages and disadvantages. However, none of those sections reached any kind of firm conclusion about which method is better or which method most developers should use. This is in part intentional because there are no firm, definitive conclusions about which, if any, method is the better or worse for this or that project. Some developers use the waterfall method, some use agile, some use a combination or variation of the two, and some use a completely different method altogether. In almost all cases, their choices can be and are justified with an appeal to legitimate and strong reasons—reasons that are logistical, technical, or economical. That being said, this does not mean there is no information here to be gleaned about which method is right for you or your project. It is only to say that the information here should be considered more of a first word rather than a last word on the matter. Some details can be concluded, and some advice can be given, and it is this advice that follows:

Note

This advice is not to be understood as hard and fast rules. Rather, it is based primarily on the decisions and decision-making processes that I make when I go about choosing which methodology to use in my development work. I stress the arguable and debatable nature of these decisions here to reinforce the idea that many different kinds of methodologies can be used for pursuing game development, and most of them can be substantiated. When choosing a methodology for your projects, be sure to consider the reasons you have made the decision that you have.

- **Contingency.** No software methodology is clearly right or wrong in an absolute sense. The decision as to which methodology should be chosen is context-sensitive, meaning it depends on the game to be developed, the developer who makes the game, and the time and resources available to that team.

- **Decide early.** Decide which methodology to use before implementation work—before developers start creating game content. Choose a methodology and apply it consistently and faithfully throughout development.

- **Know your reasons.** Do not be persuaded to use a methodology simply because it is fashionable or everybody else you know is using it. Select a methodology after impartial consideration of reasons for and against, on the basis of technical, economic, and logistical factors that are relevant for your project.

    - Use waterfall (or a variation of it) as a default model in cases where no other model seems justified or applicable. Use waterfall (or a variation of it) for all games whose content is fixed, static, or can be known ahead of time. Such games often include single-player, narrative driven games, such as adventure games or first-person shooters; side-scrolling platform games; casual games such as hidden-object games; and puzzle games such as *Tetris* or *Bejeweled*.

    - Use agile (or a variation of it) for online games, multiplayer games, social games, and Facebook games—in general, for all games in which content or features frequently change or are added based on user demand or market conditions. Such games include online RPGs, multiplayer strategy games, and multiplayer mobile games. Use agile or a variation of it for games in which users can create game content using map editors or modification tools, such as simulation games and first-person and third-person action games.

- **Do not fear being unconventional.** You can combine the waterfall and agile methods, combine or revise other methods, or invent entirely new methods if it seems appropriate to do so. Methodologies were developed largely to make software development simpler, safer, and more productive. Do not hesitate to use variations or alternatives if you think they are likely to achieve better results. Remember, there was a time when the waterfall and agile models were new, too.

RELEASE CYCLES

The main objectives of the principles of RAMS and the software-development methodologies of waterfall and agile are, despite their differences, to help developers translate a game idea into a completed and working product. The latter stages of development warrant further consideration in this section. Specifically, as a game edges toward completion, a number of common characteristics emerge for developers:

- The game will be completed enough to be playable and experienced as a game minus refinements, embellishments and some polish.

- The game will likely feature errors, mistakes, oversights, inconsistencies, and features that just don't quite work or feel right—not because of a fault in the computer, the tools, the software, or the development methodology, but simply because their human operators are fallible more generally.

- The game will be subject to scrutiny, play-testing, checks and investigations, and quality assurance to detect mistakes.

- The game will be adjusted, corrected, repaired, and altered on the basis of those tests, checks, and observations.

These operations and details during the latter part of development can be considered more carefully and summarized into a number of discrete and general developmental phases, together known as the "release cycle." These stages are so named because they refer to everything directly preceding the release or completion of the game. These phases can be identified in the order in which they occur as follows (see Figure 2.5):

- Pre-alpha
- Alpha
- Beta
- Release candidate (RC)
- Gold master

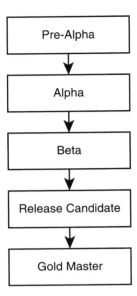

Figure 2.5
Software release cycle.
Source: *Alan Thorn*

Pre-Alpha

Pre-alpha is an umbrella term used to designate all phases of development prior to the release cycle—prior to the debugging, testing, and release stages. Thus, pre-alpha refers to design, coding, and asset creation from graphics to music, and even to the earlier and more informal testing that programmers might pursue while coding. For this reason, pre-alpha usually describes the longest and larger part of development in which most members of the team are engaged. Stages of development are not usually so precisely demarcated that it is possible to clearly identify when one stage ends and another begins, especially with the agile model, but in general the pre-alpha phase is considered to be completed when the game is in a more or less complete form such that it can be play-tested from start to finish (assuming the game is linear in this way rather than open-ended, as are many RPG games).

Alpha

The alpha phase is subsequent to the pre-alpha phase and is the first phase in the release cycle. During this phase of development, developers will have for the first time a game in a complete-enough form to be tested meaningfully. That is, the game will generally be close enough to its final form to be considered a whole game and to be genuinely reflective of the final product. During this phase, programmers and a selection of other in-house developers test the software using primarily white-box testing methods and secondarily black-box testing methods.

White-box testing requires the tester to see the game not through the eyes of a gamer but through those of a developer—to see the game not as a closed black box whose innards and workings are hidden from view, but from the perspective of an engineer who understands what is happening under the hood while the game is playing. Thus, white-box testing is generally performed by the programmers responsible for coding the game in the first place. It is they who will act as gamers in this initial phase in an attempt to find and track down errors in the game. Once found, their role is then to deconstruct those errors based on their knowledge of the game to produce solutions and repairs for them using the process of debugging.

Note

Black-box testing stands in contrast to white-box testing. This form of testing can be performed by people other than the developers. Such testing does not require an inside or working knowledge of the software. Beta-testing is often an example of black-box testing.

The exact conditions that must be satisfied for the alpha phase to end generally vary from developer to developer and from project to project. In some cases, it ends when the developers themselves can find no further errors. In other cases, it ends when only certain kinds or grades of errors can no longer be found.

Beta

The beta phase follows directly after the alpha phase during the release cycle. It marks a point in development at which the software is considered ready for exporting to a general testing party. This party consists of people (beta testers) who are not themselves developers on the project. They will be seeing the game perhaps for the first time and primarily from the perspective of gamers. Their aim, in essence, is to play the game into oblivion—to push the game to its limits, to test all of its features, and to do their utmost to break the game by all reasonable means. Their aim is not only to find errors, but to identify and record for each error the circumstances in which they occurred. Ideally, for each error, these testers will produce a clear and precise set of instructions as to how any similarly positioned user could systematically reproduce that error on his or her own system, if desired. Their list of errors complete with details and instructions are then passed to developers and programmers on the team, who work to resolve them without introducing new errors. The team then produces new revisions or patches for the software, ready to be tested again by the beta testers.

Release Candidate

The term "release" or "release version" is widely used to describe the final game, or the completed product. Consequently, the release candidate is a version of the software that integrates all the repairs and resolutions found through testing. It is proposed by the developers as the final product, subject to a further round of testing. The release-candidate phase of the release cycle thus follows the beta-testing phase, and represents the last phase of testing and the final opportunity for developers to remove errors and bugs from the game should any be found. The release-candidate stage proceeds much like the beta-testing phase, except it begins from a version of the game that has passed through beta testing and not alpha testing.

Gold Master

Game developers often issue press releases with a celebratory tone, proudly announcing to the gaming public that their game has finally "gone gold." This message is sometimes received with confusion and incredulity from some gamers who, cannot understand how a game can be declared "gold" when it is not yet even available for sale! The confusion typically arises because of the terms "gold" and "platinum," used originally in the record industries to refer to high or outstanding sales figures, which have now entered the vernacular. In the world of video games however, a game that has "gone gold" is simply a game whose development has reached the gold-master phase, or the final phase of development. The gold master phase describes a period of development when the game is considered to be completed and final. Games in this phase have left the hands of developers and entered the hands of distributers, producers, marketers, and all departments responsible for getting a completed game into the hands of customers.

Conclusion

This chapter covers a range of important ideas and philosophies that govern how developers engage in the work of game development. Considered on their own, they can sometimes seem dry and passionless because they do not relate to games directly or to their content. Nevertheless, a solid understanding of the principles of RAMS, software-development methodologies, and the software release cycles is instrumental in making the game-development process run smoothly. It is true that games can be developed without the use of any such ideas, but their absence usually signals a working practice that is anarchic, messy, confusing, and expensive—and the games that result often reflect this working practice. The next chapter moves away from the realms of design, planning, and concepts, and into the world of implementation. It begins this exploration with programming and coding.

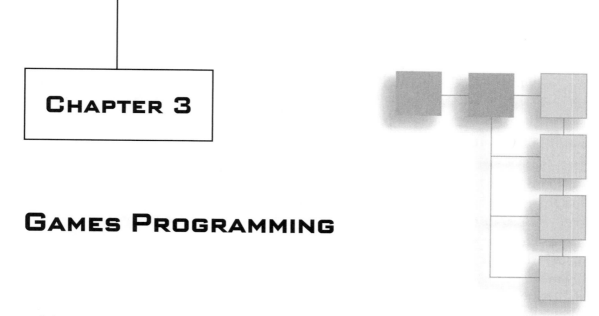

CHAPTER 3

GAMES PROGRAMMING

"There are two ways of constructing a software design: One way is to make it so simple that there are obviously no deficiencies, and the other way is to make it so complicated that there are no obvious deficiencies. The first method is far more difficult."

—C. A. R. Hoare

By the end of this chapter you should:

- Understand the role of programming in video games.

- Appreciate the distinctions between coding, scripting, and visual scripting.

- Be aware of some of the most common game-programming languages.

- Appreciate the difference between declarative and imperative languages.

- Understand object orientation and the component-based design paradigm.

This chapter is the first of several in this book that focus on the work of implementation rather than design and planning. Its primary concern is not with design documents, work schedules, development methodologies, or release cycles. Rather, its concern is with the practical—the act of getting your hands dirty turning an idea into a working and functional game. Specifically, the subject of this chapter is games programming in the most general sense—that is, the activity in which team members (programmers) sit at a computer and use a language to define game logic to bring a game to life, make it go, and put it into motion.

An analysis of games programming and of the work and concepts involved with it should begin with a clear definition and understanding of what programming *is* as it relates to games. Although this might seem obvious or trivial to the game development student, there is an important sense in which the term "programming" and the activities this connotes have a narrow and specific meaning in video games— a meaning that is in some important respects different from other areas of software development, such as in website development or business databases.

GAMES PROGRAMMING IN DEPTH

Imagining a game with all its programming removed would be the simple exercise of imagining a folder on a hard drive filled with an unordered collection of assets, including images, sounds, movies, music, databases, and other text or binary documents. This, in essence, is what a game would look like in the absence of programming. There would be no application file to run or execute, no way in which the assets would be assembled or related together, and no means of creating any kind of interactivity to allow the gamer to do anything. Thus, the act of programming is the creative act of breathing life into those assets that would otherwise remain static, unrelated, and motionless. (See Figure 3.1.)

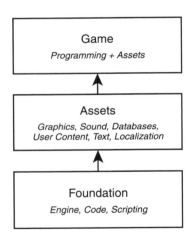

Figure 3.1
Game assets on a foundation of programming.
Source: *Alan Thorn*

When a gamer clicks the Save Game command in the main menu or presses a button on the gamepad to make a character run, jump, or punch, that gamer is relying on programming to work under the hood to ensure the game behaves as the developers intended. Thus, programming is largely about behavioral specification—about defining through a language how a video game is to act. This language is known as a *programming language*, and is a bridge between a human programmer and a computer. The role of the programmer is to write instructions in the appropriate language, and the role of the computer is to unthinkingly read and execute those instructions.

Note

Computers are often likened in popular conversation to a brain or a "thinking machine," but this analogy can be misleading in the field of programming. This is because in programming, it is the programmers who must do the thinking. It is they who must tell the computer how to think—if that term can be applied to computers at all.

Programmers have at their disposal a choice of languages that vary in both syntax and kind. They can vary in syntax in the same way that human languages vary from one another, and these variations you give names such as English, French, German, Spanish, and Chinese, among others. They can also vary in kind, or medium, much as an artist speaks in the language of shapes, colors, and lines; the musician speaks in the language of notes, pitches, and tones; and the author speaks in the language of words, sentences, and paragraphs. Of course, all these languages, despite their differences, are probably only the surface expression of a deeper system of thinking that is raw and prior to language itself.

In the world of games programming, there are three main kinds of programming languages:

- Coding
- Scripting
- Visual scripting

Within each of these kinds, there are differences in terms of syntax, which, as you will see, has resulted in a range of different languages that can be identified by name—some of which are more common than others in game development.

Coding

Coding is the first of three main kinds of programming that are commonly found in game development, and it is also the most raw or foundational of the three. For this reason, it is typically used to create game engines (refer to the section "The Engine" in Chapter 1, "Games and Game design"). The term "coding" is used here to refer more generally to compiled languages as opposed to interpreted or scripted languages. That is, coding involves programmers writing instructions in text form, using words and mathematical expressions, to control how the game behaves. A specialized piece of software, known as a compiler, will then convert those statements (code or source code) into an abbreviated form optimized for processing by the computer. (See Figure 3.2.) Once the code is compiled, the computer can then run and execute the statements at the fastest speed possible.

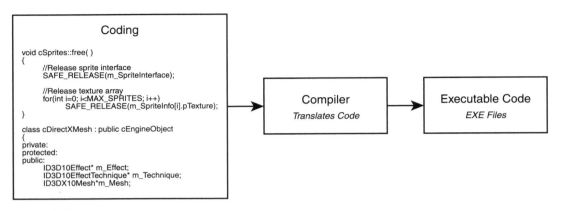

Figure 3.2
Code compiled into executable form.
Source: *Alan Thorn*

The chief advantage to programming via coding through a compiled language is performance. Compiled code typically produces the most optimal and efficient kind of code to run on a computer. Thus, game developers typically develop game engines and all other infrastructure in a compiled language, ensuring that the foundations of a game will be as optimized and efficient as possible. You might wonder, however, why—if coding is so optimized and efficient—it is not used exclusively throughout game development. The reasons for this are manifold, and include technical, logistical, and economic reasons, as you shall see.

Languages commonly associated with coding in game development include C++, Assembler, C#, Objective-C, and Java. Code in these languages is typically written using integrated development environment (IDE) software, such as Microsoft Visual Studio, Apple Xcode, or the Eclipse IDE.

Scripting

Coding, as you saw, refers generally to compiled languages. These are typically the languages of choice for programmers when developing the engine or infrastructure for a game due to speed and performance reasons. Specifically, these languages are used for the development of all the essential and architectural aspects of a game, including the following:

- **A renderer.** This is the part responsible for drawing graphics to the screen.
- **A sound framework.** This part is responsible for ensuring that sound can be played to the speakers.
- **An error-handling system.** This ensures that game errors, if they occur, are logged and printed to human-readable text files.

These are but three of potentially many features incorporated into a game engine using a compiled language, in line with the engine's abstract and general nature. But beyond these fundamentals expected of almost all games, there still remains much of the game-specific logic to be created—that is, the logic for this or that game, which rests on the foundation of the engine. Such logic for a game might include the following:

- The intelligence for specific enemy characters
- The specific win and loss conditions for the game
- The special moves and weapons that can be collected and the specific terms under which they can be used

In short, it refers to all logic associated with the game rules as opposed to the general engine code that makes the game possible in the first place. (Refer to the section "The Rules" in Chapter 1.) This logic is typically defined through scripting rather than coding.

Scripting is in many respects akin to writing a macro in Microsoft Word or a formula in Microsoft Excel, and it offers game developers the same kind of advantages. Whereas Word and Excel themselves were written in a compiled language by their developers during development, the macro, in contrast, is written much later by a user of those programs. The macro depends upon the programs as a foundation and it exists or lives within them. It needs them as a lifeline. But to create and run that macro, the user need not have any working knowledge of how the programs themselves were made. Those programs are shut to the inquiring eye (closed source), but this does not prevent you from creating macros (scripts) that can control those programs. (See Figure 3.3.) Thus, it is possible for a developer to create these programs and still enable others to customize them without disclosing the original source code or placing unnecessary technical demands on the user.

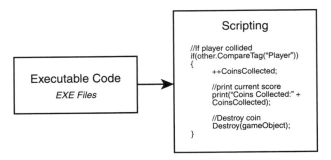

```
Scripting

//If player collided
if(other.CompareTag("Player"))
{
        ++CoinsCollected;

        //print current score
        print("Coins Collected:" +
        CoinsCollected);

        //Destroy coin
        Destroy(gameObject);
}
```

Executable Code

EXE Files

Figure 3.3
Scripted code run on top of compiled, executable code.
Source: *Alan Thorn*

Scripting games, like coding games and writing macros, involves writing instructions in a text-based form, using mathematical expressions, and in languages that are perhaps no different from those used in coding. The crucial difference between coded and scripted instructions rests on how the computer understands and processes those instructions after they are written. Compiled code is subject to further non-reversible optimization and abbreviation processes that require both time (compilation time) and knowledge to improve the performance of the code. In contrast, scripted code is in many senses left as is and is executed directly by the computer without further compilation or enhancements, just as an Excel macro or a Word macro can be run immediately after writing. The upshot of all this is that scripting can offer developers just as much flexibility as coding in terms of its power to bring about change and flexibility, but scripting comes with a performance penalty mainly because its code is left without specific optimizations. That means scripted code is typically slower than compiled code when executed in terms of time and processing cycles to achieve its end.

Scripting, however, offers unique advantages for creating game-specific logic over compiled code. First, as has been hinted, it enables non-engine developers on the team to code game-specific logic in a way that connects with and controls the engine but does not require the developer to have a working knowledge of the engine implementation itself. That means game-logic programmers need not be the same programmers who created the engine code. Rather, the programming work can be divided and separated among multiple people. This is useful for many reasons, one of which is that it makes it possible for third-party developers, such as Unity Technologies or Epic Games, to develop and market a closed-source game engine to other developers as a product in itself, known as a middleware product (or just middleware). Developers can then purchase this product and go on to make their own games based on the engine, and these games can be controlled and customized through scripting. The second reason in favor of scripting relates to convenience. Specifically, scripting is convenient because developers can make changes to game logic through changes to the script. They need not wait before testing for lengthy periods during which the script would be compiled and optimized. Rather, game logic can be scripted and tested in quick succession.

Common scripting languages used in game development include C#, JavaScript, Lua, Python, and Ruby.

Visual Scripting

Coding is a form of programming in which compiled languages are used to build an engine infrastructure for the game. Scripting, in contrast, is a higher-level form of programming in which code is written as a macro separately from the engine and is used to define the logic or specific rules for the game. Visual scripting is an increasingly popular form of programming that is seen by many as an attempt to simplify the process of programming or to make it accessible to people who are not programmers. Like scripting, visual scripting is used to define game logic. In some cases, it is used to complement standard scripting; in other cases, it is used to replace it almost entirely.

Visual scripting differs from both coding and scripting in that it does not require the programmer to write instructions into a text editor in the form of words, statements, or mathematical expressions. The script is not written line by line, statement by statement, or word by word. Rather, it is constructed visually, or diagrammatically, in a drag-and-drop editor. Visual scripting editors often look like diagram-creation tools in which the programmer assembles a macro or script by adding, connecting, and arranging blocks or modules in a diagram. The intention is to build a program that can be visualized by wiring modules together as appropriate to ensure the program flows as intended.

A number of prominent game engines feature or support visual scripting editors, including the CryEngine, the Unreal Engine (see Figure 3.4), the Unity engine, and other engines such as Construct2 and Stencyl. The use of scripting over visual scripting (or vice versa) remains in large part a matter of developer preference as well as context sensitivity.

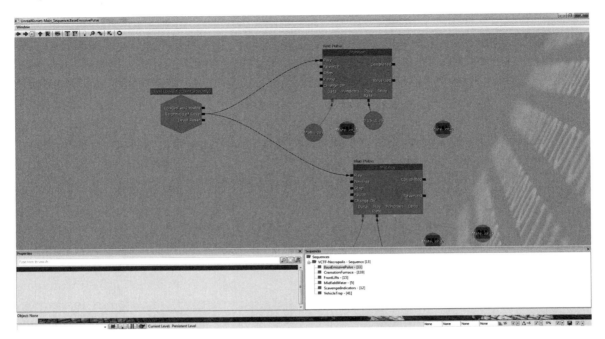

Figure 3.4
Visual scripting as featured in Unreal Development Kit (UDK) by Epic Games.
Source: *Epic Games*

GAME DEVELOPMENT WITH OR WITHOUT ENGINES?

Both Chapter 1 and previous sections of this chapter make explicit mention of the game engine as a distinct and constituent ingredient in the anatomy of a game. Together, they have emphasized and re-emphasized the genuine and important distinction between the abstract game engine on the one hand and the specific game itself on the other. The former is the abstract bedrock on which the latter is founded. The latter cannot exist without the former, but a game as we know it would not be possible without both. Thus, for a game developer beginning work on a new game, one of the first questions that arises when considering the technology to be used for development is not so much whether an engine is to be used at all, but how an engine is to be provided. How should the foundation of the game be settled?

Two main options are open for a developer in the contemporary industry regarding this matter. The first is to develop one's own custom engine in-house using a compiled language (a DIY engine); the second is to use a pre-made third-party engine—either commercial or open-source—such as C4, Unity, Unreal, etc. There are reasons for and against each choice, and which reasons are the stronger will change depending on the developer and their projects.

Note

See the appendix for a list of third-party engine and tools.

Some common reasons for and against a DIY engine are as follows:

- **Marketability.** A newly created and tailor-made engine is useful not only in-house for internal development and games, but also as a potential new product in itself for other developers. An engine can be sold as a game-development tool—a product that will have appeal to other developers interested in making games.

- **Flexibility.** Developers might be creating new and experimental games with specific and perhaps uncommon features and requirements that are not well supported by engines currently available on the market. In these cases, developers might have no alternative but to opt for developing an in-house engine.

- **Licensing.** End-user licenses to pre-made engines are typically sold to game developers much like other software is sold to companies: on a per-seat basis. This frequently means that a separate copy of the engine must be purchased for each and every workstation on which it will be installed. Some developers have found that DIY engines can in some cases be the more economical option.

- **Platform support.** Game engines support a range of platforms, including PC, Mac, console, mobile, and more. Developers often have one or more target platforms in mind when developing a game. Often, there can be a mismatch between the platforms supported by an engine and the platforms a developer is aiming to reach. This mismatch can lead a developer to favor the DIY engine route to ensure his or her game supports the full range of target platforms.

Some common reasons for and against a third-party engine are as follows:

- **Development speed.** Use of an existing engine typically saves developers time and resources over developing a DIY, which must be produced before a game can even be created. With a pre-made third-party engine, developers can dive immediately into game development and focus on game content rather than on underlying mechanics.

- **Stability.** Well-established and pre-made engines that are the work of many developers over many years often have large communities of users continually working with the software and putting it to the test in their daily lives. This often leads to bugs being caught and being repaired soon after. This can lend pre-made engines a stability and tried-and-tested edge.

- **Accessibility.** Small teams of perhaps one or two members do not typically find it economical or feasible in the long term to develop custom-made engines due to expense, time, and budget. Pre-made engines offer smaller teams a quicker and more accessible route toward developing saleable games.

- **Documentation and support.** Most engines ship with documentation and supporting help files explaining the use of the software as a game-development tool, which is often not a luxury for those pursuing the DIY route—at least not in as convenient a form. Further, well-established tools often feature unofficial documentation in the form of books, video training, and seminars. This can make the road to successful game development smoother, cheaper, and easier.

Note

For a more in-depth guide on how to create a DIY game engine, readers are recommended to consult another of my books, *Game Engine Design and Implementation* (Jones & Bartlett, ISBN: 978-0763784515).

Note

See the appendix for more information on programming languages available for game development, as well as other related tools.

Programming Paradigms in Game Development

Game developers can and do make a range of decisions regarding whether to use an existing engine or a custom-made engine. But regardless of these decisions, and regardless of whether a developer uses compiled languages, scripted languages, or visual scripting, they must still tackle the imposing problems that face game programmers generally when they go about making games. In short, the aim of the programmer when creating a game is to create a virtual world. The task of doing this can be broken into three main stages:

- Defining everything that exists or will exist in the game world

- Establishing a flow of time in that world

- Defining how everything that exists changes over time

This section focuses on the first of these three problems. Specifically, this is the problem of *referring*.

Game programming is primarily the activity of controlling how games behave by way of a programming language. Specifically, programming is a way of controlling how events, objects, people, and things inside the game operate and work together. Programming, for example, is used to control when day turns into night; when characters move, talk, and react; how doors open and close; how guns fire; and how cars explode. These are but a few of the situations that make up the whens, hows, wheres, and whys that fall within the remit of programming.

The programming language is the means by which the instructions are written, and the limits of the language determine the limits of what it is possible to do. Thus, for a programmer to have extensive control over the objects in a game using his or her language of choice, it is necessary for that language to offer some means of making the game world comprehensible—a linguistic means of understanding, identifying, defining, and describing objects within the game. Instructions on how to perform operations on things can be intelligible only to those who understand enough about what things exist and what operations are possible with those things. For example, in an everyday situation, you can ask a human friend (assuming he speaks the same language as you) to close the door, and you can reasonably expect that person to know what a door is, which particular door you want him to close, and also what the act of closing involves. Your friend who heard your request is able to understand it because he understands in the abstract what a door is and what closing involves, and in consequence he can identify particular doors whenever he sees them and can engage in particular acts of closing doors whenever he is inclined to do so. The computer, however, has none of these kinds of commonsensical intuitions, and you can rely on it for nothing in these matters. Thus, a programming language, if it is to be useful to a games programmer, must give some means of referring to objects and concepts in the world—to single out ideas and objects as being the ones in question and as being the subjects of your discourse.

It would, for example, be no good for a programmer to try coding a situation in which the player attacks an enemy if there were no means available in the language for stating clearly who the player was, who the enemy was, or what an attack is. This is because the computer itself has no intuition, and thus it has no intuitive sense of what any of these commonsensical ideas are when the programmer attempts to make reference to them. It does not know what the player is, who the enemy is, or what an attack is unless it is explicitly told. The computer needs more formal, concrete, and explicit definitions to be given for not only these three concepts, but for all concepts that are to be found throughout the game. It demands that you have a systematic and precise linguistic means of breaking down reality conceptually to say what exists. It demands that you have ontology—a way of dividing up and cataloguing the world.

The most common means of doing this in programming—of stating what exists—are known as programming paradigms. The two most common in game development include object orientation and the component-based design paradigm. These paradigms are not unique or specific to computing or computer programming. Indeed, in essence or theory, neither of them belongs to computing at all. Both paradigms make their first literary appearance in the philosophy of the ancient Greeks, such as in Plato's *Republic*. But they have since been adapted and applied to computing, where they have proven inestimably useful, regardless of their ancient origins.

Object Orientation

Object orientation (OO) is a technical term in programming for what is essentially a commonsensical view that most people have about the world—a view that can be traced back as far as the philosopher Plato (known as his "forms"). This view holds that the world is in total a collection of discrete and clearly identifiable objects, each separate from the other—one chair, another chair, a table, one car, another car, one person, another person, and so on, throughout all the potentially limitless number of things that exist. On reflecting on all of these particular objects, one can identify abstract groups or classes of objects—templates to which all similar objects belong. You can see, for example, that all the particular table objects (*this* table and *that* table) have enough of something in common (an essence) that make them all tables despite their differences—something common in them that enables you to imagine a more general idea or form of the table. You think of the table as an idea or a class, and of particular tables as being concrete instances or objects of that class.

In coming to see the world in terms of classes and instances, it is possible to refine the concept of a class in more detail based on the real and tangible differences observed in the instances. Consider the example of the table. A table can be defined further based on differences between real tables. Tables differ in color, size, weight, material, and number of legs, as well as other features. These dimensions of difference are named "properties," with each dimension being a separate property of the class. (The class that can have one or more properties.) Tables differ too in their function. Some are used as a writing desk, some as a make-shift dance floor, some as a weapon, and some as an ornament. These functions or uses of a table might be described as its methods, each use being a separate method of the class. (The class can have one or more methods.)

In sum, this way of seeing the world in terms of classes, instances, properties, and methods is object orientation. It is a method for breaking down and describing all that exists, as well as all that could exist (fiction), using a systematic and consistent terminology. This system, when applied to programming languages, is what enables programmers to create, describe, and control game worlds. Common game classes include the Player, the Enemy, the Health, and the Door, among others. These classes are the unseen and abstract templates for the concrete instances that do exist and that are experienced in the game by the player: a player, one or more enemies, a health bar for both player and enemies, and several doors. Notice too that these classes have properties. For example, the player has a name, an appearance, and a mathematical position in the level. See Figure 3.5 for an example.

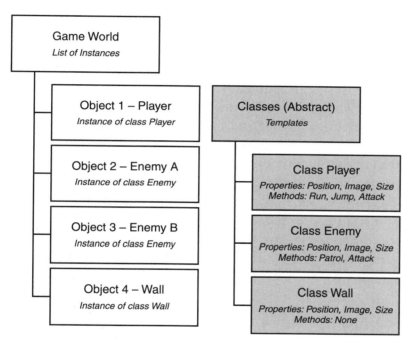

Figure 3.5
Object orientation.
Source: *Alan Thorn*

Going Further with Object Orientation

The paradigm of object orientation as stated so far sees the world as being divided into classes, objects, properties, and methods. These concepts, when used together to talk about the world, the game world, or potential worlds, construct each and every thing that exists as an instance of a class with specific properties and methods. However, this model leaves out an important ingredient that many people do perceive about objects in the world: their relationships to one another. The world is not typically seen as just a space in which objects can be itemized one by one without regard to their relationships, as ingredients might be on a personal shopping list.

Rather, objects are seen as being related to each other in subtle but important ways: a child is typically seen as having a parent, a book is often seen as coming from an author, and a ship or boat is often seen as resting on top of the water. Each of the previous statements refers to multiple objects and, although each exists independently in many respects, there are nonetheless genuine relationships to be found between objects. In response to this, the object-orientation model can be refined further to account for such relationships using the concepts of inheritance, super-class, and sub-class.

To illustrate these concepts in action in game development, consider the case of a game-development company planning to release a new side-scrolling action game for the Android and iPad tablets. This game uses object orientation in its programming. The first level of the game features a land of weak and easily defeated enemies. Specifically, these enemies are mutant frogs, all an instance of the more general class Mutant Frog. The second level features tougher and nastier mutant frogs that breathe fire known as fire frogs, all of which are instances of the class Fire Frog. These frogs, while fire-breathing and more resilient to attacks, do nonetheless share many properties found in the standard frog class—so many, in fact, that the two species of frog are clearly related. They share properties such as size, speed, intelligence, and color, among others. The programmer who sets out to use object orientation in his or her language of choice can create these frogs using the RAMS principle of recycling in at least one of two ways: one that does not use inheritance, and one that does. (See the section "Creating a Plan with RAMS" in Chapter 2, "Game Software Development" for more information.)

In the first method, the programmer could write two separate classes—one for each frog type—and then use these classes as the foundation for creating (instantiating) specific instances of the frogs throughout the levels of the game according to their type. Here, each class uses a specialized syntax to define all the properties and methods to be found in its specific frog type. And because both frog classes share many of the same properties, each frog class will therefore have many duplicate properties. The more there are identical properties among the frog objects, the more work that is duplicated in creating the classes.

In contrast, the second method, which uses the concept of inheritance and recycling, aims to remove the duplication. Like the first method, it starts by defining two classes—one for each frog—but with a subtle difference. The second class, Fire Frog, is defined using a special syntax as a derivative or a sub-class of the Mutant Frog class. The Mutant Frog class becomes known as the parent class or the super-class, and the Fire Frog class is said to inherit from the Mutant Frog class. That means the Fire Frog class specifies only the points of difference between the two classes. Fire

Frog is understood as inheriting all the properties from its parent Mutant Frog class, plus being able to extend and refine those properties. Fire Frog can go on to refine existing properties, such as increasing health, and can also add additional methods, such as fire-breathing ability, while still retaining all the properties and methods of the original Mutant Frog class. In this shorthand way, developers can derive or build completely new classes as derivatives from others. Figure 3.6 offers a different example of inheritance in action.

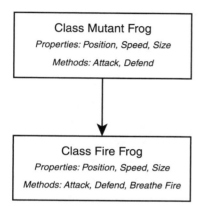

Figure 3.6
Inheritance of objects.
Source: *Alan Thorn*

Note

The exact syntax and linguistic devices for deriving classes from one another like this differs between programming languages.

Component-Based Design Paradigm

It has been mentioned already that the primary aim of software-development paradigms, whether object-oriented or component-based, is to conceive of the world—and more importantly of virtual worlds—in an easy and systematic way that can be expressed using a programming language. This is important for programmers because it affects their ability to refer to, specify, describe, and quantify phenomena in the game world using their language. Object orientation is one proposed solution for cataloguing and describing such entities—describing them in terms of classes, objects, properties, and methods, and relating them using the concept of inheritance. The component-based design (CBD) paradigm, which also traces its roots to ancient Greece (although not specifically to Plato), is another way of seeing the world and its diversity. It dispenses largely with the classic ideas of classes, properties, methods, and inheritance. Consequently, it is a solution that some see as antagonistic to object orientation (although others have come to see it more as complementary).

The component-based design paradigm encourages you to think of the world not in terms of tangible objects or structures that exist statically and concretely, such as cars, people, buildings, and trees, among others. Rather, it encourages you to see all of these things as the fleeting and changeable results that arise from energetic and lower-level functions—that is, from actions, processes, or states of doing. It conceives of entities as the product of a network of independent and functional components that are all wired together to produce something that you recognize as a working whole.

A Hogwarts archmage, for example, is what he is because that is the effect that his components produce when working together effectively. He, as a complete entity, has several working components. First among them is a physical body component, common to all humans: He has arms, legs, a torso, and a head. He has an intelligence component too, common to *almost* all humans: He is conscious and can think and reason. Further, he has a more specialized and unique spell-casting component: that thing within him that enables him to cast magical spells. This latter arcane and powerful component, when wired together with his other components, produces the celebrated and feared archmage that he is—a spell-caster extraordinaire. This archmage has just been defined in terms of the component-based design paradigm.

The component-based design paradigm is especially convenient for describing change that occurs in the world. There will come a day, for example, when the celebrated archmage will cease to be the spell caster that he is—he will lose his power or ability to cast spells. On that sad date and at that time, he can be said to have lost his spell-casting component. That component will have been removed or disconnected from his component network. Let's go on to speculate also that in even later years, this unfortunate archmage will lose both his mind and sanity; he will become unable to string together any kind of intelligent conversation. In this case, he will then have lost his intelligence component. In the end, there will come a time when he dies; on that date, all of his components will have detached themselves from the network, leaving you with a nothing or a non-network. The dissolution of the component network marks the point of death for the thing that resulted from the network. It marks the starting point of nothing, for a nothing it must be since everything that exists is defined in terms of components. In the component-based design paradigm, there can be no such thing as a component-less entity. See Figure 3.7 for a representation of the component-based design paradigm.

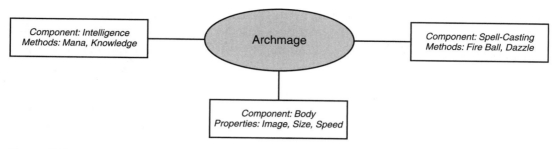

Figure 3.7
Objects made from components.
Source: *Alan Thorn*

OO Versus CBD

The previous three sections introduced object orientation (OO) and component-based design (CBD), each a different and influential method for perceiving the world and, in particular, video-game worlds. The focus of this section is on the some-times perceived antagonism between the two paradigms in game development. Its aim is to demonstrate how this perception is frequently mistaken and to help you make practical decisions about how to code your own game in a way that makes use of both paradigms. First, however, it is necessary to see the problem that is sup-posed to exist.

It is sometimes contended that the two paradigms are logically incompatible and mutually exclusive—that it is not possible to see game worlds, or any world, in terms of objects and components at the same time without contradiction. Either enti-ties are seen as objects with properties and methods or they are seen as arising from a component network, but they cannot be both. Those who maintain this view often see the component-based design paradigm as a replacement for object orientation in game development. Here, CBD is seen as a solution to the developmental problems that commonly arise from OO in video games. These problems relate mainly to the static and unchanging nature of class structure in OO.

The video-game world, much like the real world, is in a constant state of flux. Some changes relate to the properties and methods of objects, such as when players change their position or when a table is painted a different a color. These changes are easily accommodated by OO, which recognizes these dimensions of difference and change in the form of properties. Here, bringing about this kind of change demands only that you assign the same properties different values—new positions and new colors, etc. (Position = X, Color = Y). However, some changes also relate to the objects themselves. People develop new abilities and skills, vehicles undergo repairs and adaptations, and magical creatures transform themselves into entirely different beings with different properties and different methods. In short, objects are often in a state of becoming entirely new things—something that they were not. They become completely new kinds of classes, and do not simply remain the same class whose properties and states just happen to be set to new values. Here, it is not the values of properties that change, but the properties themselves. This tends to break or stress a rigid and static class structure such as is found in OO, where properties and methods are defined in advance.

Note

Some have attempted to solve this class-changing problem within an OO framework by using the concept of inheritance. (Refer to the section "Going Further with Object Orientation" earlier in this chapter.) Using this idea, for example, a Wizard class can change into a Dragon class because a programmer has derived a new and hybrid class (sub-class) that inherits the properties and methods from both the Wizard and Dragon classes. This process of multiple inheritance makes a new DragonWizard class that has all the features of both of its parents. However, this solution is often seen as inelegant in comparison to the solution proposed by the component-based design paradigm. The reasons for this are not detailed at length here. Those interested more deeply in this subject can consider the range of blogs and articles online that address the issues of object-oriented versus component-oriented design, as well as the books *Programming .Net Components* by Juval Lowy (ISBN: 978-0596102074) and *Component-Based Software Engineering: Putting the Pieces Together* by George T. Heineman and William T. Councill (ISBN: 978-0768682076).

The component-based design paradigm offers an attractive and intuitive solution to the rigidity of object orientation—one that seems to follow easily and has an immediate appeal. Any radical and constitutional change in a game object equates simply to a change in the kinds of components that are attached to the component network—to the totality of components that come together to make the object what it is. A wizard, for example, becomes a dragon not through a complex chain of class inheritance but through an adjustment in the connectivity of components—these free floating modules that can come together and move apart. The Wizard object simply loses its wizard-relevant components (torso and spell-casting powers) and instead becomes a dragon, with a dragon body component as well as a fire-breathing component, and perhaps others as relevant to the Dragon object. Changes in component constitution in essence represent a change in being—a change in what the thing *is*.

Consequently, the features of component-based design recommend it strongly and suggest that it has an important and useful role to play in games programming, especially in games where objects and entities frequently change or must allow for possible changes. But none of this appeal means that CBD must be chosen for game development at the cost of giving up on object-oriented thinking entirely. The question still remains as to what a component is in the first place as a basic unit. It is tempting to see it in object-oriented terms: as a class or module with its own properties and methods. Similarly, it is tempting to see a component as a class that can come together with other like components into a network of components that form higher-level entities that one recognizes as more complex objects such as people, cars, warriors, enemies, buildings, and others. Consequently, it is frequently the case in contemporary game development that both object orientation and component-based design will be used together in this sense: Object orientation will be used at the engine level to build a foundation of fundamental classes or objects that together make the existence of components possible. This framework is used first and foremost to create an environment that allows components to exist. But once components are thus defined, the CBD is typically used over OO to construct and define all the remaining objects and elements that exist within a game due to the paradigm's power for accommodating variation and change across time.

TIME, EVENTS, AND ACTIONS

Object orientation and the component-based design paradigm are both independent and unique linguistic methods for defining and stating systematically what exists within a game world, whether those things are visible to the gamer or not. It has further been shown how well each of these paradigms is suited for expressing and understanding changes to objects across time. That being said, neither method explicitly relies on any conception of time, meaning that it is possible to use OO or CBD to define what exists without referring to time at all. It is possible, for example, to pause a game or to take a snapshot or freeze-frame of a game at any particular moment in time and to define everything that exists in that moment using either OO or the CBE paradigms without ever talking about change. Both of them allow you to talk about the here and now in terms of the player, the enemies, the levels, and the obstacles, but neither paradigm demands that you talk about how those objects change or have changed over time. It might be easier to talk about change, should you choose to do so, in terms of the CBD rather than in terms of OO. Nonetheless, both paradigms are intrinsically silent on the issue of time and are useful primarily for stating what any object is at any moment in time, whichever moment you happen to pick. For object orientation, the status of any object at any moment can be given in terms of properties and methods. For component-based design, this is given in terms of components.

However, time is nonetheless recognized and perceived by gamers as an important factor in the game. It is a factor for bringing about change. It makes the gamer aware of time limits, races against the clock, and all the ways in which objects move, rotate, change, morph, and act as animate and active forces. For this reason, it is necessary for game developers to establish an understanding or a means of thinking about time in addition to the means that are already available for talking about states of objects at particular times, as you can with CBD and OO. Further, it is necessary to develop a means for thinking about events, which are related to time. These two concepts—time and events—are now considered in more detail.

Time

Time is a crucially important factor in video games, primarily for the changes it can bring about to ordinary game objects in terms of their properties or their component structure. Changes in the states of objects that occur over time are known collectively as "animation"; without a conception of time, no animation would be possible. To emphasize the importance of time, consider the following scenarios, each of which depends more subtly on time than the example before:

■ A game in which an explosive detonates after 60 seconds

■ A game that features day and night cycles

■ A game in which a car travels along the road at a specified speed

All three of these examples depend on a conception of time. The first most obviously depends on a conception of time because it initiates an explosion event after a specified and finite period of time has elapsed. The second depends on a conception of time because it assumes that time can be measured to know when day must transform into night and then back again on a cycle. The third depends on a conception of time because it requires that time be a factor for calculating the speed at which a car must travel along a specified distance. These three isolated examples, chosen almost at random, hint at the pervasive and critical role that time typically plays in video games. Consequently, it is generally a matter of priority for a developer when coding a video game to establish some means, programmatically, of representing time as well as the elapsing of time in both a consistent and systematic way.

Representing time in a systematic way involves putting a number on time so that meaningful comparisons and arithmetical operations can be performed from the numbers. Its aim is to enable the developer to calculate with precision at any moment the current time in the game, how much time has elapsed since any earlier time including the beginning of game time, and the difference in time between any two start and end times that might be chosen. Together, these abilities enable the developer to orientate and anchor events within a clearly established framework of time that begins from the moment the game starts running. Further, representing time in a consistent way involves establishing a basic unit of measure that applies to time when represented numerically so that all measurements of time are commeasurable— that is, can be compared directly without a conversion of units. Establishing a unit of measure that can describe time ensures that measurements are authoritative across systems and platforms. This will be a crucial factor in guaranteeing that all gamers on all systems will enjoy the same experience and timing of events. To achieve this consistency, time is usually measured in seconds or milliseconds, and not frames. See the sidebar to discover why.

Measuring Time

It is not enough to apply any kind of number to time or to use any kind of unit of measure. That's because there are some numbers and units that could be chosen that would not be appropriate for games, primarily because they lack authority. That is, they lack the power to ensure that all gamers enjoy a consistent experience—an experience such that events and actions in the game all occur at the same times and speeds for all gamers on all systems.

Consider the case of a game studio that develops a retro-style arcade game, *Rail Chase*, for the PC and Mac desktop platforms. In this game, the player is seated inside a runaway mine cart, similar to that featured in the movie *Indiana Jones and the Temple of Doom*. The player has no control over the direction of the cart itself because it simply moves along a predetermined track at a constant speed from its beginning to its end. The objective of the player is to use the mouse to aim a crosshair and shoot at approaching enemies from the discomfort of their moving mine cart until either the mine cart reaches its destination or the player is destroyed by the attacking enemies.

Representing time is critical in such a game for many reasons, one of which is to ensure that the mine cart journey starts and ends at a specified and predictable time from which the timing of all other game events can be based. Further, it is important to be certain that the unit of time to be used will ensure that time and events will be calculated to happen in the game in the same order at the same moments, for all gamers across all systems.

The developer is faced with at least two main and immediate options for representing time mathematically in this case. One option is to represent time in terms of frames. (The term "frames" here refers to a slide or image of motion that is part of a larger and linear sequence of frames played in order at a specified rate, as in a movie.) The other option is to represent time in terms of the number of seconds that have elapsed since the game began. It might seem at first glance that both options are equally suited to the task of measuring time—that it makes no practical difference which option—frames or seconds—is chosen as a unit. The programmer who chooses frame-based time might reason that if the game were to last a total of 30,000 frames, then an event (such as an enemy attack) could be scheduled to occur during the middle of gameplay by being timed for frame 15,000, because 15,000 is half of 30,000. That programmer might go on to reason that it would make no difference if he had chosen seconds as a unit because, if the same game were known to last a total of one minute, the equivalent central event would be at 30 seconds because that is half of one minute. In either case, the timing for the central event has been pinpointed with accuracy.

The frame-based solution, however, wrongly assumes that the frame rate of the game (the number of frames per second) is consistent and guaranteed across all systems, and further that it remains constant for every second even on the same system. In short, frame rates differ not only from system to system but from second to second on the same system due to variations and fluctuations in hardware and software performance. For a game whose time is based on frames, this means that a 30,000-frame game played on a high-performance PC would come to an end twice as quickly as it would on a different PC capable of only half the performance, everything else being equal. The result would be that different gamers on different systems would receive very different experiences from the same game, even if all players began playing at exactly the same time.

Measuring time in terms of seconds or milliseconds from the system clock, however, overcomes this hardware dependency because a second is an absolute rather than a relative measure. A second remains a second across all systems, for all people and at all times. Consequently, most game developers measure time in terms of seconds or fractions of a second, as counted from the instant at which the game began.

Note

In addition to the measurement of time, as discussed, developers can also code their engines within reasonable limits to have fine control over the FPS, at least in cases where the FPS is higher than desired. This is often achieved by dropping frames—that is, by counting the number of frames for each second and then ignoring any excess frames above the target FPS, waiting until the next second before processing the next frame.

Events and Actions

From the perspective of the programmer as well as that of the gamer, a video can be conceptualized as a virtual world or a virtual reality—a world in which there exists all kinds of entities and things inside the game. Statements written in a programming language, therefore, are essentially statements about a virtual world. The entities and things within that world can be referred to linguistically using either object orientation or the component-based design paradigm. Time also is a dimension of the virtual world and can be referred to mathematically using the unit of seconds or milliseconds. These two primary concepts, objects and time, can and do describe much that exists within a virtual world, but still an important ingredient is missing from the analysis. Specifically, we also recognize that objects in the world do not simply exist motionlessly or unchangeably within the stream of time as it unravels second by second.

The states of objects vary with time—and not just in any way or at any time, either. There exist specific relationships between time and the objects of the world such that objects change in specific ways and at specific times.

The player character, for example, moves in a specified direction and at a specified speed, and always in response to the player's input. That is, the player character moves whenever the player instructs it to do so by pressing, say, a directional arrow button on the keyboard. Similarly, enemies in the level do not remain motionless as the player approaches or collides with them. Rather, they respond—and usually with hostility as they seek to attack or defend themselves from the player. Thus, the enemies attack or defend whenever a condition arises that demands that they do so.

These kinds of relationships between time and objects, which bring about specific changes to objects at specific times, can all be found to have a common structure or form. This form is their essence—that which makes them what they are. It can be stated generally as follows: When X happens, then do Y. The first part of that statement (When X happens) is referred to as an "event." The second part of the statement (then do Y) is referred to as an "action." The event is a notification or moment in time that is raised when an important circumstance arises in the game world—for example, when the player presses the spacebar to fire a weapon, when an object collides with a wall, or when a specified time has elapsed. The action is invoked as a response to the event when it occurs to bring about a relevant and specified change in the game world at that time—for example, making the player character jump, the bomb explode, or the wall collapse.

This area of programming, concerned as it is with events and actions, is sometimes referred to as "event-driven programming." Its chief aim is to make things happen in the world. It is therefore the primary method used for coding or scripting the gameplay of a game—all the things that make the game tick over. Event-driven programming as applied to games, therefore is essentially the task of identifying not just *this* or *that* event and action, but all possible actions for all possible events, whether or not those events will actually happen in the game due to choices made by the player. The task of the programmer when implementing events and actions is to script all actions for all events such that the game will always have an appropriate response to all the events that could possibly happen. The task of doing this successfully and optimally can range from the simple to the complex based on the number and nature of events and actions in the game.

ERRORS, TESTING, AND DEBUGGING

The task of programming or coding games consists largely of three main stages:

- First, the programmer must define all the things that exist in the virtual world.

- Second, the programmer must establish a consistent system of time.

- Third, the programmer must implement a set of rules or relationships between objects and time that determine the time and circumstances under which specific objects can undergo specified changes.

Realizing these three stages successfully is the task of the programmer, who must go about performing it using a language and the rules of logic as his or her only tools. In performing that work, however, a programmer—being human and fallible—will typically make mistakes. These mistakes (when they occur) can be one of two main kinds:

- **Syntactical.** The syntactical mistake occurs when the programmer makes typographical errors or Freudian slips, or gets confused about proper grammar such that the instructions he or she writes in the programming language are not ultimately valid. They do not evaluate to statements that are meaningful to the computer. These kinds of mistakes are equivalent to spelling mistakes, grammatical mistakes, missing words, and jumbled up sentences. They are critical in the sense that they prohibit the programmer from completing work on the game until they are corrected. This is because the source code for the game will never ultimately make sense or be meaningful to the computer as long as it contains syntactical errors, for these errors essentially confuse meaning. Thankfully, however, the computer can always detect and alert programmers of syntactical errors when they occur so programmers can correct them.

- **Logical.** Logical errors are more nefarious than syntactical ones. These errors occur when a programmer makes a syntactically correct statement but commits an error of reasoning or logic due to an oversight. Such statements are equivalent to everyday conversations in which people use correct language to unwittingly express opinions that are factually wrong or logically impossible. They do not make a grammatical or superficial error. Rather, the error rests in the content of what is being said, and the person expressing the view is unable to see the error unless something or someone makes it clear to them. If undetected in a video game, a logical error can lead to bugs, which are essentially undetected and uncorrected logical errors. Logical errors, unlike syntactical errors, can find their way into the final game that is shipped to end-users (gamers).

Note

A famous and amusing bug in modern video games is the so-called "bucket bug" or "bucket trick" found in the RPG game *Skyrim*, demonstrations of which can be seen at YouTube. Here, due possibly to an oversight by the developers, a gamer can pick up a bucket or other container, put it on top of a shopkeeper's head, and proceed to steal all the wares inside the shop without the shopkeeper detecting the theft because the bucket blocks his light of sight. It is hard to believe that such a characteristic was intentional on the part of the developers, in which case it is a bug, arising not from a syntactical error in the programming but from a logical mistake or oversight. The bug in this case does not cause the game to crash or freeze, but some bugs do—thus, some bugs can be more severe than others.

Due to the possibility of bugs existing in a game as a result of logical oversights, programmers typically perform a rigorous bug hunt during the testing phases and release cycle of development. This bug hunt is part of quality assurance and is known as "debugging." Its chief purpose is summarized aptly by the famous computer scientist Edsger W. Dijkstra, who said "Program testing can be used to show the presence of bugs, but never to show their absence." The aim of debugging, therefore, is to search for bugs and to identify their causes. On the basis of that information, the programmer can then proceed to resolve the problem. It is important, however, to keep in mind the limitations of debugging that are hinted at by Dijkstra: Debugging cannot be used to show the absence of bugs. To give an example, an exterminator searching a house for an infestation of wasps might, in fact, find no wasps at all. Even then, the exterminator is not in a position to claim there are no wasps in the house; there could still be wasps, only in a place she has not looked. The absence of evidence is not to be mistaken for evidence of absence. The process of debugging carries with it the same risk of missing out on some bugs. This explains why even some of the most famous and expensively made games contain bugs. It also explains why a programmer can never be in a position to claim that his or her software is bug free (unless "bug free" is understood in a relative rather than absolute sense, such as "free from error so far as our technologies, time, and budget have allowed us to be").

CONCLUSION

This chapter introduces the basic idea behind programming as the act of using a language to control behavior in a video game. It attempts to approach the subject of programming not from the perspective of a programming student starting out to learn a specific language, but from the perspective of a game developer in general considering the abstract principles related to programming. It presents the act of games programming as the act building a virtual world. This consists of three main stages: defining everything that exists or will exist in the world, establishing a stream of time, and creating a framework for events and actions that can change the status of objects across time. The chapter concludes with an examination of debugging as the process of bug-hunting—the search for errors in order to correct them. In total, the picture should emerge from this chapter that programming in the form of coding, scripting, and visual scripting is a foundational step in game development. The game cannot exist without some form of programming to act as an infrastructure or frame for all the remaining pieces. The assets, such as graphics and sounds, are also important, but together can be seen as a kind of dressing that hangs on the frame of programming. The next chapter explores programming further through the related field of mathematics as it pertains to games.

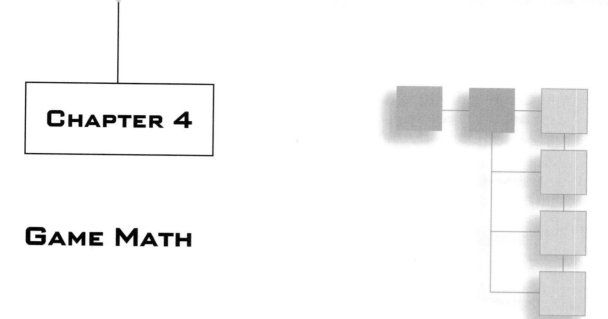

CHAPTER 4

GAME MATH

"The essence of mathematics is not to make simple things complicated, but to make complicated things simple."

—S. Gudder

By the end of this chapter you should:

- Understand the importance of mathematics and physics for game development.
- Understand 2D and 3D coordinate spaces.
- Have a basic understanding of translation, rotation, and scale.
- Understand transformation and other mathematical properties such as size and color.
- Be familiar with mathematical ideas, including vectors and matrices.

One can describe a video game as a virtual world. As demonstrated in the previous chapter, programming and its associated concepts are what make the creation of virtual worlds possible. The term *virtual world* is used loosely here to draw a distinction between the real world in which we exist on planet Earth as physical people and gamers, and the fictional world of a video game that exists digitally in the computer. This virtual world is home to the many characters, cities, objects, and stories that all gamers experience through their senses whenever they play video games.

The relevant differences between the real and fictional worlds that make them separate and distinct places are matters for philosophers and scientists, and are beyond the scope of this book (even though the differences might at first glance appear obvious). Regardless, it is not difficult to spot many of the similarities between the two worlds, including the following:

■ Both worlds are populated with distinct entities that exist in time and space, such as characters, weapons, vehicles, and nations. These entities have properties, including color, size, position, orientation, and others.

■ Both worlds feature relationships between entities. Those relationships are governed by generally identifiable and explicable rules or laws, including gravity, inertia, and causation (cause and effect).

In typical everyday settings, most people have no difficulty talking to one another about what goes on between entities in the real world—and even in virtual worlds—in a commonsense language. But a problem arises for game developers when they try to communicate these sorts of goings-on to the computer to make those things happen in the game world, even when the developer has a programming language available to facilitate the communication.

People often make general statements about the world in such terms as, "The apple is large and red," or "The car was traveling very fast in a northeasterly direction," or "The attacker assaulted the victim and then turned and ran away." These sorts of statements make sense to most human beings because we hear them in an interpretative framework of assumptions. That is, we do not simply hear the statements; we fit them into what we already know with a background of knowledge or common sense. We have a rough sense of what "very fast" means for a car as opposed to a missile or tortoise. People can visualize what "large" means when it is said about an apple, as opposed to a skyscraper or microscopic bacteria. This background of knowledge common to most of us is critical to the way in which we make sense of such commonsense statements that do not state their assumptions explicitly.

The computer, however, has no comparable background knowledge or database of assumptions that enables it to make sense of such general and commonsense statements. For the computer, such statements lack precision and clarity and are therefore meaningless. The upshot of this is that game developers cannot instruct the computer to make things happen in the game world with vague and commonsense statements, even though their ideas about what should happen might begin in those terms. To make things happen, the developer must resort instead to a rigorous, precise, and systematic method for describing how entities in the game world behave and appear. The method must be one that could, in theory, make sense to an alien beamed down to Earth with no previous knowledge of human languages or about how life on this planet is conducted or understood. This is why developers typically turn to the universal language of mathematics and, indirectly, to physics to quantify, measure, describe, and explain. In effect, game developers use mathematics to say to a computer what they can say to each other in commonsense terms over a cup of coffee.

THE LANGUAGE OF NUMBERS

The commonsense statements given in the previous section, as well as almost all similar statements, rely on a range of more fundamental and critical concepts that are amenable to mathematical description. These include the following (among others):

- Position
- Size
- Scale
- Color
- Orientation
- Rotation
- Direction
- Speed

For example, the apple has a color and a size; the car changed its position on the road as it traveled in a specified direction at a certain speed; the attacker turned away and changed his orientation from the victim.

One of the main roles of the game programmer is to translate these commonsense statements into a mathematically precise form in terms of these fundamental concepts. These concepts and the methods for representing them mathematically are discussed later in this chapter. This section focuses on an even more fundamental concept on which all the aforementioned concepts rely—a concept on which people's common sense, too, relies when you think about objects in the world. Namely, this is the concept of space—not outer space or the stratosphere, but the more general concept of space in terms of space and time, or the idea that all entities in the world, despite their differences, inhabit a unified space or environment. For example, every object in a restaurant (tables, chairs, people, doors, etc.) is a distinct and separate thing, but all of those things share the common space of the restaurant. They all exist in the restaurant. More widely, every entity that exists in the game world shares that single space. Space in this sense is expressed mathematically as a coordinate space.

COORDINATE SPACES

A coordinate space, when applied to video-game worlds, is a mathematical construct or system that enables developers to put a number onto the position and the size of every object in the world. Coordinate spaces come in two main forms, 2D (two-dimensional) and 3D (three-dimensional), depending on whether the game in question is 2D or 3D respectively. Consider the two coordinate spaces in Figure 4.1 and Figure 4.2.

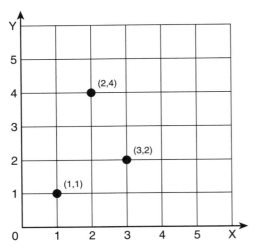

Figure 4.1
2D coordinate space, in which positions are measured from the origin as 2D coordinates in the form (X, Y).
Source: *Alan Thorn*

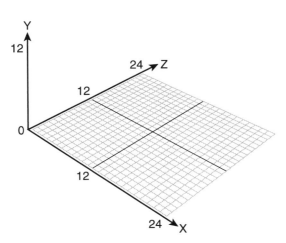

Figure 4.2
3D coordinate space, in which positions are measured from the origin as 3D coordinates in the form (X, Y, Z).
Source: *Alan Thorn*

Note

Most examples in this book focus on 2D coordinate spaces because such spaces are more clearly represented on paper and in diagrams. However, everything that holds for 2D coordinate spaces remains true for the 3D kind, except that the 3D kind involves an extra axis.

COORDINATE SPACE FUNDAMENTALS

The 2D coordinate space works by drawing two straight intersecting lines (three lines for 3D spaces) that stretch entirely across the extent of the game world, from one side to the other. These lines are known as the *axes* of the world, with each line being called an *axis*. A point, called the *origin*, is marked at the intersection of the lines. The origin represents the starting point for all measurements within the coordinate space. (See Figure 4.3.) Each axis is then subdivided from the origin into equally spaced divisions to create a system of units, known generally as *world units*. (See Figure 4.4.)

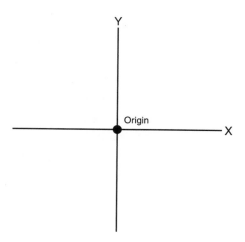

Figure 4.3
World axes of a coordinate space X and Y, with the world space origin at (0,0).
Source: *Alan Thorn*

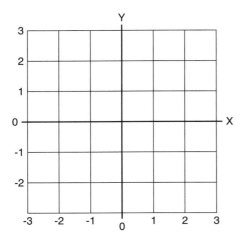

Figure 4.4
World space divided into units.
Source: *Alan Thorn*

After the units are established, any point within the coordinate space can be measured and stated precisely. That is, it can be stated without any confusion arising as to which point in the space is intended. Points can be expressed in terms of a special kind of number, known as a *coordinate*. Most coordinate spaces label their axes using the letters X and Y (and Z for the third axis in 3D spaces). Therefore, any point in the space can be expressed using the notation (X,Y) or (X,Y,Z) as a relative offset or movement from the origin. You can arrive at any point within the system by following a journey from the origin along the axes according to the coordinate, in the order of the numbers. Move first along X (horizontal) and then up along Y (vertical). (See Figure 4.5.)

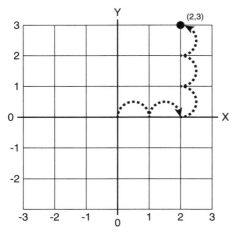

Figure 4.5
Coordinates specify positions and are measured as an X,Y offset from the origin of the coordinate system.
Source: *Alan Thorn*

Measurements made through coordinates are convenient because they are both authoritative and consistent. They are authoritative because every point within the coordinate space can be uniquely identified by its coordinate. That is, no two different points share the same coordinate. Two different coordinates will refer to two different points within the coordinate space. The measurements are consistent because they are all specified in the same system of units, just as a range of weights given in kilos would all be consistent because they were all specified in kilos. This consistency has two main advantages. First, coordinates can be compared to each other. For example, using the Pythagorean theorem, as you will see later, the linear distance between any two points to the origin can be compared to see which point is nearer to the origin. Second, coordinates can be combined using arithmetical operations (such as addition, subtraction, multiplication, and division) to produce meaningful results in the form of new coordinates. (See Figure 4.6.)

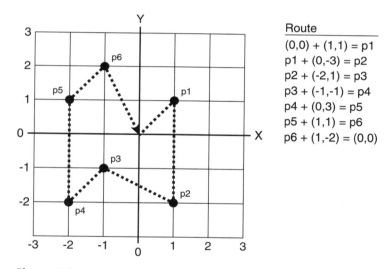

Figure 4.6
Coordinate addition and subtraction results in new coordinates.
Source: *Alan Thorn*

WORLD AND LOCAL COORDINATE SPACES

As you have seen, coordinate systems offer a precise and systematic means of defining the positions for objects in the game world with coordinates, or measured offsets from the origin. From this, it follows that the width and height of objects (as well as depth in 3D) can be calculated or estimated in world units using coordinate arithmetic, as was demonstrated in Figure 4.6.

Based on these concepts, game developers typically rely on two different types of coordinate systems working together to specify the position and size of objects in the world: *world space* and *local space*. These are not mutually exclusive systems, but are used in different circumstances to define position and size in different terms. The difference between them lies crucially in the location of the origin of the coordinate space.

In world space, coordinates are measured from the *world origin*, a point in the game world that is designated as the center of the world. Positions measured from this point could potentially be anywhere throughout the game world. The coordinate (0,0) refers to the world origin—a point at the world center—and the position (5,3), for example, refers to a measured offset from that origin of 5 units along the X axis and 3 units along the Y axis. World space is useful therefore when the position of an object or event must be specified absolutely in the world—that is, when the position must be given in terms that have meaning relative to the world origin.

Note

This might at first sight seem the only sensible or correct way in which position can and should be understood in a game, but an example will serve to demonstrate why this is not always so, and why it can be convenient for developers to think of position differently.

Consider a game with a world featuring a vast and populous city of many buildings and people, not unlike any major city in the real world in which millions of people can be found today. In this city, each building, person, and thing will have its own unique world-space position because no two objects can occupy the same space at the same time. Their position is measured from the world origin, wherever that might be—at the Equator, the North Pole, the South Pole, etc. Each building in the city will also have many contents within, including walls, doors, tables, chairs, sofas, and more; each of these furnishings will also have its own world-space position, an offset from the world center. However, although all these furnishings can and do have world-space positions, it is not always convenient for a developer to think about their positions in world-space terms. For example, suppose a level designer wants to position a sofa at an exact position at the center of a room on the third floor of a building. In that case, the designer will typically measure the position of the sofa relative to a point closer than the world center, such as the corner of the room, the edge of a door, or maybe even as far as the entrance of the building. The designer does not typically measure the position from the distant origin of the world (although he or she could do so). Measuring the sofa against the world origin is possible but inelegant because it fails to satisfy a fundamental tendency of humans to specify positions from a near point of reference.

A better solution is to measure the position from a point somewhere within the room in which the sofa will appear. Thus, the position of the sofa is defined as an offset from a nearer point or origin. Using this technique, the sofa is positioned in local space, because its position is measured from a point in the world other than the world origin. The origin of local space is sometimes called the *object center, anchor point,* or *pivot.* (See Figure 4.7.)

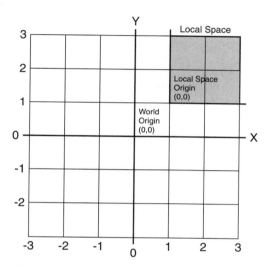

Figure 4.7
A coordinate system within a coordinate system (local space).
Source: *Alan Thorn*

Game developers make use of both local- and world-space coordinate systems when specifying the positions of objects in a level. The systems are not mutually exclusive, but are chosen for convenience based on circumstances. That means developers will specify positions using both systems.

This might initially seem to be incorrect on the grounds that the local- and world-space systems are incompatible. They must surely be different systems, and coordinates in one system will not hold true for those in another. If a sofa is 10 units away from the corner of a room, it will not be 10 units from the world origin (unless the world origin and room corner happen to be in the same place). But the local-space coordinate system still exists within world space. For this reason, all local-space positions can ultimately be converted into world-space positions, provided the origin of the local space is known in world-space terms. Converting between coordinate systems using arithmetical processes as shown in Figure 4.8 gives developers the convenience of specifying coordinates in one system while knowing they can ultimately be resolved to coordinates in another.

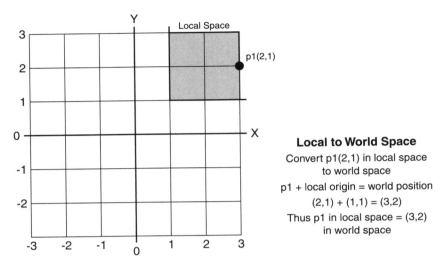

Local to World Space

Convert p1(2,1) in local space to world space

p1 + local origin = world position

(2,1) + (1,1) = (3,2)

Thus p1 in local space = (3,2) in world space

Figure 4.8
Converting local space to world space.

Source: *Alan Thorn*

Note

The differences between local- and world-space coordinate systems will emerge again later in this book, when we consider the subject of meshes and 3D geometry for games.

POSITION, ORIENTATION, AND SCALE

The placement of an object (any object, whether a car, a person, a gun, etc.) and its appearance in the game world is essentially a function of three critical and independent properties that belong to that object:

■ **Position.** As you have seen, the object's *position* is its location within the game world expressed in terms of coordinates as either an absolute world-space position or a local-space position (the latter being resolvable into the former). The position of an object is the exact coordinate at which the pivot or center of an object will be aligned.

■ **Orientation.** The orientation of an object is the direction in which it is facing in the world. It specifies whether the object is facing up or down or over here or over there. Orientation is independent of position, meaning that any one of these two properties can change without affecting the other. The object can turn to face a new direction without changing its position, just as a person can turn on the spot to face new directions and sights. Orientation, as you will see, can be expressed mathematically using a variety of different kinds of numbers, including Euler angles (using the traditional degrees measurement), matrices, radians, and quaternions.

- **Scale.** The scale of an object influences its size or mass in terms of width, height, and depth. It is represented mathematically as a decimal number and acts as a multiplier—a factor used to multiply an object's height, width, or depth to grow or shrink its dimensions. An object remains at its standard size whenever its scale is 1 because any value multiplied by 1 remains unchanged ($S \times 1 = S$). An object scaled by a factor of 2 is doubled in size ($S \times 2 = 2S$), and an object scaled by 0.5 is halved in size ($S \times 0.5 = S/2 = ½$).

Together, these three properties—position, orientation, and scale—define the placement of an object in the world and thus affect how it appears to the gamer.

TRANSFORMATION

The term *transformation* conjures up images of change and motion. Indeed, in biology, it frequently refers to alterations in the cells of an organism. Similarly, in video games, transformation refers to any combination of changes over time in the position, orientation, or scale of an object. Thus, a car that travels (moves) along the road is transformed; a periscope or propeller that rotates around its center is transformed; and a tiny rabbit that eats a biscuit to increase its size is transformed. All these are examples of transformations at work, and a typical video game will perform tens, hundreds, or perhaps even thousands of these kinds of transformations per frame.

Transformation consists of three smaller and constituent processes:

- **Translation.** Translation is the process of moving an object, or changing its position.

- **Rotation.** Rotation is the process of turning an object, or changing its orientation.

- **Scaling.** Scaling is the process of stretching or shrinking an object, or changing its scale.

Applying one or more of these three processes to an object in a game at any one time forms a transformation (singular).

Transformation can be represented mathematically—that is, as a data structure—in many different ways. One way is to keep track of three different types of numbers to represent translation, rotation, and scaling. Another is to encode all the transformation data together in a new hybrid kind of number known as a *matrix*. The former method is considered in more detail first.

Translation

Translation can be represented as a coordinate that specifies the relative movement to make from an object's current position. Hence, a translation coordinate of (2,3) means simply to move 2 units along the X axis and 3 units along the Y axis from the object's current position (not from the world origin). (See Figure 4.9.)

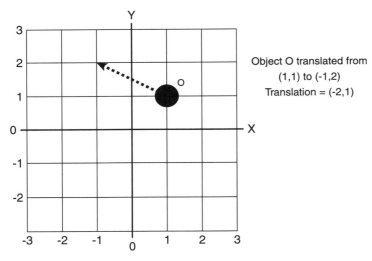

Object O translated from
(1,1) to (-1,2)
Translation = (-2,1)

Figure 4.9
Translation refers to movement, typically expressed as a coordinate offset.
Source: *Alan Thorn*

Rotation

Rotation can be represented in 2D space in terms of Euler angles, or degrees (°), where 360° represents one complete turn, or *revolution*; 180° is a half turn; 90° is a quarter turn; and 0° represents no turn at all. In 3D space, the representation of rotation would require three numbers for degrees, because an object could turn potentially in many directions. It could turn around the local X axis (pitch), the local Y axis (yaw), or the local Z axis (roll). Figure 4.10 shows a local space origin and set of axes passing through the center of the object.

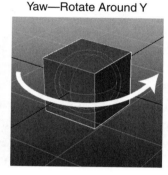
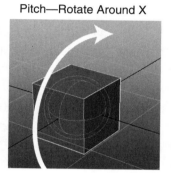

Figure 4.10
Rotation of an object in 3D space.
Source: *Alan Thorn*

Scaling

Scale can be represented using the decimal number method discussed earlier, where a factor of 1 retains the object's size (S × 1 = S), a factor of 2 doubles the object's size (S × 2 = 2S), and a factor of 0.5 halves the object's size (S × 0.5 = ½S). In 2D space, two separate decimal numbers would be required for scale, for width and height (X, Y). Three decimal numbers would be required for 3D space to specify the scale of the object in each of its local axes, for width, height, and depth (X,Y,Z).

Scaling is defined on a per-axis basis, where a unique scaling factor in the form of a decimal number is specified for each axis of an object. It enables you to stretch or shrink an object separately on each axis. That means any scaling operation can be one of two types:

- **Uniform.** Uniform scaling—the most common form of scaling—ensures that an object is stretched or shrunk by the same factor on all of its axes, such as (2,2,2) to double the size of an object.

■ **Non-uniform.** Non-uniform scaling refers to all other forms in which a different factor is used on at least one axis, such as (2,0.5,0.5) to double the width of an object and to halve both its height and depth.

Uniform scaling always results in an object looking larger or smaller overall while retaining its original proportions. Non-uniform scaling results in an object appearing distinctly larger or smaller in at least one dimension such that it no longer has the same proportions as before. For example, uniform scaling could be used to inflate the size of a character in a game—for example, a rabbit that magically grows into a giant. This giant rabbit will maintain its height-to-width-to-depth ratios. That is, it will look no slimmer or fatter than before, just generally larger overall. Non-uniform scaling, however, can make the rabbit appear taller but not fatter, or fatter but not taller. It tends to make an object look noticeably stretched or shrunk in one dimension. (See Figure 4.11.) Uniform scaling is more commonly used in games than non-uniform, primarily because of its proportion-preserving function. Non-uniform scaling frequently causes a distorted effect. That is not to say, however, that non-uniform scaling is wrong, dangerous, or errant. There are times when developers *do* want to create a distorted look in their games—for example, for comic effect, to create an atmosphere of surrealism, or to create the effect of a character under the influence of an intoxicant or drug.

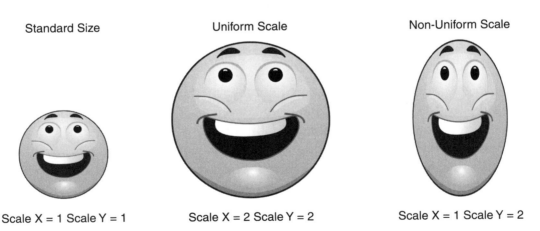

Figure 4.11
Uniform and non-uniform scaling.
Source: *Alan Thorn*

Transformation with Matrices

Transformation is composed of the three smaller processes of translation, rotation, and scaling—movement, turning, and stretching and shrinking. As you have seen, each of these can be represented mathematically as separate numbers of different kinds: translation as a coordinate offset (X,Y,Z), rotation as a decimal number measured in degrees (for example, 90°), and scaling as a decimal number expressing a fraction (for example, 0.5). These methods of expressing transformation can be used successfully and repeatedly on a per-object basis for every frame of the game to describe the totality of transformations applied to all objects in the game world over time. However, developers more commonly rely on another, arguably more elegant mathematical structure for encoding transformations in the form of numbers. This structure is known generally as a *matrix* (plural: *matrices*), but in the context of transformations is known more specifically as a *transformation matrix*. The mathematical details and specifics of a matrix are beyond the scope of this book; it is necessary here only to describe in a commonsense way the purpose and overall benefits of a matrix—the justifications for using them as the main means for expressing transformations.

The transformation matrix is, in essence, a data structure formed by a four-by-four grid of decimal numbers. These numbers are arranged systematically into columns and rows, and the entire structure is surrounded by large bracket symbols, as shown in Figure 4.12. Together, these numbers can encode all the transformation data for an object (rotation, scaling, and translation), just as regular coordinates and decimals can do independently.

$$\begin{matrix} X \\ Y \\ Z \\ {} \end{matrix} \begin{bmatrix} 2 & 0 & 0 & 0 \\ 0 & 2 & 0 & 0 \\ 0 & 0 & 2 & 0 \\ 0 & 0 & 0 & 1 \end{bmatrix}$$

Figure 4.12
A matrix structure can be used to encode transformation data. This matrix scales an object (increases its size) by 2 on the X, Y, and Z axes. Thus, the matrix encodes a uniform scale operation.
Source: *Alan Thorn*

The matrix, however, has two benefits over the standard method:

- It is a single structure as opposed to multiple structures. In other words, it is a method of consolidating related transformation data into one standalone structure.

- The matrix is so ingeniously configured that it is amenable to a range of arithmetical operations. That is, it can be multiplied by another matrix (matrix-to-matrix multiplication), and can even be multiplied by a single decimal number, or scalar (matrix-to-scalar multiplication).

More on Matrix Multiplication

Matrix-to-matrix multiplication is the process of combining two or more transformations. For example, suppose a game character, such as Sonic or Mario, performs a combined run-and-jump manoeuvre to cross a large abyss between two moving platforms. This process of running and jumping combined involves two main translations: one on the X axis as the character runs and one on the Y axis as the character jumps. Matrix multiplication can come to the rescue by combining the translations into one structure. A matrix A could encode the transformation for running; matrix B could encode the transformation for jumping; and the combination of the two through multiplication could produce a single matrix C that encodes the combined transformation—the run and jump.

Similarly, matrix-to-scalar multiplication allows for the scaling of matrices. A matrix A might encode a rotation of 180°, and multiplication of this matrix by the decimal 0.5 will result in a new matrix B that encodes half the transformation—thus, a rotation of 90°.

Most game engines and game-development tools provide access to languages and libraries with out-of-the-box support for matrices, for representing transformations as matrices, as well as most for other mathematical concepts discussed in this chapter. The upshot of this is that although the mathematics behind these structures is useful and interesting in itself, many game engines hide a lot of the associated math so that developers can simply concentrate on using them to make games—even if they have only a cursory knowledge of how they work. This, of course, should not be taken as a recommendation to avoid learning the details of matrices and matrix arithmetic, but only as a restatement that such knowledge is not to be considered among the fundamental and core principles of game development. It is possible to make video games without understanding exactly how matrices work.

VECTORS: DIRECTION AND MOVEMENT

Previous sections explained how coordinate systems provide a systematic and mathematical means of dividing and charting space such that every unique point within that space can be expressed as a number in the form of a coordinate—either (X,Y) or (X,Y,Z). This is made possible by establishing a single point as the world center (origin) and then by thinking of every other point as a measured offset from the origin. Using this system, it is clear and simple to see how every point can be uniquely identified in space. Further, it provides an intuitive means for expressing translations—for moving objects from one point to another in the same coordinate system. Object X can be moved from point 1 (0,10) to point 2 (2,15) by simply adding a coordinate T (2,5) to point 1 to reach the destination. Thus, coordinate arithmetic makes it easy to understand how translations are supposed to work.

A problem arises, however, for the developer regarding translation or movement in more complex cases. To illustrate, consider a game world that begins with the player character standing at the origin, looking forward along the world Y axis. This game will be 2D and seen from an overhead view, looking directly downward on the characters. (See Figure 4.13.)

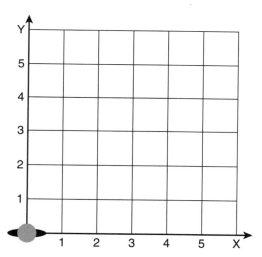

Figure 4.13
The player begins at the origin.
Source: *Alan Thorn*

Moving this character forward at a certain speed (say, 3 world units per second) is not a problem. After 1 second, the player will have moved to position (0,3) (1 second × 3 world units per second = 3 world units), as shown in Figure 4.14. So far so good.

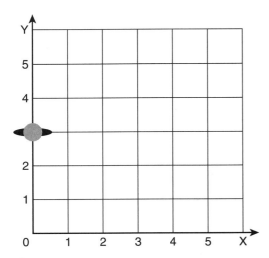

Figure 4.14
The player moves to (0,3).
Source: *Alan Thorn*

When the player arrives at the destination, he turns (rotates) 33.5° to face in a new direction. (See Figure 4.15.) The aim now is to keep the character moving at the same speed in the direction in which he is now facing rather than along the Y axis, where he was facing before he turned. How, then, does one calculate the position of the player after a further 2 seconds?

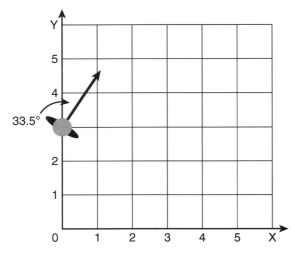

Figure 4.15
The player rotates 33.5°.
Source: *Alan Thorn*

This question brings to the surface a single mathematical problem that manifests itself in a wide range of other situations that a game developer might encounter. Indeed, this mathematical problem is at the root of several questions that a programmer might ask during development, such as the following:

- How can I keep the character moving in the direction in which he is facing?
- How do I know which direction the enemies are looking?
- Is the player in the line of sight of the enemy sniper?
- How far does the player need to rotate to be looking at the enemy?
- Can the player see the enemy monster from where he is standing?
- Is enemy 1 nearer to the player than enemy 2?

These questions all pertain to the concept of direction. They ask how it is possible to travel in specific directions, whether particular sights can be seen by the gamer or enemies when looking in specific directions, or how far an object must turn to be oriented toward a specific direction. The concept of direction plays a pivotal role in all of these problems, and developers attempt to solve them directly or indirectly by making use of the mathematical structure of a *vector*.

"What's Our Vector, Victor?"

The vector is a mathematical structure that game developers use to represent direction. It is the mathematical equivalent of a person pointing in a direction and saying, "This way!" or "That way!" If you draw a straight line of any length and in any direction on a sheet of paper, and then add an arrow head to either end of the line so that it points in a specific direction, you will have successfully drawn a vector. The concept of direction is, in essence, the concept that one attempts to capture in numbers when one uses the vector as a mathematical structure. A vector is written in exactly the same form as a coordinate (X,Y,Z), and comes in both 2D and 3D varieties. (See Figure 4.16.)

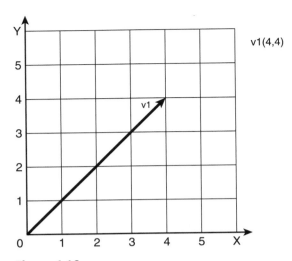

Figure 4.16
A vector.

Source: *Alan Thorn*

A vector differs from a coordinate even though it is written using the same basic form or structure. A coordinate always specifies a point within a coordinate space as measured from the origin. In contrast, a vector does not represent any specific point or position in the coordinate system. Rather it encodes a direction. The vector is assumed to begin at the origin and its X, Y, and Z components always specify the point of the arrowhead from the origin—the direction in which you would be looking if you were standing at the origin.

In addition to its direction, a vector has a *magnitude*. The magnitude of a vector is the length of the straight diagonal line in world units—that is, the line that could be drawn directly from the origin to the hypothetical point expressed by the vector arrowhead. This line is the equivalent of the hypotenuse of a right-angled triangle and expresses the amount of distance to travel in the specified direction. As you shall see, however, the magnitude of a vector can often be ignored—generally in cases where you care only about direction. (See Figure 4.17.)

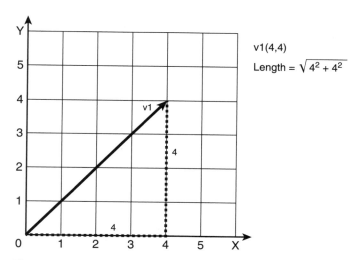

Figure 4.17
Vector direction and magnitude.
Source: *Alan Thorn*

Vector Addition and Multiplication

Like matrices and most mathematical structures, vectors can be combined through arithmetical operations (addition, subtraction, multiplication, and division) to produce new vectors that have meaning and value in relation to the originals. Thus, vector arithmetic is essentially about creating new directions from existing directions. When you ask the question, "Where will I be facing after turning 45°?" you are ultimately seeking to produce a new direction on the basis of various inputs—namely, your current direction and the amount of rotation that you are to undergo. The aim here is to take those inputs and create a new vector that will specify your direction after the turn. For this reason, vector arithmetic can be seen as the process of answering questions about direction. Let's consider the two most common vector arithmetical operations: addition and multiplication by a scalar (decimal number).

Vector addition is the process of adding two or more vectors (sequence S), adding all X components, Y components, and Z components, as shown in Figure 4.18. The result of the addition is a new vector that expresses the shortest and most direct route from the origin to the final vector of the sequence S. Vector addition is equivalent to laying out all the vectors to be added in a sequence, where the tip of the first vector touches the tail of the next vector. It treats all vectors in sequence S as a sequential tour or detour that must be followed from start to end. On reaching the end vector in the sequence, a direct diagonal line is traced back to the beginning. This line represents the output vector, the result of the addition. Thus, the result tells you how to reach the end of the sequence directly, tracing the shortest and most direct route from the origin.

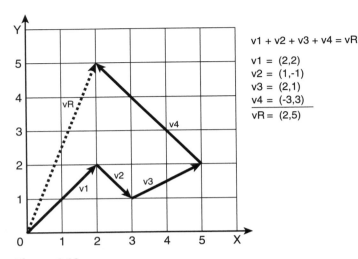

v1 + v2 + v3 + v4 = vR

v1 = (2,2)
v2 = (1,-1)
v3 = (2,1)
v4 = (-3,3)
─────────
vR = (2,5)

Figure 4.18
Vector addition results in a direct route.
Source: *Alan Thorn*

Vector multiplication comes in two main forms: vector-by-vector multiplication and vector-by-scalar multiplication, the latter of which is considered here. You can think of vector-by-scalar multiplication as the process of *vector scaling*, just as a decimal number can be used to scale the size of objects along their local axis. The scalar 1 (*vector* × 1) maintains the magnitude and direction of the vector. The scalar 0.5 (*vector* × 0.5) halves the magnitude of the vector but maintains the direction. Likewise, the value of 2 (*vector* × 2) doubles the vector magnitude and still maintains the vector direction. In contrast, a scalar of −1 (*vector* × −1) maintains vector magnitude but reverses the direction. A final example of −2 (*vector* × −2) both doubles the magnitude and reverses the direction. These basic arithmetical concepts as related to vectors will prove instrumental in making objects travel a specified direction, as you shall soon see. (See Figure 4.19.)

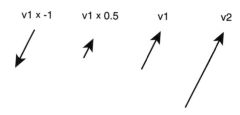

Figure 4.19
Vector by scalar multiplication.
Source: *Alan Thorn*

Vector Normalization

The vectors considered so far in this chapter have denoted both a direction and a magnitude or length. That is, they all tell you a direction in which to travel and how far you are to travel it. This is undoubtedly a useful construct when you know in advance both the direction and the distance. However, there are often cases in games, such as when the player is running along a corridor, when you are concerned with direction only, not distance. In these cases, you want an object to travel at a specified speed and in a specified direction, but for an unknown distance. The distance is "to be determined" or left open until such time as you decide for the object to stop.

In these cases, where you want to remove the magnitude from a vector or adapt the vector such that its magnitude no longer has significance, you must perform the process of normalization. *Normalization* is an arithmetical operation that takes as input a standard vector with direction and magnitude, and outputs a new vector with the same direction but whose magnitude is always 1. This vector, known as a *unit vector*, is special because it indicates direction only. Unit vectors can easily be made to have any magnitude that you wish through vector-by-scalar multiplication. For example, you can multiply a unit vector by 2 to give it a magnitude of 2, or by 3 to give it a magnitude of 3, and so on. The formula for normalizing a vector is given in Figure 4.20. Normalizing a vector is an important concept whose significance for traveling in directions will become clearer later in this chapter.

Normalize Vector v1

$$v1 = (4,3)$$

$$\text{Magnitude} = \sqrt{4^2 + 3^2} = 5$$

$$v1.x = 4 \,/\, \text{Magnitude} = 4\,/\,5 = 0.8$$
$$v1.y = 3 \,/\, \text{Magnitude} = 3\,/\,5 = 0.6$$

$$\text{Normalized } v1 = (0.8, 0.6)$$

We know this is a unit vector because:

$$\sqrt{0.8^2 + 0.6^2} = 1$$

Figure 4.20
Normalizing a vector.
Source: *Alan Thorn*

Vector Dot Product

When dealing with vectors, developers often need to know the angle or amount of turn between any two vectors. For example, a game might feature an enemy character poised and ready with his rifle by the window of a building, looking and aiming at a distant doorway, ready for the player to enter through it. Suddenly, and completely by surprise, the player enters from a different doorway behind the enemy location. Here, the enemy should turn to face the player. You can calculate the direct line of sight between the player and the enemy, who are now both in the same room, by subtracting the player position from the enemy position, leaving you with a vector pointing from the enemy toward the player. This vector represents the amount of translation that would need to occur to travel from the enemy position to the player position. Once normalized and stripped of its magnitude, this vector is in essence the direction in which you want the enemy to face—to rotate from his current direction at the window to a new direction in which he will be facing the player to engage him in combat. You want to know, in short, not only how much you must rotate the enemy in terms of degrees (to turn him from his current direction to his new direction), but also how you can calculate a new vector representing the new direction on the basis of your current direction and an angle. Thus, you want to know the angle between the old direction and the new direction (the angle between vector A and vector B) and how to generate a new vector that is the result of rotation by a specified angle.

The angle between two vectors can be calculated on the basis of a number known as the *dot product*. Also known as the *scalar product* or *inner product*, the dot product is a scalar (a decimal number) that can be generated by performing a set of arithmetical operations on two vectors. This number does not give the angle between vectors, but it does express some relationships about the angle. Once the dot product is generated, you can plug that number into an inverse trigonometric function acos (arccosine) and finally produce the angle in degrees between the two vectors. The process for calculating the angle between two normalized vectors is given in Figure 4.21. Given a direction vector V and an angle A that specifies an arc, you can also generate a new direction vector that will be the result of rotating V around angle A. (See Figure 4.22.)

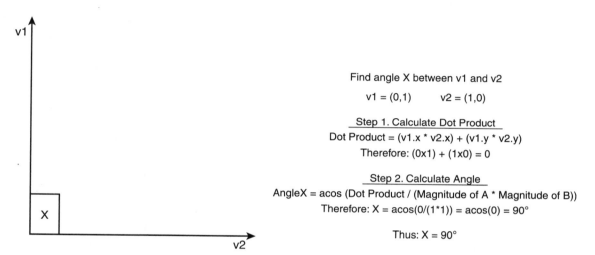

Find angle X between v1 and v2

v1 = (0,1)   v2 = (1,0)

Step 1. Calculate Dot Product
Dot Product = (v1.x * v2.x) + (v1.y * v2.y)
Therefore: (0x1) + (1x0) = 0

Step 2. Calculate Angle
AngleX = acos (Dot Product / (Magnitude of A * Magnitude of B))
Therefore: X = acos(0/(1*1)) = acos(0) = 90°

Thus: X = 90°

Figure 4.21
Calculating the angle between two vectors.
Source: *Alan Thorn*

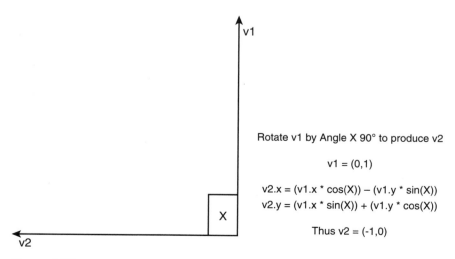

Rotate v1 by Angle X 90° to produce v2

v1 = (0,1)

v2.x = (v1.x * cos(X)) − (v1.y * sin(X))
v2.y = (v1.x * sin(X)) + (v1.y * cos(X))

Thus v2 = (-1,0)

Figure 4.22
Rotating a vector around an arc.
Source: *Alan Thorn*

SOLVING PROBLEMS WITH SPEED, DISTANCE, AND TIME

This section combines much of what you have learned about vectors with some fundamental ideas in Newtonian physics—specifically, speed, distance, and time—to address the practical problem stated earlier that got us thinking about vectors in the first place. That problem was, how can you calculate the movement of a character or thing inside the game world when it travels routes that do not rigidly conform to the world axes? For example, how can you calculate the position of a character on each frame of animation as that character moves frame by frame along a diagonal route from the world origin to his destination? This question will be answered here in a step by step style, and the method used can be applied to answer all kinds of similar questions about the position and movement of objects using vectors in a coordinate space.

The first step in solving an applied mathematical problem with programming such as this one is to make sure you understand the problem as clearly and entirely as possible. The problem before you might be stated in this way: Given an object, person, or thing in the game world (object O), and given its speed (S) and trajectory expressed in the form of vectors and angles, how can you calculate the position of the object at any subsequent time T? Figure 4.23 shows a sample route you could use for object O. You want, in effect, for your object to start at the origin and move (translate) at a constant speed toward point P1. Once there, you turn (rotate) 45 degrees, and then travel at a constant speed and in a straight line toward point P2. The following steps demonstrate how to calculate this route using only the concepts discussed so far.

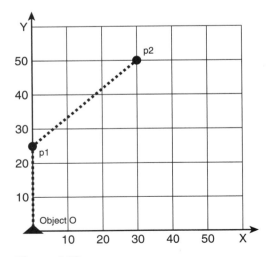

Figure 4.23
The route to travel.
Source: *Alan Thorn*

Object O begins positioned at the world origin, or (0, 0). But although its position is (0,0), it is facing in a forward direction looking along the Y axis. This direction can be expressed in the form of a normalized vector (0,1). Again, this example will be 2D and feature an overhead view looking downward on the characters. Note that the direction of object O (0,1) is a normalized vector because its length or magnitude is 1.

Object O will travel at a speed of, say, 5 world units per second. That means after every second of constant and uninterrupted motion, object O will have traveled a further 5 world units from its current position. This is because distance = speed × time; thus, speed (5 world units per second) × seconds (1) = 5 world units. Because of this, you can determine that the position of object O after 5 seconds will be (0,25) provided it moves from the origin in an upward direction as we have specified it must. Note that this position could also be calculated by multiplying the direction vector (0,1) by the distance to travel, and the distance calculated by multiplying the speed by the time. (See Figure 4.24.)

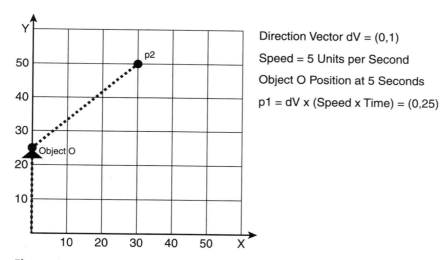

Direction Vector dV = (0,1)

Speed = 5 Units per Second

Object O Position at 5 Seconds

p1 = dV x (Speed x Time) = (0,25)

Figure 4.24
The object moves along the Y axis in the direction it is facing for 3 seconds, at a constant speed of 5 world units per second.
Source: *Alan Thorn*

When object O arrives at position (0,25), it rotates 45° to face a new direction. Thus, the direction vector is rotated 45° to produce a new direction vector using vector-rotation arithmetic, as shown in Figure 4.25. The resultant direction vector can then be normalized to express only direction—the direction of the diagonal.

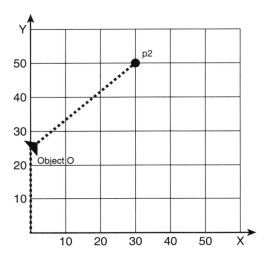

Figure 4.25
Rotate direction vector.

Source: *Alan Thorn*

Object O then continues to travel forward along its direction and at its specified speed until the gamer issues a command to stop. Thus, its position after 15 seconds can be calculated by multiplying its direction vector by the distance traveled, and then by adding this position to its former position at (0,25), as shown in Figure 4.26.

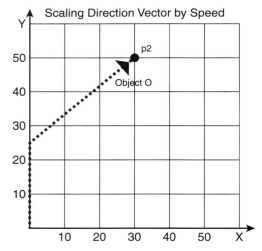

Figure 4.26
Traveling to the destination.

Source: *Alan Thorn*

In short, then, a general formula for calculating the position of object O at time T given its position, direction, and speed can be stated as follows:

New Position = Current Position + (Normalized_Direction × Speed × time)

CONCLUSION

This chapter focused on a selection of the key mathematical concepts and ideas that underpin video games and their development. The aim of almost all of these concepts is to systematize and put numbers on general and everyday ideas that you rely upon to talk about actions and events within the real world, so you can then replicate that behavior believably in the video-game world. These concepts include coordinate systems, angles, vectors, coordinates, positions, and vector arithmetic.

However, one problem quickly arises as a block to progress for many students. It relates specifically to confidence with mathematics and with mathematical thinking generally. Some people, when presented with a cold and clinical chart, formula, or graph, tend to shut down. They see mathematics and numbers as an obstacle—something they were never very good at and would rather avoid. This frame of mind usually reflects an attitude more than a truth. Looking at mathematics as an insoluble mystery appears to trace its roots back to as far as ancient Greece, where many thought numbers to be sacred and mysterious things, predating human civilization. For them, "progress" in mathematics was seen as the process of making discoveries of truths that already existed rather than as the act of inventing new conventions. This awestruck attitude toward numbers is frequently destructive for game developers—destructive in that it often cultivates a dislike or fear of mathematics and reinforces a frequently mistaken belief that one is somehow cursed with an innate and unchangeable inability to work with numbers.

This chapter, in contrast, has tried to introduce key mathematical ideas from a fundamentally different perspective that aligns more closely with the view taken by John von Neumann, who said, "In mathematics you don't understand things. You just get used to them." It has sought to present mathematics first and foremost as a tool for getting things done—as something that is there to be used to achieve a purpose rather than as something to be understood for its own sake. This advice should not be taken to mean that mathematics is entirely devoid of meaning or beauty or anything worth researching or understanding. Neither should it be taken as the stronger claim that the ancient Greeks were wrong in their beliefs about the transcendent properties of mathematics and numbers. Rather, it is intended only as a gentle reminder for those not confident with mathematics that progress and confidence can frequently be attained simply by seeing mathematics less as a mystery to be solved than as a tool or convention to be practiced for solving practical problems. In short, do not fear the numbers, but start to make them your friend on the simplest terms available.

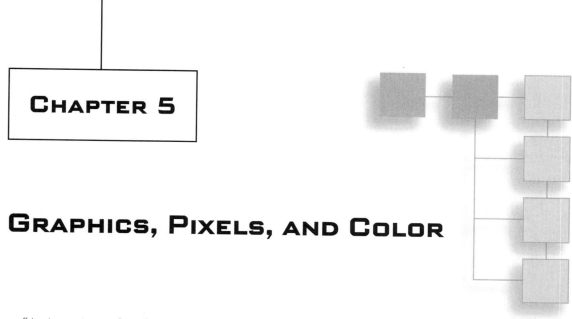

CHAPTER 5

GRAPHICS, PIXELS, AND COLOR

"A picture is worth a thousand words."

—Unknown

By the end of this chapter you should:

- Understand raster graphics and pixels.

- Appreciate primary colors, secondary colors, and tertiary colors.

- Understand concepts such as hue, saturation, value, and gamma correction.

- Become familiar with color channels, alpha channels, selections, and masks.

- Understand image formats and compressions methods.

There was a time in the late 1980s when the word *graphics* was a fashionable and technical buzzword, much like the words *cloud computing* are today. Now, however, the word *graphics* is generally considered to be commonplace—a household word that most people understand. This is primarily because video games have found their way through PCs and consoles into more homes than ever before. In the world of video games, *graphics* refers to the things inside a game that can be seen or that can appeal to the sense of sight. If a thing is in a video game and you can see it, then it falls squarely within the remit of graphics.

It is not necessary here to provide a justification of graphics; practically nobody disputes their importance for video games. For people with the ability to see, graphics, like most visual phenomena, are very influential and important both psychologically and emotionally. There are, however, debates among some gamers and game designers about exactly *how* important graphics are for games in comparison to other game elements such as gameplay and sound. From the game developer's perspective, it might seem that graphics are simply a matter for artists and graphic designers. They're the ones who create the original graphical content for a game—animations, 3D models, menus and buttons, sprites and characters, and videos and marketing. This is generally a mistaken view, however, because graphics are relevant to other developers, too, including programmers, game designers, and scripters. Programmers, for example, must place constraints and restrictions on artists to ensure the graphics they create are compatible with the game that has been coded. Programmers must also work with the graphics made by artists to integrate them into the game in an optimal and performance-conscious way. Thus, graphics—and the fundamental game-development principles surrounding them and their creation—are relevant for almost all members of the game-development team.

PIXELS: THE RAW UNIT OF GRAPHICS

Graphics refers to all visible things in a game: images, animations, and videos. These are seen by gamers on a screen after having been processed and manipulated by a computer, whether a PC, a console, or a mobile device. This might seem so obvious that it is hardly worth mentioning at all—until you question how a computer, which works only in numbers, could present a non-numerical image on the screen. How can a photographer or an artist feed an image from the real world into a computer, and have it display that image on a screen with such fidelity and accuracy that we recognize it to be the same image? The answer is that the computer uses a system to convert visual data into numerical data. The basic unit of this system is the *pixel*, which is a contraction of the more complete name: *picture element*. (See Figure 5.1.)

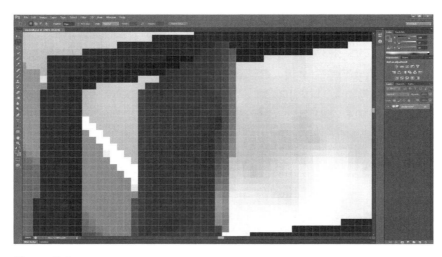

Figure 5.1
An image full of square pixels, as shown in Photoshop.
Source: *Adobe Photoshop*

Note

Pixels come in various shapes and sizes, but this book concentrates on the square pixel, the most common type used in video gaming.

The computer divides the width and height of the display (the screen) into equally sized divisions or squares, and each square is termed a pixel. Thus, the surface of the screen represents a grid of pixels. Each pixel in the grid represents only one solid color. Using this basic system, complex images can be formed from a sufficient number of pixels crammed together in a grid, like the tiles of a mosaic. This works because images can be conceived systematically to be a collection of colors—a composition that emerges from tiny blocks of color arranged in rows and columns in which there are no separations or gaps between pixels.

Resolution

The width and height of the screen in terms of pixels are known as the dimensions of the pixel grid, the pixel dimensions of the screen, or more commonly as the resolution. The *resolution* is used to express the size of the pixel grid and thus the amount of detail that can be shown on the screen or in an image—the more pixels, the more detail. A number of common resolutions are used in video gaming, including 1,024×768 (that is, 1,024 pixels wide and 768 pixels high). This resolution is used for many older desktop games, the original iPad, and some phones. Other resolutions include 800×480, 640×960, 1,280×720, and 1,920×1,080. The latter two resolutions are known as *HD*, short for *high definition*.

Aspect Ratio

The relationship between the width and height of the screen in pixels can be expressed as a ratio, called an *aspect ratio*. You generate this ratio by writing the width over the height as a fraction and then by reducing the fraction into its simplest terms. For example, if the resolution is 1,024×768, the aspect ratio, or AR, is 4:3. If the resolution is 1,920×1,080, the aspect ratio is 16:9. The latter aspect ratio is commonly known as *widescreen*; for every 16 pixels in width, there will be 9 pixels in height.

The Problems of Resolution and Aspect Ratio

In short, the resolution of an image or of the screen tells you how many pixels there are in total in the system, and the aspect ratio tells you how those pixels are distributed in terms of width to height—that is, the proportions of the image. When taken together, these two properties of the pixel grid are especially significant for game developers (as well as for those working in other fields such as movies and television). They hint at a potential challenge faced by game developers, which arises due to differences in the design and manufacturing of computers, mobile devices, and televisions.

Specifically, different devices support different resolutions and aspect ratios. Some televisions, for example, support high definition (1,920×1,080), while others do not. Some mobile phones support the 4:3 aspect ratio, some support 16:9, and some support a different ratio altogether, depending on the size and shape of the screen. The result is that a developer who creates a game for only one resolution and only one aspect ratio cannot expect that game to look the same on the screen of a device whose resolution or aspect ratio is different. Because resolution and ratios differ widely across devices, the game will inevitably differ greatly in how it looks across devices.

With respect to differences between a game's design and the target device, there are in essence two smaller problems: cases in which the resolution differs, and cases in which the aspect ratio differs.

Differences in Resolution

Consider the first and simpler case of a difference in resolution. Suppose a developer creates a game for the 16:9 HD resolution of 1,920×1,080 pixels. (The resolution for which the game is made is known as the *target resolution*). However, the gamer who plays the game has a computer that can show only the 16:9 HD resolution of 1,280× 720 pixels (the *user resolution*). In this case, there is a mismatch between the target and user resolution, but not in the aspect ratio. The target is simply too large for the user resolution.

Here, the developer is faced with at least two possible solutions, both of which are used in the contemporary games industry. The first and least popular solution is simply to deny the user the pleasure of experiencing the game, claiming it supports only a resolution of 1,920×1,080 and no other. The second and more popular solution is to have the game *downscale*, or resize the graphics to a smaller size to fit lower resolutions in cases where the user hardware leaves no other alternative.

In cases where only the resolution differs, downscaling is not typically problematic. This is because the aspect ratio of both resolutions is identical despite their difference in dimensions. Consequently, the image can be scaled down uniformly and still maintain its original proportion of width to height. Thus, the graphics can scale down and still extend across the entire surface of the screen just as they did when shown at the target resolution. In this example, both the target and user aspect ratios are 16:9, so for every 16 pixels in width there are 9 pixels in height.

Differences in Aspect Ratio

The alternative case is where both the resolution and the aspect ratio differ between the target and user resolutions—for example, when the target resolution is 1,920× 1,080 and the user resolution is 1,024×768. The first resolution has an aspect ratio of 16:9 while the latter has an aspect ratio of 4:3. In these cases, scaling down the pixels of the target resolution to fit those of the user resolution will involve shrinking the image out of proportion—at least, if the image is still to extend entirely across the screen in both width and height. Shrinking in this way involves changing the relationship between the width and height of the image. The result is that the resized image is stretched or shrunk non-uniformly and appears distorted or skewed, being wider or taller in one dimension without any corresponding increase in the other dimension. (See Figure 5.2.)

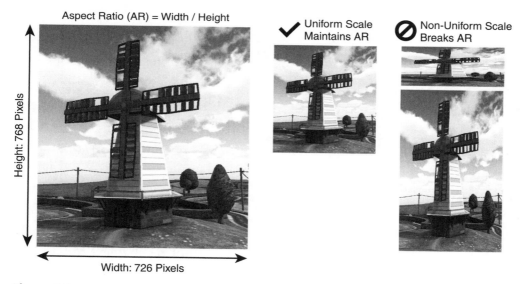

Figure 5.2
Image dimensions, aspect ratio and image scaling.
Source: *Alan Thorn*

There are two main solutions to the problem of maintaining aspect ratio across different resolutions. The first is *letterboxing*. This involves downscaling the original image uniformly (by the same factor in both width and height) until either the width or height of the image matches the width or height of the user resolution, respectively. Because the image is scaled uniformly, the aspect ratio does not change. The result is that the resized image maintains aspect ratio and extends entirely across the screen surface in one dimension only, but leaves black bars or margins at either the top or sides of the screen. These cover the vacant space that could not be filled in the other dimension so as to maintain aspect ratio. The second solution is to produce multiple versions of configurations of the game that are tailored to work at different aspect ratios, just as Web pages can be constructed to respond differently to different browsers and screen resolutions.

Conclusions About Pixels for Games

In short, the following information and advice can be gleaned from this section:

- All game graphics are ultimately translatable into pixels.
- A pixel is a square block of color.
- Pixels are arranged in a pixel grid to form images.
- The dimensions of the pixel grid are known as the resolution of the image.
- The ratio between width and height is the aspect ratio of the image.
- Graphics can be scaled without distortion between two different resolutions of the same aspect ratio.
- Graphics cannot be scaled without distortion to fit the screen across two different aspect ratios.
- You can use letterboxing or multiple game configurations to support different aspect ratios.
- Decide on your supported resolutions and aspect ratios *before* making your game. Pixel-based graphics made at one aspect ratio cannot be converted to alternative aspect ratios without quality loss, either by non-uniform scaling or letterboxing. An 800×600 image, for example, cannot be changed to 1,920×1,080 without involving upscaling and non-uniform stretching to fit the extra width space.

COLOR: THE QUALITIES OF IMAGES

Each pixel is in fact a square block of color, expressed in a digital or mathematical form (even though we do not see the pixel on screen with our eye in terms of mathematics). Thus, a pixel is essentially a number. The question arises, then, how numbers are used to represent in the computer the range of colors that we see around us with our eyes. In other words, how can numbers be used to build colors? After all, the phenomenon of color does not in any clear way seem amenable to mathematical or systematic representation.

To answer this question, it is worthwhile considering a scenario from the real world in which colors are created artificially: the example of an artist who uses oil paints to build colors for his paintings. To create realistic-looking paintings, the artist must make use of an extensive range of colors. These colors are not purchased individually from the art store as separate paints. That is, the artist does not buy 100 different tones of red. Instead, they are made manually by the artist from a mixture of a more narrow set of color paints that he already has. These original colors with which the artist begins are known as the *primary colors*. They are said to be primary because by mixing and combining them and all their derivatives, the artist can produce every other color he needs. Colors that result from mixing two primaries are known as *secondary colors*. *Tertiary colors* result from mixing either one primary and one secondary color, or two secondary colors. By this process of combining and mixing, the artist can produce every color he needs in a complete color set. Every color in the color set is ultimately traceable to the original primaries, the ultimate ancestor colors, because it is from these colors that every other descends. The artist need not buy separate paints for every shade of every color, and he need not know every color that has ever existed. Rather, he can make all he needs from only a limited set of colors.

Creating colors in the real world through the mixing of oil paint has a strong parallel in the world of game development, where mathematics is used to build colors. Specifically, numbers can be used to build colors by establishing the convention of a color space. A *color space* is the mathematical equivalent of the color set for oil paints. It is an ingenious and (in my view) exciting system whereby monitors and displays are manufactured so that certain pixel numbers show certain colors on the screen.

The color space makes two things possible for developers:

- It ensures every unique color has its own unique number.
- It ensures that the arithmetical operations between color numbers (addition, subtraction, division, and multiplication) act as forms of color mixing. That is, arithmetical operations produce results describing new colors that are a mix of the original two.

Today, there are two main color spaces used in computer graphics: RGB (red, green, blue), used almost exclusively in games and movies, and CMYK (cyan, magenta, yellow, black), used almost exclusively in printing and document design. (The letter K is used for black in CMYK because B is used in RGB to mean blue.) These systems take their names from the primary colors of the space—that is, the colors that can be mixed to make all other colors. RGB is the focus of this chapter, although the same basic principles underpin each system. (See Figure 5.3.)

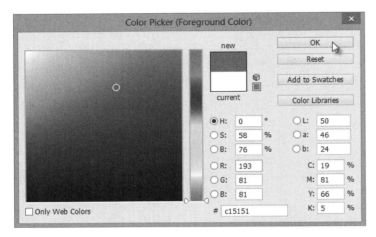

Figure 5.3
Selecting color from the Photoshop Color Picker dialog box. Notice the R,G, and B values for specifying color.
Source: *Adobe Photoshop*

RGB: Color Does Not Exist?

One of the most shocking ideas taught to many students on the first few days of their graphic arts courses is that there is no such thing as color. This idea runs entirely against the grain of common sense and seems to be refuted easily by our everyday experiences in which we do, in fact, see color. However, there is a limited sense in which this notion is true, provided its meaning is made clearer. This more limited meaning is important for understanding how contemporary pixel-based graphics work.

The RGB color space is a system of numbers in which every unique number expresses a unique color. Each color is written as a three-component number in the form (R,G,B). For example, the color red is (255,0,0), the color green is (0,255,0), and the color blue is (0,0,255). Each component in the number is called a *channel*. It expresses the strength of the associated primary color in relation to the other primaries, where 0 means fully off and 255 (or sometimes 1—see the upcoming sidebar for more details) means full strength. So, for example, RGB (255,0,0) represents red because the red channel is set to full strength while all other channels are turned off. In contrast, green would be (0,255,0), with the green channel fully on and all others fully off. Black would be (0,0,0), with all channels fully off, meaning there is an absence of color. Green, for example, would be (0,255,0), because the green channel was fully on and all others were fully off. Colors can be mixed, too; yellow would be (255,255,0), because an equal mixture of red and green results in yellow. And the color white would result from each component being fully on: (255,255,255).

Normalized Values

In this discussion so far, colors have been expressed using their absolute RGB values, which range from 0 to 255. In this case, as well as in others throughout game development, the developer must deal with ranges of numbers from a minimum to a maximum. Often, when dealing with these ranges, the developer wants to talk about specific positions or values within the range. In the case of colors, you might want to refer to the "middle value" color, to a shadow, or to a highlight. Now, all these expressions refer to values somewhere within the range, but between the extremes.

You can, of course, express these values in absolute terms: The middle value is 128, the shadows are below 100, and the highlights are above 200. However, all of these values are meaningful only for this scale, and as long as you know what the minimum and maximum values are yourself. If the range were to change, however—perhaps because more colors were added to it—then suddenly the maximum value would become greater than 255. The consequence would be that the highlights and shadow values specified earlier would take on different positions within the range. Thus, you'd need to go back and revise any absolute color values you had specified previously, before the amendments to the range occurred. This is because, after the amendments, the previous values are invalidated.

Developers often seek to avoid these kinds of problems concerned with absolutes by using a *relative* form of measure, called normalized values. This technique works wherever you have a range of numbers. In short, it maps the absolute range to the decimalized values of 0–1. In the case of colors, it maps 0–255 to 0–1. In RGB terms, 0 maps to 0 in the normalized scale, and 255 maps to 1. Thus, the 0–255 range can be specified in normalized terms as 0–1. The mid value is at position 0.5, the shadows at 0.39, and the highlights at 0.78.

You can convert these normalized values to their absolutes by simply multiplying them by the absolute range. So $0.5 \times 255 = 128$ (approximately) (the middle color); $0.39 \times 255 = 99$ (shadows); and $0.78 \times 255 = 198$ (highlights). Now, if more colors are added to the range, it's not a problem. Your normalized measurements still refer to the same proportions as before, because they were not tied directly to the absolute values. So, for example, 0.5 still *refers* to halfway along the scale, however long the scale might be; 0.39 still refers to the shadow limits; and 0.78 still refers to the highlights. In short, normalized values are a powerful technique, and I recommend using them whenever you are dealing with ranges of values.

Note

You can try creating colors of your own using RGB. To do this, open Photoshop or any similar image-editing program and access the color selection dialog box for choosing the color of brushes. Figure 5.3 shows Photoshop's Color Picker dialog box; note the RGB fields for entering the values of an RGB color. Also, notice how, when you select colors from the dialog box using the mouse, the RGB color fields are populated automatically with numbers, showing the RGB values for the selected color.

So how does this discussion of RGB values and channels relate to the more fundamental idea that color does not exist? To see this, open Photoshop or any similar image-editing software and examine any RGB image—perhaps one captured with your digital camera. The image, being in the RGB color space, will have three distinct channels: red, green, and blue (See Figure 5.4). Each of these channels appears to contain three separate, distinct, and complete versions of the same image, but in black and white, or grayscale. Every pixel in the channel is a single, grayscale value between 0 (black, or *shadow*) and 255 (white, or *highlight*), and the value in the middle is 128 (gray, or *midtone*). In short, each of these channels contains all the strength values (grayscale numbers) for a specific channel for every pixel in the image. Thus, the complete RGB values of the image result only when all the channels are overlaid onto each other and their values for each pixel are combined into complete RGB values on a pixel-by-pixel basis. For example, the top-left pixel of the red channel will be combined with the equivalent pixel of the green and blue channels to complete a final top-left pixel specified in RGB.

Figure 5.4
Red, green, and blue channels compose the image.
Source: *Alan Thorn*

Even when a final RGB value is produced in the form of a three-component number, however, it still effectively encodes only three channels of grayscale or strength values, with each channel ranging from 0 to 255. It is in this sense that RGB is said to show that color does not exist. That is, color does not exist in the number itself, or in the computer itself, or in the digital image itself because the numbers express only three channels; the image is really only three channels of grayscale. Rather, the color emerges at the level of hardware: the monitor or display, which is manufactured to activate specific diodes at certain frequencies, which our eyes and brain recognize as the appropriate color.

The result is that the colors of digital images are *never* constant, but are always device dependent. That is, an RGB pixel of a specific value always has the potential of looking slightly different on different devices, depending on their manufacture. This helps to explain our memories of visiting an electronics or TV store and witnessing the dramatic differences in color and image quality between stacks and rows of TVs all showing the same TV show. Differences like this might initially seem a troubling prospect, especially for perfectionists who want to ensure their graphics appear totally consistently across all devices. Thankfully, much has been done to ensure that many displays show colors as consistently as possible. But even now, differences do exist. Sometimes these differences can be minimized at the level of software through image-adjustment processes such as gamma correction, as you will see later in this chapter. But sometimes these are unavoidable differences for which we can do nothing but learn to live with them until new solutions are invented and become affordable for the majority of consumers.

Note

More information on RGB spaces and working with RGB images can be found in my *Game Development Principles RGB* video on my YouTube channel, located here: http://www.youtube.com/user/alanthorngames.

Hue, Saturation, and Value: Tints, Shades, and Tones

An RGB color wheel represents in chart form the complete range of colors that can be represented in the RGB color space—at least where all channel values range from 0 to 255. Variations of this basic color-wheel display are found in the Photoshop Color Picker dialog box and other similar dialog boxes found in general image-editing software. Because such colors are in the RGB color space, each one has its own unique RGB number. With these numbers comes a range of technical terms borrowed from the world of art that are used to describe various changes in the numbers of a color, or the ratios and proportions of a color between the different RGB channels. These relationships have importance for how the color will look because its appearance is determined by the RGB values. The terms are hue, saturation, and value, and they are used frequently in game development.

Note

Because the illustrations in this book are printed in black and white as opposed to color, the RGB color wheel cannot be meaningfully shown here, relying as it does on showing the full range of colors. Before proceeding further, I recommend using the search engine of your choice to search for "RGB color wheel." This wheel demonstrates the full range, or palette, of colors that can be used in a digital image.

Hue

The word *hue* means what we commonly mean by the everyday term *color*. Blue is a hue (0,0,255), green is a hue (0,255,0), and red is a hue (255,0,0), as are the colors yellow (255,255,0), magenta (255,0,255), periwinkle (170,170,255), and all the others. If you substitute the word hue in all cases where you would typically use the word color, then chances are you will be using the word hue correctly. The hue of an RGB color is determined by the value of all three of its color channels and arises from the balance between them, or their mix of strengths. As long as all three RGB values are not equal, the pixel will have a hue. If all three channels are equal, then the pixel will be a grayscale value, termed a *neutral*, because the equal strength of each channel has a cancelling effect in terms of color. Thus, "ideal gray" in RGB form is (128,128,128).

Note

With reference to the color wheel, changes in hue can be conceived as rotating around the color wheel.

Saturation

Saturation describes the intensity or strength of a hue. A neon sign or a bold, bright playroom hue are said to be fully saturated. The closer to a neutral a hue becomes, the more desaturated it is. For example, a bold red color (255,0,0) is a fully saturated red, while a weaker red (255,100,100) is a desaturated red. The duller and weaker pastel shades of a color are considered desaturated hues. Saturation results from a specific kind of balance between the color channels of an RGB pixel. In short, the nearer all three RGB channels are to being equal, the more desaturated the pixel becomes because neutral pixels are those in which the RGB channels are equal. The greater the difference, the more intense the saturation. Graphic artists typically opt for pastel tones instead of bold, unabashed primaries when designing graphics for a game because such tones are most commonly found in the real world. Thus, saturation plays an important role for generating believable colors.

Note

With reference to the color wheel, changes in saturation can be conceived as moving in or out along the diameter of the color wheel.

Value

Value, frequently used interchangeably with *brightness*, refers to how close to fully black a pixel is. Value is measured by the highest or strongest channel in the RGB pixel. Hence, the value of red (255,0,0) is 255 because the red channel is the highest of all three channels. The value of periwinkle (170,170,255) is also 255 because value is taken from the strongest channel in a pixel. Pixels with a value of 210 or more are generally classified as highlights—the brightest colors of an image. Pixels with a value lower than 100 are classified as shadows—the darkest colors of an image. Values in between are often labeled midtones.

Tint, Shade, and Tone

Three additional terms also crop up frequently in connection with hue, saturation, and value: tint, shade, and tone. Sometimes these terms are used loosely and interchangeably to mean the various colors in an image or graphic. Other times they are used more narrowly and specifically. In their specific senses, *tint* refers to any pixel that has been whitened, or had white mixed with it. In short, it refers to the pixels that result from a process of desaturation. *Shade* refers to any pixel that has been mixed with black, or darkened or reduced in value. The term "a shade of red," then, refers to a red that has been darkened—whose strongest RGB channel has been reduced. Finally, *tone* refers to any color that has been both desaturated *and* darkened.

Bit Depth

RGB images specify their colors in the RGB format—a three-channel number (R,G,B). As you have seen, the values of each channel typically range from 0 to 255, yielding a total of 256 different luminance levels, or tones (including 0, which is black). That means an image can show a total range of 16,777,216 different colors (256×256×256=16,777,216), which is known as *true color*. Whenever a digital camera takes a photo, for example, it must ensure that all colors it records from the lens are mapped to the closest color it has within the RGB range (or the dynamic range) when the image is stored in a file. However, the range of each channel need not be 256 (or 0 to 255). It could be higher, in which case even more luminance levels or tones could be shown in the image—although that image would potentially require much more storage space in memory. Figure 5.5. shows a digital image being edited with the Info panel open in Adobe Photoshop. You can use this panel with the Eyedropper tool to sample pixels and check out their RGB values.

Figure 5.5
Using the Eyedropper tool and the Info panel (F8) to view the RGB colors in a Photoshop image.
Source: *Adobe Photoshop*

The total number of values that can be expressed in a single color channel (red, green, or blue) is determined by the bit depth of the channel. *Bit* is an abbreviation of the more complete phrase binary digit (0 or 1). Thus, *bit depth* refers to a collection of binary digits. The bit depth of a channel with 256 values is 8 bits. This is because eight binary digits can be combined and recombined to produce a total of 256 unique combinations. (We know this to be so because $2^8=256$.) Thus, a standard RGB image used in video games (most JPG and PNG images) features channels with a bit depth of 8 bits, or 8 bits per channel (bpc). This means that in total, the image is a 24-bit image, or has 24-bits per pixel, because $8\times3=24$ (the image has three 8-bit channels). Consequently, any single pixel can be any color from within a 16,777,216 color range, because $2^{8*3}=16,777,216$.

So what practical advice can be gained here? Practically all textures and graphics for contemporary video games are 24-bit (or less) images, having a bit depth of 8 bits per channel. This default setting is applied to most images in Photoshop and other image-editing software. However, this does not mean that the artists who produced these images using tools such as Photoshop always work with the image with that bit depth. It is possible to change the bit depth of an image. (See Figure 5.6.) Artists frequently work on images at 16 bits rather than 8 bits per channel to gain extra precision and accuracy when performing color operations and applying effects. Their working practice is based on an important tip in mathematics: Your answer can never be more accurate than your unit of measure and degree of rounding; only round your final answer, and never round your intermediate calculations. When an artist applies hue-saturation adjustments, blur and color-correction edits, or other kinds of changes in Photoshop, they are adjusting the color values of pixels in the image. These colors are the result of mathematical operations between colors. The 16-bit depth allows for more colors and thus a greater degree of precision in color operations. The artist can always work in this color mode and then round their final answer when saving their image, converting to 8 bits per channel when saving the final image file.

Figure 5.6
Setting the bit depth of a Photoshop image.
Source: *Adobe Photoshop*

Alpha Channels and Masks

RGB images can contain extra, optional channels in addition to the three essential channels of red, green, and blue. These optional channels are known as *alpha channels* or *masks*. They are useful for making selections in an image—especially to mark out regions that should be transparent or hidden when shown in a game. They do not contribute directly to the final colors of the image, but they can be used to modify how the image will appear.

Like the standard RGB channels, the pixels of the alpha channel map directly in a 1:1 correspondence to the pixels in all other channels. Further, the pixels of the alpha channel are also in grayscale. Their values do not contribute to the color of the image directly, however. Instead, they specify strength of selection. That is, the value of a pixel in the alpha channel indicates whether the pixel at that position in the image is selected, and if it is, the strength of that selection. Black pixels express "no selection" and white pixels express "fully selected," with values in between varying the strength of selection from black (weakest) to white (strongest). In short, pixels in the image that are fully selected will appear fully visible when shown in a game. Pixels that are unselected will be hidden entirely from view, while semi-selected pixels will appear at a degree of opacity or transparency whose strength matches the extent of selection. (See Figure 5.7.) Alpha channels are used commonly in video games to mark out regions of pixels that will be hidden from view, such as the background pixels of a sprite character image.

Image with Transparency

Alpha Channel

Figure 5.7
Images made transparent from an alpha channel.
Source: *Alan Thorn*

Image Formats: Lossless Versus Lossy

Pixels, images, colors, and alpha channels represent just some of the fundamental data that constitutes an image. However, there will inevitably be a point at which the digital artist will want to save all that important image data to a file on his or her hard drive or network drives. This is to protect the data from harm, to retain all of his or her work, and to have an asset or file that can be imported into a game engine for inclusion into a game.

Saving a pixel-based image involves recording all of its pixel information to a persistent file on the hard drive, which will remain intact even after the computer has been switched off and which can be retrieved and edited at a later time. The format of a file refers to the way in which the pixel data is structured, listed, and arranged inside the file. There is a wide—almost intimidating—selection of image file formats available to artists for saving their work: BMP, JPG, GIF, PNG, TGA, and TIFF, to name but a few. Different formats lead to different arrangements, and some arrangements are more suited for different purposes. However, practically all common file formats, including TIFF, PNG, and JPG, use some form of compression—that is, some technique for shrinking or abbreviating the image data so that only the minimal amount of information is recorded to the file. This reduces the hard-drive space consumed and makes the file easier to transfer across Internet connections.

There are two types of compression:

- **Lossless.** Lossless compression ensures that the image data is compressed into an abbreviated or shrunken form in the file that will always retain the quality and detail of the original data. The lossless format always allows the original image to be reconstructed without data loss from the saved compressed form. If you save your image in a lossless format, when you open it up again in an image editor, you will access the original data. Lossless image formats include BMP, TGA, TIFF, and PNG.

- **Lossy.** Lossy compression compresses the image data to a file with size and hard-drive space in mind, but at the expense of image quality and fidelity. For this reason, only an approximation of the original image can ever be retrieved from the compressed data. Consequently, if you save your image in a lossy format, when you open it up again in an image editor, you will get only an approximation of the original—a lower quality version. This problem is magnified on each resave because for every save operation, the compression method will generate yet another approximation. (See Figure 5.8.) The primary lossy image format is JPG.

Original   Repeated Lossy Save

Figure 5.8
Repeated saving in lossy formats can reduce image quality.
Source: *Alan Thorn*

The lossless formats of TIFF, TGA, PNG, and PSD are the formats of choice for most game artists primarily because such formats both compress data and retain the original quality.

Gamma and Gamma Correction

Earlier in this chapter, the section "RGB: Color Does Not Exist?" discussed how color is not something in a digital image but is something produced by a monitor or display device when it shows an image based on its grayscale values in the RGB channels. This explains how there can be differences in color when the same image is shown on different monitors. The monitor works essentially by converting RGB pixel values into a range of voltages between 0 and 1 that are sent to the monitor display, where they are seen as color. Thus, the color black would convert directly into 0, and the value 255 (white) would convert into 1.

An interesting, hardware-specific problem arises during the color-conversion process, however: The relationship between the values in the image and the colors on the display is not linear. Specifically, colors shown on the monitor are subject to *gamma*, or to a *gamma curve*.

The result is that pixels sent directly to the display always look darker than intended. This is because of the gamma curve, which, on most modern monitors raises all values to the power of 2.2. Thus, the value of 0.9, when taken from an image and subjected to the gamma curve, will actually result in a darker value of approximately 0.793 on the monitor because $0.9^{2.2}=0.793$. Similarly, the exact midtone value of 0.5 will result in the darker 0.218 because $0.5^{2.2}=0.218$.

The hardware compensates for the gamma curve by artificially increasing the values of the image before they are sent to the display, a process known as gamma correction. Its aim is to ensure that a linear relationship is maintained as closely as possible between the luminance levels in the image and their appearance on the monitor. It also aims to make midtones in the image appear as midtones on the monitor, as well as to make highlights and shadows in the image appear as the same highlights and shadows on the monitor. (See Figure 5.9 and Figure 5.10.)

| Gamma-Corrected Image | Without Gamma Correction |

Figure 5.9
Image with and without gamma correction.
Source: *Alan Thorn*

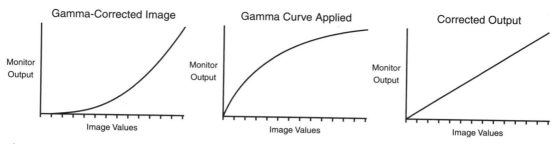

Figure 5.10
Gamma-correcting images.
Source: *Alan Thorn*

So what is the practical relevance of gamma correction to game development? In most cases, there will be little or nothing to do regarding gamma, as almost all digital images are already automatically configured with the correct gamma settings to show appropriately on most display devices. That being said, there are two main specialized cases in which gamma could become an issue and might need to be tweaked. The first is when a rendering system, such as 3DS Max or Maya, or a game engine renderer applies gamma correction to its renderings. In this case, it is important to either remove gamma correction from the textures or to indicate to the renderer that textures already have gamma correction applied to them. This is to prevent gamma correction from being applied twice to the textures. The second situation is when your game will be played on non-standard display devices—devices whose gamma differs from the conventional 2.2 standard. Figure 5.11 shows how the gamma of an image can be viewed and edited in Photoshop. In most cases, however, the gamma setting can be left as is.

Figure 5.11
Editing gamma using the Levels Adjustment layer.
Source: *Adobe Photoshop*

Color Blending: Color Arithmetic

An artist who produces paintings creates his or her colors by mixing different paints of primary colors. Mixing white with black produces gray, mixing red with blue produces purple, and so on. This mixing process—the process of making new colors from existing ones—has a parallel in the world of digital images: color blending. Color blending is important for creating materials and shaders, as you shall see.

Color blending is essentially color arithmetic. It is the process of combining two color values in RGB form arithmetical operations (adding, subtracting, dividing, and multiplying) to produce a new color that is a mix of the original two. These color-mixing processes are what enable enemies in game to turn red when damaged or angry, for defensive laser beams to appear partially transparent, or for GUI buttons to become dimmed or grayed when disabled. All these operations, and countless more, involve a transformation in color that is the result of color blending.

Photoshop provides a range of features that work with color blending, known as blend modes. These modes control how overlapping colors on different layers in the stack are blended into a composite result. They are an excellent visual demonstration of color blending at work, and are essentially no different from the color blending found in video games. (See Figure 5.12.)

Figure 5.12
Using blend modes in Photoshop.
Source: *Adobe Photoshop*

Note

For more information on blend modes, see the companion videos for this course on my YouTube channel (http://www.youtube.com/user/alanthorngames) in the Game Development Principles group.

In short, the two main blend modes are as follows:

- **Multiply.** The color value for black is 0; hence, RGB (0,0,0) is black. When any number is multiplied by 0, the result is 0. For example, $5\times0=0$, and $3\times0=0$. The color value for white is 255, or 1 (when represented as a multiplier). When any number is multiplied by 1, the result is itself. For example, $5\times1=5$, and $10\times1=10$. It follows, then, that the Multiply blend mode (multiplying colors) is a process of darkening a color. Multiplying color X by white (1) results in color X; multiplying color X by black (0) results in black; and multiplying by grayscale values in between will darken the result to that extent. Multiply mode is especially useful in game development. For example, you can give your main character in the game a white T-shirt, and then multiply it by the color red to turn the white T-shirt to red. Or, you could multiply the alpha channel values of an image over time by decreasing shades of gray, moving from white to black. The result: The image will gradually become transparent.

- **Screen.** Screen blend mode is in many respects the opposite of the Multiply blend mode—at least in terms of the results. Screen blend mode division is often seen as the inverse or flip side of multiplication, but the screen blend mode does not involve division. It is the opposite of the Multiply mode with regard to its results: brightens rather than darkens on the basis of two colors. It works by negating all color values, multiplying them together, and then negating them again. The result is that color X, when multiplied by black (0), results in color X. Color X multiplied by white (1) results in white. Screen blend mode is useful for ghosting effects, bright particles in a particle system (like magic sparkles), and other situations in which colors must glow and brighten.

Note

There is a wide range of blend modes available, each involving different steps of calculation—that is, different algorithms for mixing colors to produce meaningful and predictable results. For more information on Photoshop's blend modes, as well as many encountered in video games, visit http://help. adobe.com/en_US/photoshop/cs/using/WSfd1234e1c4b69f30ea53e41001031ab64-77eba.html.

Image Resampling

Image resampling is about changing the size or dimensions of an image. Simply put, an image is resampled whenever it is enlarged or shrunk. You can change the dimensions of an image in Photoshop by choosing File > Image > Image Size and entering the new dimensions in the width and height fields.

The process of image resampling and image quality are related. This relationship must be made explicit here because its importance is often not entirely appreciated due to the poetic license taken by popular TV dramas such as *CSI Miami* and *NCIS*. These shows often feature a "techie guy" or "techie girl" who somehow enlarges (or resamples) images of a crime scene to grandiose proportions to observe the finer details and clues, which would not otherwise be seen—for example, the face of the criminal in the reflection of the rain drops. This kind of enlargement is not the way most digital imagery works, however. In reality, you cannot enlarge a pixel-based image without incurring a loss of quality. For example, enlarging a 100×100 pixel image to $7,000 \times 7,000$ pixels does not retrieve extra detail present in the original image, because 100×100 pixels was all that the original image contained. Instead, the existing image is stretched to the new dimensions and the computer fills in the extra pixels using averaging techniques that are part of the resampling process.

My advice: Never resample upward (upscale) unless doing so is unavoidable or unless you want to create a blurry, low-quality look. Always try to create or capture images at the highest dimensions necessary, and then resample downward (downscale) where appropriate. Before creating a graphic, ask yourself, "Will this image ever need to be larger than these dimensions I have planned?" If the answer to that question is yes, then create the image at the larger size so that the image will never need to be enlarged for your purposes.

Vector Images: Vector Versus Raster

All digital images, no matter what their construction or source might be, can be reduced to pixels without exception, because it is pixels that are rendered to the display or monitor. Even so, digital images are nonetheless divided into two main kinds:

- **Rasterized images.** Rasterized images are standard pixel-based images of the kind opened and edited in Photoshop or other images editors—the kind discussed in this chapter so far. In these sorts of images, the artist works directly with the pixels themselves, with low-level control over how each pixel appears using brush tools, selection tools, color adjustments, filters, and more.

- **Vector images.** These are images such as those created in Adobe Illustrator, Flash, or Inkscape. They can be reduced to pixels but do not offer the artist direct control at the pixel level. That is, the artist does not create or edit these kinds of images by painting pixels. Instead, the artist creates vector images mathematically by controlling a set of points or anchor points that can be plotted and connected to mark out the regions of a shape. (See Figure 5.13.) By plotting points to create the boundaries of shapes, two distinct properties of the vector graphic emerge: stroke and fill. *Stroke* refers to the inked outline or boundary of the shape that is created by a set of connected anchor points. *Fill* defines the pattern or color that fills the interior of the shape.

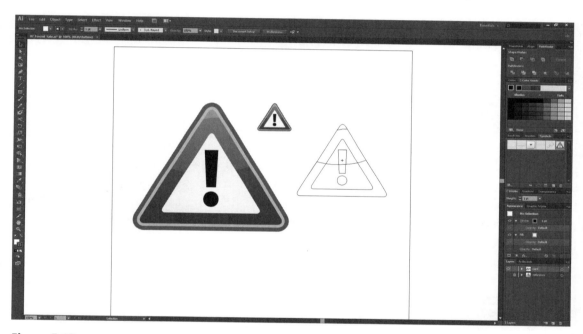

Figure 5.13
Vector-based images are constructed from lines, shapes, and anchor points. Notice the wireframe version of the sign composed from an enclosed shape.
Source: *Adobe Illustrator*

The mathematical nature of vector graphics gives them two distinct advantages over raster images:

- They can be upscaled infinitely without quality loss. You can create a small vector graphic and then enlarge it to any higher dimension without losing any of its original quality. This is because the graphic is generated from a mathematical set of anchor points, and these numbers remain intact at every size. The vector graphic is simply regenerated to fit the larger dimensions.

■ You can easily edit the vector graphic, without having to make pixel selections, because editing a vector image is the process of changing its original mathematical properties.

The chief disadvantage of vector graphics for game developers is that they do not easily capture photo-realistic data, or graphical information that must vary continuously on a pixel-by-pixel basis. Vector graphics are, however, especially suited to creating GUI widgets (buttons, arrows, and other elements), as well as icons, logos, and cartoon characters and scenes. Having said this, artists will typically convert vector images into a rasterized form (that is, turn them into pixel-based images) before importing them into a game engine because most game engines do not recognize vector graphics.

IMAGES AS TEXTURES: TEXELS AND UV MAPPING

Let us now consider pixel-based images as applied in 3D games in the form of textures. Figure 5.14 shows a 3D cube primitive—the kind that could be found in any 3D game, along with any other 3D object. (3D objects and their composition will be discussed in greater detail in Chapter 6, "Meshes, Rigging, and Animation.") The cube, as it stands, is dull and grayish in appearance, looking entirely computer generated and offering little aesthetic interest. To make a 3D cube or other 3D object appear to be made from real-world materials such as wood, brick, skin, or steel, developers resort to the use of textures in combination with materials and shades. (The latter two are discussed further in Chapter 7, "Lighting and Rendering.")

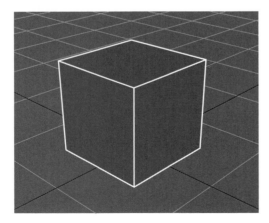

Figure 5.14
Cube in 3D space.
Source: *Alan Thorn*

A *texture* is in essence a pixel-based image that is projected onto or wrapped around a 3D model to "paint" its surface, like wrapping paper on a gift. Photos of brick walls make good textures for brick structures and models, photos of grass make good textures for hill and landscape models, etc. Although the texture is a pixel-based image, its pixels are referred to as *texels* (short for *texture pixel*). This is because the texture, when applied to the surface of a 3D model, will appear in perspective; its pixels no longer have a direct 1:1 correspondence with the pixels of the screen or display. The pixels of the screen continue to be called pixels; the word texels is reserved for the pixels of a texture. Thus, each term refers to pixels in two different kinds of coordinate systems or spaces. The pixels of the screen are measured in terms of X and Y, and the texels of a texture are measured in terms of U and V, where (0,0) refers to the top-left corner of the texture, and (1,1) refers to the bottom-right corner. The center of the texture is always at (0.5,0.5).

Note

> The problems of aspect ratio and resampling apply to the world of textures when projected onto 3D models. Consider the problem of aspect ratio. If a 3D surface, like a plane, differs significantly in proportion to its texture, then its texture will be stretched disproportionately across the model to fit the surface. This will happen if, for example, you try to fit an 800×600 pixel texture onto a 1,920×1,080 pixel surface. Then there is the problem of resampling. If a small 100×100–pixel texture is applied to a large 7,000×7,000 unit wide surface, shown on an HD screen, the texture will be upscaled or stretched across the surface. This will result in quality loss at your intended resolution because the renderer must fill in the missing pixel data when upscaling. Thus, you must ensure that textures are appropriately sized and proportioned for their intended use to avoid quality loss in your graphics

The technique used for projecting or wrapping textures onto the surface of a model is known as *UV mapping*. UV mapping is discussed in more detail in the next chapter, but is stated in summary here: A 3D model marks points across its surface, and each point is given a UV value that corresponds or maps to a position in the texture. The texture is then wrapped around the surface of the model so as to be consistent with the UV values specified by the model. Consider the case of the cube in Figure 5.15. Note how its corner points refer to UV coordinates in the texture, indicating how the texture is to be projected across the surface.

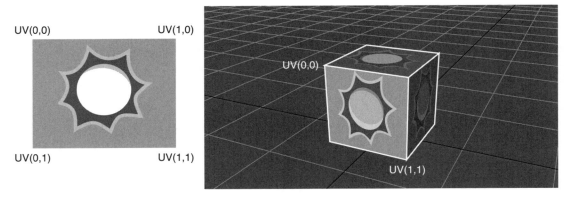

Figure 5.15
A texture UV mapped onto cube faces.
Source: *Alan Thorn*

Several industry-standard guidelines apply to the creation of texture images, and these can be given as follows:

- Textures should be of power-2 dimensions to ensure they perform well on most hardware devices. That is, their width and height in pixels should be only from among the following sizes: $2^2=4$, $2^3=8$, $2^4=16$, $2^5=32$, $2^6=64$, $2^7=128$, $2^8=256$, $2^9=512$, $2^{10}=1,024$, $2^{11}=2,048$, and $2^{12}=4,096$. The textures need not be square, so valid sizes include 512×256, 1,024×2,048, etc.

- Although textures need not be square, square dimensions are often ideal for lower-powered hardware such as mobile devices. For this reason, square textures are preferred where possible.

- Textures should be saved in lossless and not lossy formats—that is, in formats such as PNG, TIFF, TGA, and PSD, but not JPG.

Conclusion

This chapter is jam-packed with critically important information regarding game development—specifically, about the creation of graphical assets for games. It familiarizes readers with the concepts of pixels, aspect ratio, pixel dimensions, resampling, compression, hue, saturation, and value. Learning and applying these concepts can have significant benefits for the quality of your images and textures. Ignoring these concepts can potentially be disastrous.

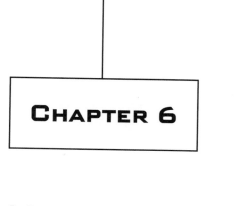

CHAPTER 6

MESHES, RIGGING, AND ANIMATION

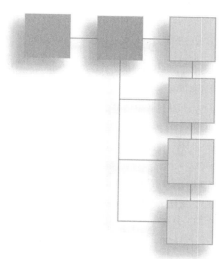

"Animation is not the art of drawings that move but the art of movements that are drawn."

—Norman McLaren

By the end of this chapter you should:

- Understand the differences between meshes, UV mapping, rigging and animation.
- Understand the constituents of geometry: vertices, edges, and polygons.
- Appreciate the importance of topology: edge loops and quads.
- Understand the modular building method.
- Understand culling and occlusion.

Perhaps one of the most common terms in video-game development is the term *mesh*, or *model*. If you have played practically any contemporary AAA game, then you likely have seen many meshes. In short, *mesh* refers to any 3D model in a game, and the plural, *meshes*, refers to them all: cars, buses, guns, trains, enemies, characters, walls, floors, trees, leaves, birds, blood splatters, and more. This understanding of a mesh is both accurate and appropriate in many ways, but it is nonetheless general and vague because it does not make clear many of the finer details and properties associated with the concept. The aim of this chapter is to take a closer and more detailed look at the mesh—to examine its parts and pieces as well as to offer some general dos and don'ts when it comes to creating, importing, and working with meshes for your own game projects.

THE MESH: FOUR CHANNELS OF INFORMATION

The mesh is a game asset in the sense that it is a model created or digitally sculpted by an artist in a modeling package (such as Maya, 3DS Max, or Blender), and is then imported into a game engine, where it appears in the final game. The general workflow for an artist and level designer in creating and using a mesh is as follows:

1. Build the mesh in modeling software.

2. Export the mesh to a file.

3. Import the mesh from the file into the game engine.

4. Insert the mesh into a level.

Steps 1 and 2 are typically performed by the artist, and steps 3 and 4 are typically performed by the level designers or programmers.

This workflow shows that the mesh is created and then exported to a file. This encodes the mesh. If the file could be opened and examined, it would be seen to contain all of the information that is required to reconstruct the mesh, just as an image file—such as a JPG or PNG file—contains all the data required to rebuild an image.

Like an image file, a mesh file features several different channels, or tracks of information. Specifically, there are four, all of which are integral to defining the mesh. Unlike image files—which do have the industry-recognized RGB color channels—mesh channels do not have similarly standardized names or clearly stated purposes. That being said, most meshes encountered in game development feature enough of the same kinds of critical data and channels that it makes sense to talk about them as though they were standardized. I refer to the four main and most common channels of the mesh as follows (see Figure 6.1):

Mesh channel data
for windmill model

UV mapping channel
data for windmill model

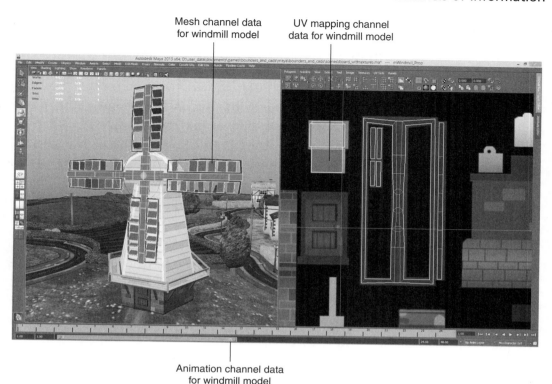

Animation channel data
for windmill model

Figure 6.1
A mesh may feature four channels of information: geometry, UV mapping, rigging, and animation.
Source: *Autodesk Maya*

- **Geometry.** The geometry channel is the only compulsory channel of the mesh. It defines the construction or constitution of the mesh.

- **UV-mapping.** The UV-mapping channel describes how materials and textures are wrapped around the surface of the mesh, as defined in the geometry channel.

- **Rigging.** The rigging channel is related to animation. It specifies the joints, hinges, and underlying skeleton of the mesh in a way that is useful for understanding how the different parts of the mesh can move (if they move at all).

- **Animation.** The animation channel describes the actual motions and animations that are applied to the mesh, according to the constraints of the rigging information.

These four channels are now discussed in further detail in sequence.

THE GEOMETRY CHANNEL

The geometry channel, together with the UV-mapping channel, answers the question, what does the mesh look like? Both of these channels provide half of the answer. The geometry channel defines the form, substance, or constitution of the mesh. It describes how the mesh is built. If the information in the geometry channel were converted into commonsense statements, they would, for example, be of the kind: The mesh has two arms, cylindrical in shape, each with a diameter of 20 cm. The geometry channel does *not*, however, explicitly define how the mesh surface appears or responds to light and shadow, nor does it define how a material or texture is wrapped or patterned across the mesh surface. These details are the remit of materials and UV mapping, respectively.

The geometry channel defines the form of the mesh using a variety of mathematical structures or constructs—namely, vertices, edges, and polygons (hence the reason meshes are sometimes referred to as *polygonal meshes* and the process of making them as *polygonal modeling*). Together, these industry-standard constructs can completely specify the mesh structure and form. To see how, consider the triangle in Figure 6.2, defined using these three constructs.

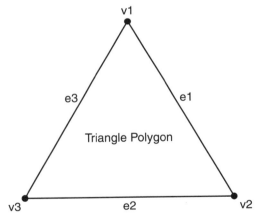

Figure 6.2
A triangle composed of vertices, edges, and a polygon.
Source: *Alan Thorn*

The triangle has three corners, or corner points. Each of these points appears at the intersection of two or more lines. Each point has its own unique coordinate space position, defined mathematically in the form of (X,Y,Z). Each of these points in 3D space is known as a *vertex* (plural: *vertices* or *vertexes*). Thus, the triangle has three vertices, one for each corner: v1, v2, and v3.

The triangle is a shape composed of three sides or three connected lines, where the beginning and end of a line is defined by a vertex. Thus, a line is a straight edge drawn between two vertices. The triangle therefore has three edges: e1, e2, and e3. Each edge is defined mathematically using two vertices—one to mark each end of the edge.

The edges of the triangle are arranged in a connected way so that the end point of the last edge touches the starting point of the first edge, forming an enclosed space. The enclosed space is the triangle, which is an example of a *polygon*, or *face*. The triangle is the simplest or most basic kind of polygon; no other polygon can exist with fewer sides, and every other polygon or shape can be formed by arranging together multiple triangles.

A polygon or face is created whenever a sequence of edges connects back on itself to form an edge ring, marking an enclosed space. The polygon, however, refers not to the edge ring itself but to the area or surface of space inside the ring. Vertices and edges are the constituents of a polygon, and one or more polygons arranged together form the geometry of the mesh. Vertices and edges do not appear themselves to the gamer; that is, the gamer will not see edges and vertices during the game. Their purpose is to form polygons, which can be seen by the eye, because polygons can be shaded or textured.

The triangle itself is a simple shape when compared to the complex and intricate meshes and details that appear in most contemporary video games in architecture, cartoon characters, weapons, and more. In a sense, however, a game's meshes consist of nothing but triangles for defining their shape, despite the appearance of greater complexity. Indeed, the intricate meshes of a game are simply intricate arrangements of triangles, angled and hinged together in strips and fans to form more complex models. By arranging triangles inventively and in highly tessellated networks, it is possible to produce all of the mesh detail for a game. Consider the rectangles of the mesh in Figure 6.3, formed from two right-angled triangles aligned together in a triangle strip at the hypotenuse. Notice the regular and structured arrangement of polygons to create the detail for the house, shown here in a wireframe view (a view that shows the geometry of the model—its edges and polygons—on top of its texture).

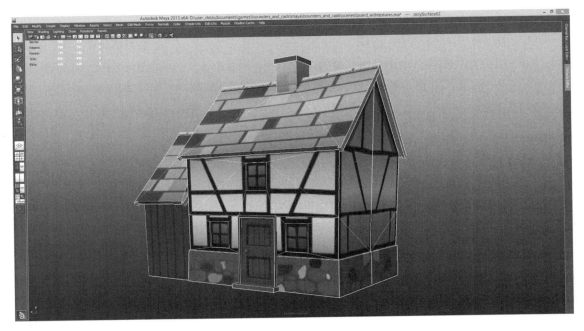

Figure 6.3
House model: an optimized arrangement of triangles and polygons.
Source: *Autodesk Maya*

THE UV-MAPPING CHANNEL

When working with flat, two-dimensional shapes such as triangles, squares, rectangles, and circles, which can be drawn on a sheet of paper or shown directly onscreen, it is a comparatively straightforward matter to shade or color them. Photographic textures, for example, can be overlaid directly onto the shape to alter its color and appearance because the shape itself already exists in two dimensions. A photo of, say, a brick wall can be pasted in Photoshop into the interior of a shape to make that shape take on the appearance of the photo. But meshes existing, as they do, in three dimensions and appearing in perspective pose a technical problem for the artist regarding how their surface should be shaded. This problem exists because of a discrepancy between coordinate spaces—specifically, between the three dimensions of the model and the two dimensions of the flat image textures that are to shade the model. To wrap or project a two-dimensional texture around the surface (polygons) of a 3D mesh in a predictable and manageable way, additional information is required to map between the two spaces. This information is contained in the UV-mapping channel of a mesh.

To visualize the concept of UV-mapping, consider the creative crafts of young children who are encouraged to draw the six sides or polygons of a cube on a sheet of paper, connected together in a T-like shape. The child then cuts around the T shape using scissors and finally folds the paper at each edge of the cube to assemble the cube in three dimensions. In effect, they convert a 2D schematic into a 3D model. (See Figure 6.4.)

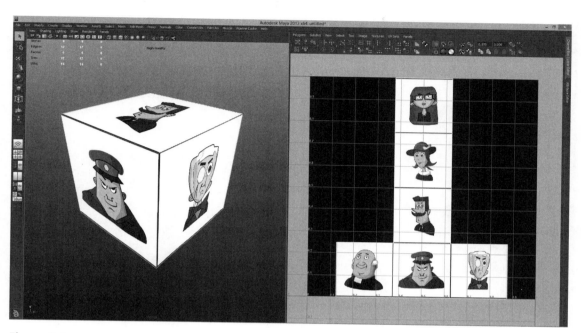

Figure 6.4
Cube unwrapped into two-dimensional texture space.
Source: *Autodesk Maya*

This process can in theory be reversed for any 3D object to map the object into two dimensions. That is, if the object were cut or sliced in enough places, it could be unfolded and flattened out onto a plane. This correspondence between coordinate spaces is, in essence, what UV mapping seeks to achieve so that each part of the mesh surface can be accessed or covered directly by a standard image texture. It achieves this result by using UV coordinates, usually abbreviated to simply UVs. UV coordinates are a specialized coordinate system; the letters U and V are used instead of X and Y to avoid confusion with naming.

UV coordinates start by defining a coordinate space for the flat, 2D texture in terms of 0 and 1. The top-left corner of the texture is position UV(0,0), and the bottom-right corner is position UV(1,1). Thus, the center texture pixel (texel) of the texture is at coordinate UV(0.5,0.5). Consequently, when the 3D mesh is cut apart (metaphorically speaking) and flattened into UV space, every vertex in the mesh is projected to have its own unique UV coordinate. In this way, each vertex is assigned a UV value; thus, the texture can be projected or painted appropriately onto the mesh polygons so as to be consistent with the UV values of the vertices. (See Figure 6.5.)

Figure 6.5
Object mapped into UV space. Notice how the mapping on the plane is reversed because of the UV-mapping coordinates associated with each vertex.
Source: *Autodesk Maya*

Note

UV channels often encode two subchannels. The first (UV map channel 0) defines how a texture is to be projected onto a mesh (2D to 3D). The second (UV map channel 1, or light map UVs) defines how lighting information, such as shadows projected onto a mesh, can be mapped, baked, or flattened from the mesh into a 2D texture (3D to 2D). The latter channel is relevant for the process of lightmapping, discussed in more depth in the next chapter.

THE RIGGING CHANNEL

The rigging channel, together with the animation channel, answers the question, how does this mesh move (if it moves at all)? Like the geometry and UV-mapping channels, the rigging and animation channels are related but distinct. The rigging channel is created by the artist using modeling software. It defines not movement or animation per se, but all the valid and constraining ways in which the mesh *can* move when it does move. It specifies the underlying skeleton or framework of bones, hinges, and joints hidden under the surface of the mesh—how its various appendages and pieces will move and rotate when animated. The rigging for a human or bipedal character, for example, would be the familiar human skeleton, with its network of bones connected at hinges and joints, allowing them to move and rotate in specified directions and to limited extents but forbidding them to rotate or move in other directions. That is, arms cannot bend backward, and heads cannot turn 360 degrees.

The fact that the rigging channel is separate and distinct from other channels, especially the animation channel, is significant. It means that the rigging information for a specific mesh, such as a bipedal character mesh, can be extracted and singled out independently to be reused and recycled for similarly structured meshes. Think back to Chapter 2, "Game Software Development," which discussed the principle of recycling. Because of this, artists can create many meshes that have a similar skeleton—many characters and enemies, for example—and have them all share the same rigging to ensure consistent movement in their animations.

THE ANIMATION CHANNEL

The fourth and final mesh channel is the animation channel, again created by the artist or animator using 3D modeling and animation software. This channel is responsible for defining how a mesh moves or changes over time. Thus, it encodes a relationship between change on the one hand and time on the other. The animation encodes two fundamental types of properties: first, the kind and extent of change to make; and second, the time at which the change should be made. If a mesh walks, runs, jumps, explodes, mutates, rolls, moves, or changes over time, then it is likely to incorporate animation data from its animation channel.

There are two main kinds of animation that can be applied to a mesh, and their differences have implications both for the runtime performance of the game and for the kinds of effects and animations that can be achieved. These animation types are as follows:

- **Rigid body animation.** Rigid body animation (RBA), also called skeletal animation, represents a list of changes or transformations to make to the rigging of the mesh over time in terms of translation, rotation, and scale. RBA is used for walking, running, jumping, flying, and other kinds of animations in which parts of the mesh must move or change. RBA transforms the bones and joints of the rigging directly; the mesh geometry animates indirectly because it conforms to the underlying rigging. The majority of mesh animation in most games will be of the RBA variety because of its close connection to mesh rigging and because it is comparatively cheap to process. Typically, developers record RBA from real-life subjects through motion-capture hardware and software and then import that animation into the mesh to animate its rigging according to the recording.

- **Morph-based animation.** Also called vertex-based animation, morph-based animation (MBA) works independently of mesh rigging, working directly on the mesh vertices themselves—that is, on mesh geometry as opposed to mesh rigging. It is useful for organic-like animation or animation that does not depend directly on bones or rigid structures such as facial expressions, mouth movements, eye blinking, waving flags, pulsating alien egg sacs, and more. Morph-based animation starts by recording the positions of mesh vertices at key times or on key frames and then plays back the animation by morphing the mesh vertices between states over time.

Working with Meshes: Performance Optimization

The mesh asset typically has four main channels of information: the geometry channel, the UV-mapping channel, the rigging channel, and the animation channel. Of these four, only the first is technically essential. That is, without a geometry channel, a mesh cannot be a mesh, just as without a body, a person cannot be a person. However, meshes usually feature more than just the geometry channel.

Here, let us consider further the general but important issues surrounding meshes—specifically, best practices and performance issues for games. Doing so is critical because meshes are so prevalent in games and because, given their complexity and detail, mesh assets pose a number of logistical problems for game developers. It is not uncommon, for example, for a contemporary video game to display, or render, a scene featuring many models—characters, cars, houses, and guns—whose total polygon count reaches hundreds of thousands of polygons (perhaps even more). These will have to be shown and processed onscreen, perhaps up to 100 times *per second.*

The sheer vastness of the information pumped out of a typical game many times per second for processing by the hardware (graphics data, sound data, animation data) can seem both impressive and intimidating. However, given that computing hardware is finite and limited in its capacities, there is a definite limit or bottleneck as to how much data the hardware can process or manage (although this limit varies according to hardware and circumstances). When that bottleneck (wherever it is) is reached, the game will stutter or lag, freeze, or even crash altogether because the target hardware simply cannot consistently sustain the performance.

It is one of the duties of the game developer, then, to engage in a delicate balancing act called *performance optimization.* In this way, the complexities and details of the game are calibrated—carefully arranged and optimized so that the whole performs acceptably on the target platform, as free as possible from lag. Because meshes are so common and plentiful in games, and because meshes are so complex and detailed (with thousands of polygons), they have a critical role to play in performance optimization. Indeed, there is a range of guidelines or working practices to which developers typically adhere creating meshes to ensure that those meshes work optimally when rendered during the game. These practices, as you shall see, conform to the principles of RAMS outlined in Chapter 2—in particular, to the principles of recyclability and simplicity. The following sections detail these guidelines further. Together, they amount to several main rules for creating and working with meshes.

Minimize Polygon Count

The word *topology* often emerges when discussing meshes, and it has important implications for the run-time performance of games. Topology is shorthand that refers to the total number of polygons in a mesh and to their structured arrangement throughout the model. Questions about topology center on how triangles compose the mesh—or rather, the exact pattern of their tessellation.

Consider the rectangles in Figure 6.6. Both A and B are rectangles (also known in 3D terminology as *quads* or *billboards*), but they are composed of two different topologies. Specifically, A is composed of just two right-angled triangles aligned along the hypotenuse, while B is composed of many triangles fitted together like pieces in a jigsaw puzzle. The same mesh ultimately emerges from the arrangement of both A and B (namely, a rectangle), but their internal arrangement or topology differs.

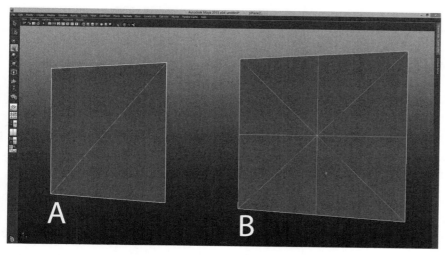

Figure 6.6
Rectangles and topology.
Source: *Autodesk Maya*

Topology in this sense is an issue primarily for the graphics artist who must make the mesh, but it is important for games generally. This is because some topologies are preferred over others, for strong reasons: order and simplicity. Order is discussed in the next section, while simplicity is examined here.

Creating a mesh with simplicity in mind means creating a mesh with as few polygons as possible—*without* compromising on your original design. The total number of polygons in a mesh is referred to as the resolution or detail of the mesh, defined by the polygon count (poly-count). A mesh with more polygons is said to be of a higher resolution because it can potentially contain more details. High-resolution meshes are sometimes referred to as high-poly meshes, and low-resolution meshes are termed low-poly meshes. High-poly meshes are computationally more expensive than low-poly meshes because they contain more data in the form or polygons, edges, and vertices. The exact number of polygons that separates a high-resolution mesh from a low-resolution mesh is not clearly defined and varies from platform to platform, as well as across time. That being said, an important prop mesh (perhaps a weapon) with 500 polygons is generally considered a low-poly mesh on most platforms and by most developers' standards for most kinds of games. Thus, in Figure 6.6, rectangle A is preferable to rectangle B because A produces the same result but with fewer polygons, simply because of the optimized arrangement of the rectangle's topology.

Note

The exact number of polygons that constitute a high-resolution mesh rather than a low-resolution mesh is not clearly defined and varies from platform to platform, as well as across time. That being said, an important prop mesh (perhaps a weapon) with 500 polygons is generally considered a low-poly mesh on most platforms and by most developers' standards for most kinds of games.

Game artists should always strive for the most optimal arrangement consistent with their requirements. It is not enough just to make the mesh; you must make it with optimized topology. Optimizing the poly-count of meshes is no trivial issue, even with the powerful hardware on the market today. An optimized mesh can make the difference between a game that crashes under the burden of expensive meshes and one that performs well.

Optimize Topology

The principle of simplicity demands not that you create a mesh simply with the fewest number of polygons possible (because that would always give you a triangle), but that you create a mesh with the fewest number of polygons that is still consistent with your design or intention. The principle of simplicity does not work in isolation, however. The principle of order dictates that artists should also take care with the arrangement and tessellation of the polygons within a mesh, especially if the mesh will deform, animate, or change over time. In short, the vertices and edges of the model should be arranged, insofar as it is possible, in ordered and neat columns and rows so that the tessellation of the model is predictable.

Figure 6.7 depicts a cylinder object. In that figure, cylinder A is preferred over cylinder B because of the orderly tessellation of its polygons. In A, the edges stretch horizontally and vertically around the hull, creating a clearly identifiable and ordered flow of edges. Connected edges running in a sequence around the model are known as an *edge loop*, because they frequently loop around on themselves. In contrast, parallel edges that run in a line or loop across the length of the model are known together as an *edge ring*. Edge loops and rings mark parts in the mesh where it can fold, bend, or deform. This is because meshes can animate or move *only* in places where there are vertices. Consequently, cleanly ordered topology typically leads to predictable and ordered animations that behave as intended. In contrast, messy topology with unstructured edges and vertices will often lead to unpredictable and unclean animations—animations that deform and contort the mesh out of shape.

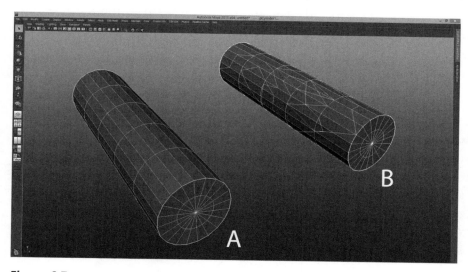

Figure 6.7
Optimizing topology using edge loops and edge rings.
Source: *Autodesk Maya*

Note

Real-time game meshes should typically be modeled to feature only three or four-sided polygons, known as *tris* and *quads*, respectively. That is, no mesh should contain any polygon that has more than four sides. Polygons with more than four sides are commonly referred to as *N-gons*; most game engines do not recognize or process them, meaning they do not render correctly or at all. To ensure best performance and maximum compatibility for your mesh files, use only three- and four-sided polygons.

Reduce UV-Mapping Seams

UV mapping, as you have seen, is the process that allows a 3D model to be flattened into two dimensions so that its surface can be mapped directly onto a standard texture. The process of UV mapping, however, requires that the model be metaphorically cut apart or sliced in several places so that it can be unfolded and flattened mathematically into two dimensions. You cannot, for example, flatten out a sphere, a ball, or an orange skin without first cutting a line somewhere along the length or breadth of the object. The lines or edges of the model along which cuts are made are known as *seams*. The more seams a model has, the easier it is to unfold and flatten it without distortion. The seam, however, introduces two main problems—one for the artist and one for the programmer.

The problem for the artist is that a seam inevitably marks a breaking point in the texture—a line at which the continuity of the texture stops because the edges on the seam mark a place where two connected polygons on the mesh have been split apart when unraveled onto texture space. The seam is the line or edge at which the texture, when applied to the mesh surface, will wrap around to meet itself. If the pixels are too dissimilar on either side of the edge or seam, they will highlight the seam in the mesh due to the contrast they create when meeting side by side. (See Figure 6.8.) Artists use a range of devices to solve this problem, including editing the texture to minimize the seam (making a tileable texture), arranging the model in the level so that the seam is hidden, and finding ways to minimize the number of seams in the UV mapping itself.

Figure 6.8
Texturing issues caused by UV seams.
Source: *Autodesk Maya*

The problem for the programmer regarding seams relates to computational expense. For game engines, such as the Unity engine, there is a price to be paid for each UV seam in the mesh. The result is that, due to the way current hardware processes and renders 3D models, there is often a duplication or doubling up of vertices along the seam. Consequently, each seam increases the number of vertices in the mesh when the mesh is displayed in the game. In short, the primary means of solving this problem is to reduce the number of UV seams in the mesh to the fewest possible (in addition to making careful use of texture space, discussed in the next section).

Recycle Texture Space

After reading the previous section, it might seem that given the number of problems they raise, UV seams are ultimately a bad thing, to be avoided where possible. It is of course not possible to avoid them entirely, however, because all 3D objects must be cut apart somewhere to be unwrapped into texture space. Nevertheless it may seem initially as though UV seams should be minimized just as polygons should be minimized, and for the same reason: to reduce avoidable complexity.

However, UV seams can also offer performance benefits with regards to texture space. *Texture space* is used here to refer to the amount of space in terms of megabytes to hold or store all the textures used for a game in video or system memory while the game is running. Texture space or texture usage is increased when a game uses more textures or larger textures. Benefits to texture space are those features that can reduce the amount space required to hold texture data. That is a benefit because fewer resources are used to hold the same texture data.

Specifically, UV seams can reduce texture space through texture recycling. If extra seams or cuts are inserted into a mesh to break apart the mesh's mapping into several independent and separate islands (called *UV shells*), the islands can then be overlapped in texture space to share the same section of texture. That is, the islands can be overlaid on top of one another in texture space to refer to the same texels. This is, in effect, the practice of taking advantage of the way UV mapping works to reduce the number of texels a mesh would otherwise require.

Figure 6.9 features a standard box with four sides, and each side has the same texture applied. Notice from its mapping, however, that the box has not been unwrapped or unfolded using the standard cube unwrapping, in which each side of the cube is laid out forming a T shape and where each side requires its own unique texture space. Rather, each side has been cut apart and separated in the mapping, and then overlapped in UV space so that the texture and all of its pixels are mapped onto each side identically. In this way, each side recycles the same texture space. Thus, each side does not need separate texture data—meaning the model actually requires fewer texels.

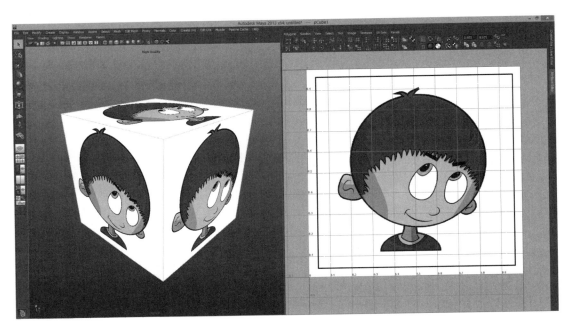

Figure 6.9
Optimizing texture space using recycling with overlapping UVs. Each face of the cube shares the same texture space.
Source: *Autodesk Maya*

In short, the benefits and disadvantages of UV seams show that it is good practice to use them judiciously. You should minimize them in cases where they can be minimized and no appreciable benefit can be gotten from otherwise having them, but use them in cases where the savings in texture space will be substantial.

Establish Texel Density

Texel density, an abbreviation of *texture pixel density*, expresses a ratio or relationship between the size of any mesh or surface in 3D and the number of texture pixels applied to that surface through UV mapping. In short, the texel density of a scene or level helps you judge the number of texture pixels packed onto the surface of all 3D models through their textures, regardless of whether the model or mesh is actually seen by the gamer. Texel density is important because the amount of pixel data that the graphics hardware must process on any one frame has a significant bearing on a game's run-time performance. More pixel data means greater complexity, and thus greater computational expense.

It is important to remember that the size of a mesh and its texture are independent variables. One can change without a corresponding change in the other. The texture, whatever its size, will always appear either stretched or shrunk to a greater or lesser degree as it maps to fit the surface of a 3D model according to its UV mapping. Thus, the subject of texel density becomes an issue for game developers.

Consider the case of a textured rectangle object (or quad) in 3D, as shown in Figure 6.10. The texel density of the object increases whenever the object itself maintains its size but the texture increases in size in terms of its pixel dimensions. In contrast, the texel density decreases when the object maintains its size but the texture decreases in size. The texel density changes in these cases, and all like cases, because there is a change in the relationship between the size of the texture and the size of the surface onto which it is projected. An increase in texel density means that more pixels are squashed onto the surface of a model, and a decrease in density means that fewer pixels are stretched onto the surface of the model.

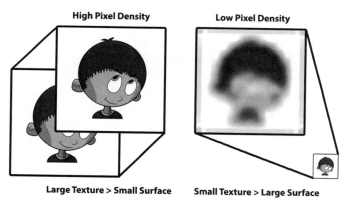

Figure 6.10
Packing textures onto a primitive, increasing and decreasing texel density.
Source: *Alan Thorn*

Having too low a density or too high a density can pose problems for a game. Having too low a density (too few pixels) can make the textures for a game look blurry and pixilated because fewer pixels are upscaled to fit the mesh. (Remember from the previous chapter that upscaling is generally to be avoided.) Too high a density (too many pixels) can cause pixel artifacting as well as performance problems, such as stuttering and lag. So what should the pixel density be for a game?

Finding that magic balance point for correct pixel density in a game is primarily a practical issue. It is something found on a case-by-case basis through repeated testing and checking, depending on the game and target hardware. It is often found using a general two-stage process. The first step involves ensuring consistent pixel density among all objects in the level. The second step involves testing the pixel density of just one object on your target hardware to reach a general conclusion about what will and will not look good for your game. What does this all mean in practice?

Consistent Pixel Density

In step 1, an artist maps and models all meshes for the game at a consistent size and scale using established units and conventions (such as meters and centimeters) that were decided upon by developers beforehand. In this way, you indirectly ensure that all objects share a consistent pixel density. How is this so? For example, a door object might be modeled to be approximately 2 m in height based on general real-world proportions for domestic doors, and this might turn out to be around 1.5 times taller than the main game character should be. To ensure consistent sizing between these two models, then, the main character will be modeled to be around 1.333 m in height because the door is 2 m.

This kind of consistency will apply not only to model size but to its mapping. That means the door should typically be UV-mapped to have 1.5 times as many pixels to its height than the main character—that is, the UV mapping for the height of the door should be 1.5 times larger than the UV mapping for the height of the character. By UV-mapping objects directly in proportion to their actual size in the game level, developers can ensure that a single and consistent pixel density or ratio is applied throughout all models of the game.

This solution does not in itself concretely answer the question as to the correct pixel density for a specific level, but it makes the task of answering it simpler. This is because when all objects in a level share a single pixel density, the question as to which density is correct need only be asked once for all objects as opposed to once for each object in the level. One answer will be correct for all.

Calibrating Pixel Density

In step 2, developers establish the correct pixel density for their level, assuming all objects have a consistent pixel density. They do this mostly by trial and error—specifically, by focusing on only one isolated object in the scene such as a door, the game character, a weapon, or some other object the player can move close to. They put this object into the game and then play the game on their target system to see how the object appears—to see whether it looks good or bad, pixilated or too detailed at the current resolution. They usually start with larger textures than required, creating a high texel density, and then proceed by incrementally downsizing textures until arriving at an appropriate density for their target platform and resolution.

There is no hard and fast right or wrong answer as to correct pixel density. It varies between games and systems. Some developers designing for PCs and consoles use a density of 64–128 pixels per world meter, meaning that for every square meter of geometry in the level there will be around 64×64 (4,096) texels. For lower-powered mobile devices and legacy hardware, such as previous generation PCs and consoles, texel density can sometimes be as low as 16 texels per meter or world unit. Notice, however, that the density is usually specified in texels per world unit and is of a power-2 size, as is consistent with texture sizes generally (as discussed in the previous chapter). The advice to be gained here is, once again, to have the foresight to plan ahead before creating a game and its assets—in this case, to establish a system of units that is to apply consistently for all models to arrive at a texel density that is calibrated for your target hardware.

Optimize Models for Culling and Occlusion

In video-game development, the terms *culling* and *occlusion* have very specific meanings, but both are related to the simple maxim, "Keep it simple." Most scenes in a video game feature a complex and expansive world that the gamer can explore, and it is demanding and expensive for the computer to process and render that data. Massive role-playing games allow the gamer to crawl through tunnels, find secret passageways, visit the beach, examine forests, reach highly guarded fortresses, and more. These locations usually feature computationally expensive graphical effects: leaves rustling in the trees, animated shadows, water ripples and splashes, burning fire and torches, and all kinds of textures, reflections, highlights, and shines—not to mention all the models and meshes themselves. There is typically a lot to see and do in most game worlds, and the computer performs thousands and even millions of calculations per second to make it possible to see and experience those worlds.

One thing, however, remains constant both in the game world and in the real world: the gamer, no matter where he is standing, has a limited field of view based on the game camera. For example, he cannot see behind himself because he does not have eyes in the back of his head; he cannot see beyond the horizon because he does not have remote vision; and he cannot see through solid objects such as walls, doors, rocks, and trees because he does not have X-ray spectacles. All of these conditions place limitations on how much of the world can be seen by the gamer at any one time. This limitation, however, has been exploited since the earliest games and game engines to create what is one of the most important optimization tricks, and one of the most important techniques for reducing the computer's workload to make the rendering and drawing of complex game worlds possible. In short, the game engine will ignore or exclude from processing any objects not directly observable by the gamer.

If the gamer cannot see it, then the game engine will not bother drawing it to the screen or calculating how it should be drawn. Thus, if an object is hidden or occluded, then it will be culled, or removed from the list of objects that must be calculated and rendered.

This optimization trick typically has implications for how artists model or create meshes. In short, artists must make sure that objects, which will appear distant from one another during the game, are imported into the engine as separate meshes or files. That is, they must not group meshes that are spatially remote from one another. A house mesh, for example, should not be grouped with a car mesh that appears on the other side of the game world. This will make it easier for the engine to detect what is and is not seen and to cull or exclude objects appropriately on a per-object basis. If both a car mesh and a distant house mesh are grouped together into a single mesh, then both will be rendered and processed even if only one of them is really in view of the camera because both objects are detected or recognized by the engine as being the same mesh.

Create Meshes as Modules

Did you ever play with Lego or similar building blocks when you were a child? Such toys give you abstract blocks with connection points so they can be combined together and used to assemble all kinds of complex and larger-order constructions such as houses, trucks, and even life-sized characters. It is often useful for game developers to think of meshes in this way—as bricks or blocks that can be arranged side by side to make larger constructions. This approach to meshes is known as the modular building method. This name is appropriate because it makes use of the RAMS principle of modularity. (The RAMS principles were outlined in Chapter 2.)

To illustrate the modular building method, consider the case of a space-station environment for a science-fiction game. This kind of environment and its architecture often features incredible consistency and sameness in its control rooms, observation decks, sleeping bunkers, medical facilities, and long mechanical-looking corridors. The doors are usually of the same style, as are the windows, floor plates, and even the room shapes.

At least two methods are available for the artist modeling this kind of environment:

- The traditional method is to sculpt out the environment complete and intact as a single rigid mesh, ready for import into the game engine as a single piece.

- The other is to first identify in the environment all of the areas of repetition, pattern, and abstractness, and then to break down that environment according to its repetition so that each repeating element is modeled as a single mesh that can be reused and recycled many times, like a building block.

This latter approach to modeling the environment involves thinking in terms of its smaller constituent pieces. The environment features many instances of the same basic door model, a control console, a standard window, and sections of corridor, such as a corridor intersection piece, a corridor long piece, a corridor T intersection piece, a corridor dead end, and so on throughout the level. Identifying the level in terms of smaller pieces and importing those into an engine and level-editor software enables you to assemble the larger and more complex whole level simply by recycling and reusing the smaller pieces together.

There are two main advantages to this latter method, which generally justifies its use in game development:

- Modular building is optimized.
- Modular building is easily extensible.

Modular Building Is Optimized

The modular building method essentially requires the graphics artist to atomize the basic constituents or pieces of a scene and to focus on making those pieces separately, whether they are walls, doors, whole sections of corridor that can be fitted together, or even whole rooms whose doorways can be fitted or connected to the corridor pieces. (See Figure 6.11.) The pieces, whatever they might be, are ultimately used as building blocks for assembling the larger scene and level.

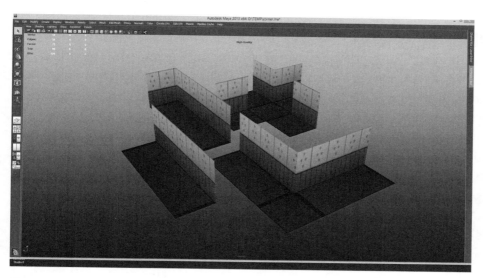

Figure 6.11
Creating levels using the modular building method. Different corridor sections in this figure can be combined to produce different arrangements: a corner piece, an intersection piece, a straight-through piece, and a dead-end piece.
Source: *Autodesk Maya*

There are two main senses in which this method has notable advantages: the first for the developer and the second for the game itself. For the developer, the modular building method saves the artist from having to duplicate work—from having to model the whole environment in terms of every individual piece including every door, every window, and every corridor section. Instead, the artist models *a* door, *a* window, and *a* corridor section, and reuses them as duplicates for building larger environments. For the game, the modular building method is advantageous because, with it, it is not necessary to hold a giant texture that must span across the entire environment as a whole piece. Rather, each unique building block has its own texture applied, and the texture is recycled along with each piece.

Modular Building Is Easily Extensible

The modular building method is extensible because of the way an environment is divided into reusable pieces. If the designer wants to change the level arrangement as a result of story-line changes or in an attempt to increase or decrease the game's level of difficulty, it is not a problem; level adjustments simply consist of rearranging the level pieces. If the testers or gamers demand expansion packs or additional down-loadable content in the form of new levels or environments, these can be created through creative reuse and rearrangements of the same building blocks. In short, the modular building method is essentially the process of playing Lego bricks with meshes, and therein lies its power: the power to use basic ingredients to produce a more complex whole with the potential for almost limitless customizability.

Reduce Animation Keyframes

The final mesh-optimization technique considered in this chapter for real-time 3D games relates to mesh animation—specifically, to all the data inside the animation channel that describes how the mesh changes over time. Much of the animation data contained there is encoded in the form of keyframes. A *keyframe* is a record or snapshot of the state of the mesh at a specific time (a key moment) during the animation. An animation can contain one or more keyframes. A 100-frame animation for a rotating ball, for example, might feature four keyframes of animation: one at the start, recording the starting orientation of the ball; another at frame 25, recording a 25% turn; another at frame 50, recording a 50% turn; and so on, until the final frame, recording a 100% turn.

On the basis of the information recorded in the keyframes, a computer can automatically generate all intervening frames using interpolation. This is a mathematical technique that plots the values of keyframes on a graph, draws a continuous curve that runs through them, and then uses the curve to read off the values for frames between the keyframes. In this way, a smooth and continuous animation can be produced from the first frame to the last in which each and every frame has an appropriate number for all the values recorded in the keyframes.

It follows from this that the more keyframes an animation has, the greater the degree of control an animator has over the course of the animation because there are more user-defined keyframes as opposed to interpolated frames. But, as is often the case, that gain in control comes at an expense: More keyframes means more data, and more data means a greater performance hit. Consequently, animation developers must engage in the same type of balancing act as when optimizing meshes for polygons and textures for pixels. The aim here is to keep keyframes to a minimal while also achieving the results intended for your project.

CONCLUSION

This chapter considers the other side of graphics—specifically, 3D graphics. Here, an object is seen as being a mesh. A mesh is composed of four channels of information: geometry, UV mapping, rigging, and animation. The geometry channel defines the form, shape, or constitution of the object in terms of vertices, edges, and polygons. The UV-mapping channel defines how a two-dimensional texture is projected or flattened out onto the surface of the model. The rigging channel defines the underlying skeleton or bone structure for a model, marking its hinges and joints and the limits of its movement. And the animation channel defines how that mesh changes over time within the limitations specified by the rigging. Together, these four channels constitute a mesh, and a mesh is the one of the raw materials for 3D scenes.

This chapter also offers some practical advice as to how meshes can be created, optimized, exported, arranged, and otherwise handled to get the most from them and to maximize the performance of your game when working with them. These techniques included minimizing the number of mesh polygons, optimizing mesh topology to feature only tris or quads arranged in edge loops and rings, reducing the number of UV seams, exploiting UV seams to recycle texture space, establishing consistent texel density, optimizing models for occlusion and culling, and reducing animation keyframes wherever possible. The next chapter builds on knowledge from both this chapter and the previous, exploring the world of lighting and illumination for real-time 3D graphics.

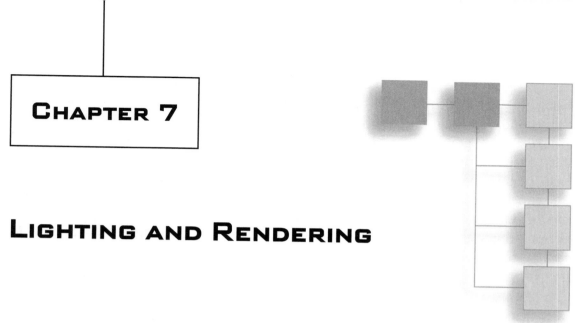

CHAPTER 7

LIGHTING AND RENDERING

"There is a crack in everything. That's how the light gets in."

—Leonard Cohen

By the end of this chapter you should:

- Understand the importance of lighting for real-time games.
- Understand direct and indirect illumination.
- Understand materials, normals and normal mapping.
- Appreciate the difference between forward and deferred rendering.
- Understand vertex-based and pixel-based lighting.

This chapter is in many respects a continuation of the previous in that it relies and expands on all the information contained there. Specifically, it considers the subject of lighting and rendering for 3D scenes.

In the previous chapter, I used the terms "render" and "rendering" loosely to refer to the process of drawing 3D polygonal objects to the screen as pixels—cubes, triangles, meshes, and others composed from the basic ingredients of vertices, edges, and polygons. In this chapter, to be more precise, "rendering" refers primarily to the process converting a 3D scene (with its meshes in 3D space), as seen from the perspective of a camera, into a 2D form that can be projected onto the flat surface of a monitor, where it is presented to the user in pixels as a final image complete with lighting information and special effects.

This final image of the 3D scene, which will be seen by the gamer, is referred to as the "rendered scene" because it is the result of the render process. Consequently, for real-time 3D video games, rendering is something that typically occurs once per frame. Thus, for a game running at 30 frames per second, there will be 30 renders per second. Rendering is therefore the video-game equivalent of using your camera to take a photograph of a real-world scene, developing the photo yourself, and then showing your friends the final photo—the final photo being the rendered image. The focus of this chapter, then, is to offer a basic overview of the mechanics underlying the render process—the process of "taking the photo" and "developing it" in the context of real-time 3D graphics. This is a subject of the upmost importance for all games programmers and artists, and especially so for programmers planning to develop their own homemade game engine.

If you have already used asset-creation software such as 3DS Max, Blender, or Maya, or if you have used game engines such as Unity or the UDK, you will likely be familiar with the term "rendering" and with how these programs take care of most rendering work automatically. Indeed, they ship with pre-made render systems (renderers) that do the calculation and rendering work for you on the basis of your 3D scene. You simply put your meshes into the scene, and it is rendered automatically!

Using this software, you might be led to believe that only those who must create their own render system from scratch need to learn about how rendering works, just as one need not know how a car is made in order to drive it. But a sound working knowledge of rendering and renderers can help you to optimize your work, even if you never plan to make a render system. It can help you work better with whatever renderer you *are* using, whether pre-made or custom made. Indeed, the performance gains and workflow improvements to be had by finding out more about rendering should not be underestimated. This knowledge can help you increase the run-time performance of your game, work faster and more easily with your game-development tools, and offer guidance and instruction about the optimal way to create special effects and implement other game features. In short, you should learn about rendering. It is important.

THE COMPONENTS OF SHADING

If an artist gave you a blank sheet of paper and asked you to "render it," you couldn't do it because you would have insufficient data with which to work. You'd have to hand back the paper unchanged. An empty scene produces an empty render because nothing comes from nothing. If, however, an artist sketched only the outlines of a cartoon character and asked you to "render it," or "shade it," you could do so—but only after asking several relevant questions. These questions might be as follows:

- What color should the character be?
- What is the object made of? Skin? Fur? Metal?
- Where is the light source in this image?
- In which direction is the light facing?
- Where should the shadows be?

The answers to these questions, in combination with the outline or shape of the object, are sufficient to produce a rendering. In short, they are the components of *shading*.

To render an image, you need the following ingredients for all objects in the image:

- Form
- Material and texture
- Lighting

Together, these three components (form, material and texture, and lighting) determine the shading of an object. Because rendering is the process of shading, these components are therefore instrumental in rendering.

Form: Shape, Outline, and Structure

In the world of 2D, the form, or structure, of an object can be defined through shapes and outlines. In the world of 3D, it can be defined through a mesh, as built from vertices, edges, and polygons. The geometry channel of the mesh defines its form—the extents of the object itself, the amount of space it occupies, its mass, its shape, and its structure. (See Figure 7.1.)

Figure 7.1
The outline or form of a house mesh, in wireframe. This model is untextured and unshaded.
Source: *Autodesk Maya*

Material and Texture

Together, the material and texture of an object define the properties of its surface—
that is, whether the surface is rough, smooth, hard, soft, shiny, dull, transparent, or
opaque. They define all the nuances of the surface that change or affect how it
responds to lighting or illumination—almost all the things that make it appear as it
does to the human eye. Questions of material and texture relate strictly to the surface of the object, and not to the object structure or to the properties of lighting.
(See Figure 7.2.)

Figure 7.2
Material applied to a form, without lighting applied.
Source: *Autodesk Maya*

Lighting

Objects do not typically exist in isolation from each other in some abstract nowhere place. Rather, they exist inside a coordinate space and world along with other objects and with light sources that cast illumination in the form of directed rays. Light in the form of photons is emitted from a light source and travels from the source to an object. The photons then bounce and scatter from the surface of the object, after which they continue traveling until they hit your eye. When the photons reach your eye, your brain decodes the frequency into the sensory experience of sight; through it, people perceive colors, shapes, and forms. The more light an object receives, the brighter it appears.

Notice that both the form and material of the object influence how the object is affected by light. The material, or surface, controls how light bounces and is scattered when it strikes the object. The form determines whether it receives light at all and whether it blocks or occludes other objects from receiving light. (See Figure 7.3.)

Figure 7.3
Lighting applied to a form on the basis of the material. Notice the shadow from the chimney.
Source: *Autodesk Maya*

LIGHTING: DIRECT AND INDIRECT ILLUMINATION

It is necessary to continue this analysis of rendering by considering lighting in more depth. Lighting is in many respects the most fundamental ingredient of any visual phenomenon. Without light, people would not be able to see. But light is more than simply a Boolean property that enables you to see when it is "switched on" as opposed to when it is "switched off." Light does not enable you to see the world as it actually is, right now; rather, it gives you a sensory experience that is meaningful to you based on the movement of light in relation to your eye, regardless of whether your vision corresponds to what is really there.

For example, light from the sun travels in rays. It is estimated that, after bouncing from the moon, the rays travel to the earth in 1.3 seconds, at which point the light enters your eye. The upshot of this is that the moon you see with your eyes is always 1.3 seconds old. You do not see the moon as it is right now. If an alien battleship were to eradicate the moon, you would not see the effect of the explosion until 1.3 seconds after it actually occurred. This interesting factual aside is not directly relevant to video-game graphics, but it hints at the nature of light—the way it travels in rays and bounces, resulting in your seeing a thing only when the light enters your eye. This ability has fundamental significance to computer graphics and for any video-game artist interested in creating realistic scenes. Specifically, it enables you to make a distinction between two main kinds of light: direct illumination and indirect illumination.

Direct Illumination

"Direct illumination" refers to light rays that have travelled from a light source (the sun or an artificial light) to a target object—any object—with no bounces in between. If you were to place a chair directly under a spotlight, most of its illumination would be direct illumination. That is, most of the light hitting the chair would come directly from the spotlight source. (See Figure 7.4.) This is significant for two reasons. First, direct illumination is more intense and will illuminate the subject more strongly. Second, direct illumination will color the subject more strongly with the color of the light. Green lights will add green tints to any objects they illuminate directly, blue lights will add blue tints, and so on.

Figure 7.4
An object affected by direct illumination. Notice that shadows are black, as are walls not directly illuminated.
Source: *Autodesk Maya*

Indirect Illumination

Try the following experiment: Walk into your bedroom, turn on the light, and take a look at the floor underneath the bed. The floor is not itself in the direct path of the light source, but is still visible to the eye. That is, it does not appear completely black. True, it is darker than other areas of the floor that *are* directly exposed to the light source; fewer rays are reaching the destination. Even so, it is still visible—albeit dimly. The floor underneath the bed is illuminated by indirect illumination. This refers to light that has been emitted from a source and that has bounced one or more times from other objects before hitting the subject—in this case, the floor under the bed.

Note that light bounces not only from smooth and specular objects such as mirrors, metal, and glass, but from practically any object, including diffuse objects such as walls, sheets, carpets, bricks, doors, and people. Light that has bounced from the latter type of objects is called a "diffuse inter-reflection," and light bounced from the former is called a "specular inter-reflection." Light—whether direct or indirect—that actually touches an object is called an "incident ray." (See Figure 7.5.)

Figure 7.5
Indirect illumination at work. Notice the subtler effects of lighting from light bounces.
Source: *Autodesk Maya*

Indirect illumination loses intensity with each bounce, and thus its intensity on a subject is less than if it had been direct. In addition, a bounced ray inherits just a shade of the color of the surface from which it bounced. If light bounces from a red brick wall, then the bounced light will inherit a desaturated shade of red.

Rules for Lighting

Together, direct and indirect illumination are responsible for creating lighting in a 3D scene. From these two kinds of light, six basic rules emerge for lighting and rendering believable scenes:

■ Objects that receive neither direct nor indirect illumination should appear black.

- Objects that receive both direct and indirect illumination will typically be the brightest and will feature the highlights (bright points) of the scene.

- Objects that receive only indirect illumination are said to be in shadow and will typically appear darker and dimmer than other objects receiving direct illumination.

- Objects receiving indirect illumination will receive color splash. That is, they will be tinted with subtle coloration because indirect illumination inherits the color of the surface from which it bounced.

- When, for example, a coffee mug is placed on a table, a small sliver of space forms on the underside edges of the mug where it meets the table that is inaccessible to light, creating a tight but dark shadow. This is known as a "contact shadow," and the overall effect is called "ambient occlusion." (See Figure 7.6.)

Figure 7.6
Ambient occlusion produces contact shadows found here around the wall edges and where the box meets the floor.
Source: *Autodesk Maya*

- The material of an object determines how much or little light is received on a surface pixel basis. Shiny materials (like glass and mirror materials) intensify the effects of light because they absorb fewer rays and reflect more. Diffuse materials (such as brick and cloth materials) diminish the effects of light because they absorb more and reflect less. The variation in tones across the surface of the object based on its material and on the lighting in the scene contributes to how rough or smooth the object appears. Rough objects feature high levels of contrast and variation in the light levels across the pixels of their surface; jumbled patterns of lights and darks emphasize ruggedness and roughness. Smooth objects feature continuous tones of light levels; predictable gradations between lights and darks emphasize smooth surfaces.

LIGHT SOURCES

Lighting, whether direct or indirect, is emitted into an environment from one or more light sources. In computer graphics, a light source is essentially a place from which light is cast. Unlike the real world, where light is cast from bulbs and the sun and other tangible objects that can themselves be affected by light, the light sources in video games are primarily substance-less mathematical constructs. The video game light source is where light begins—something that can send out light but cannot receive light. In the real world, the brightest light source in the solar system is the sun. Light sources also include light bulbs, candles, flashlights, reflections, fires, and more. In computer graphics, we have far fewer types of light sources to work with, but all of these must be used and combined in imaginative ways to simulate real-world light sources.

Note

It should be noted that, from here onward, I shall use the term "light source" to refer to the primary light sources discussed next—the originators of light in a scene. It shall not be used to refer to indirect light sources, such as when a wall allows light to bounce from it, unless otherwise stated.

In the world of computer graphics and games, a pre-determined set of mathematically precise light sources is used to simulate or approximate real-world light sources. These are summarized here. Most game engines and 3D modeling software support these lights sources and offer additional specialized types. Support for light types differs from engine to engine and software to software, however.

- **Directional light.** A directional light is typically the cheapest form of light, computationally speaking. That is, the presence of a directional light in a 3D scene places the least demand on both the graphics processing unit (GPU) and central processing unit (CPU) compared to other standard light types. A directional light can be defined mathematically by a direction vector D. This expresses the direction in which the light source is facing. The directional light typically has no limitation on its range, and thus acts metaphorically as an infinitely large wall that casts light along its direction vector for an infinite distance. Directional lights are frequently used in video games for simulating large and bright light sources—most notably the sun for daylight scenes and the moon for nighttime scenes. (See Figure 7.7.)

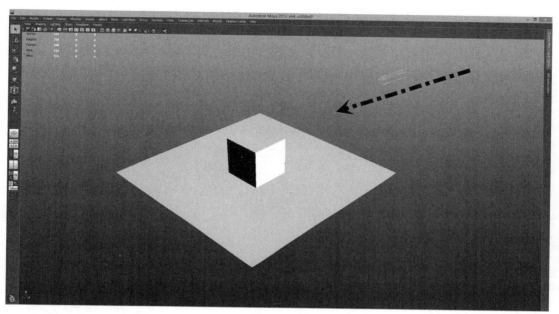

Figure 7.7
Directional lights in a 3D scene cast light infinitely in a specified direction. This figure demonstrates the direct illumination effects of a directional light in Maya. Notice the darkness of the cube faces pointing away from the light.

Source: *Autodesk Maya*

- **Point light.** The point light is widely used in games as a light source for various artificial kinds of light including wall lights, ceiling lights, explosions, flares, fireworks, torches, magical effects, and more. In essence, the point light casts rays of light in all directions radially from a single and infinitely small point in 3D space. This point is expressed using a coordinate value. The cast illumination is limited in its effects by two radius values: the inner radius and outer radius. The inner radius specifies where the light begins to fade out. The outer radius marks where the light terminates completely. Any object in the scene beyond the point light's outer radius is unaffected by the light. The point light can be represented mathematically in at least two distinct ways, and some engines use one over the other depending on their requirements. As a result, the point light can be the next most computationally expensive light after the directional light or sometimes the most expensive of all lights, depending on the method used. (See Figure 7.8.)

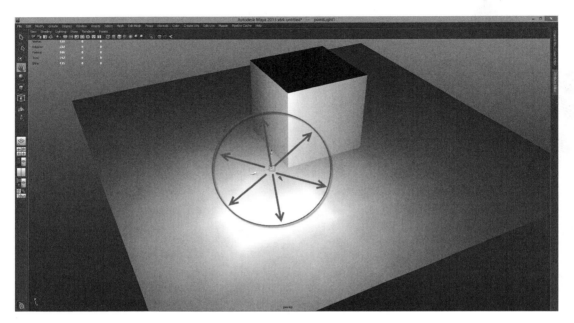

Figure 7.8
Point lights cast light in all directions from a single point out to a specified radius.
Source: *Autodesk Maya*

- **Spot light.** A spot light is typically used for directional lights whose limits or range must be carefully specified. The spot light is used for car headlights, flashlights, stage lights, various kinds of cone-like or tube-like magic spell effects, and more. The spot light is often the most computationally expensive light and is thus used sparingly, when no other light type can be applied. (See Figure 7.9.)

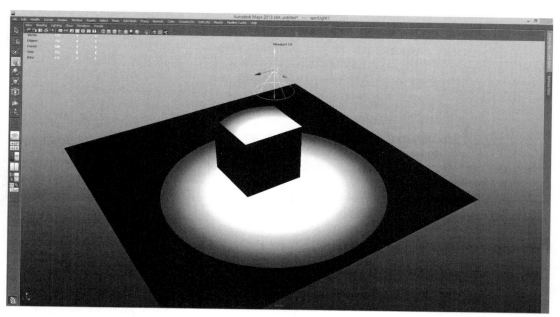

Figure 7.9
Spot lights cast light from a single point within a conic volume. This figure demonstrates the effects of a spot light using direct illumination. Note the darkness of faces not directly facing the light source.
Source: *Autodesk Maya*

CALCULATING DIRECT AND INDIRECT ILLUMINATION

The combined effects of the direct and indirect illumination of a scene, as discussed earlier, are referred to as its global illumination (GI). In short, "global illumination" refers to all the lighting ingredients of a computer-generated scene that make it look realistic. These include highlights, shadows, reflections, ambient occlusion, color splash, and more.

Calculating accurate GI is computationally expensive—phenomenally so. In fact, it is perhaps the single most expensive calculation a video game must make regarding its graphics, at least in terms of time required. This is because the computer must first trace out all light rays from each light source, then determine their points of contact with objects in the scene, then trace out their bounces based on each object's material, then trace out the points of contact for the bounced light rays, and then repeat this process for however many bounces are permitted from each ray.

In the real world, an infinite number of rays and bounces are allowed (for all we know). But for developers interested in competitive run-time performance for their games, a strict limit must be set as to the number of light bounces permitted to enter the lighting calculations to prevent infinite looping and recursion. Even with such concrete limits in place, calculating realistic-looking lighting for a 3D scene is still too much for real-time graphics, at least on current consumer hardware. That is, GI cannot yet feasibly and practically be calculated on a per-frame basis (for each render) on consumer hardware, such as gaming PCs and consoles (although each generation of gaming hardware and engines brings it closer to reality).

Note

Note that this limitation is a practical and not a logical one. It is not that GI cannot be calculated in real time because of some logical incompatibly or requirements of the method, but only because the limitations of current consumer hardware make it impractical.

So what can be done to simulate or fake realistic lighting in games? Clearly something can be, because most contemporary games do look very realistic (comparatively speaking). They feature the hallmarks of direct and indirect lighting, ambient occlusion, reflections, shines, and color splash, not to mention rough and smooth-looking surfaces.

There are, of course, a range of tricks and techniques that developers use to create realistic-looking lighting in games. Almost all of them relate to hacks or changes made to the rendering process, or to specific rendering methods. One of these is light-mapping (discussed next) and another is deferred rendering (discussed later in this chapter).

Both are particularly important in rendering and affect the way artists and developers go about building their levels, meshes, and scenes. Essentially, they demand that you see 3D graphics and video-game worlds from a perspective that is fundamentally at odds with the way people typically see and understand the world around them. Even so, it is a perspective that you must understand and appreciate in order to design games that look impressive and perform optimally.

LIGHT-MAPPING: ILLUMINATION THROUGH TEXTURES

One of the most pressing problems with lighting for real-time 3D games is its computational expense. There are just too many variables, complexities, details, and intricacies involved to calculate realistic lighting on a frame-by-frame basis given current consumer hardware. Light-mapping is one attempt to work around that problem, but although it has proved largely successful and is widely used in games, it still has some significant limitations, as you shall see.

The term "light-mapping" refers not to a specific thing or entity, but to a process or technique that game developers use. Light-mapping is something that developers *do*.

Specifically, light-mapping is the process of baking lighting into textures. That is, it is the process of having a render system calculate the lighting for a scene once and ahead of time, and then saving that lighting information in the form of regular textures, which are blended or layered onto the existing textures of the scene when the game is running for the models to appear as though they are really being illuminated by lights in the scene. In practice, this means that the output of the light-mapping process is a set of textures, called "light-maps." These textures record all the lighting for the meshes of the scene based on the position of the lights and the form of the meshes. Shadows are rendered as darker pixels, and highlights as lighter pixels. These textures can then be blended onto the existing textures of models to brighten and darken them in specific areas to imitate the effects of the shadows, highlights, and indirect illumination that would have been created from the lights if they had been calculated in real time.

Light-mapping is essentially the following three-stage process:

1. **Calculating the lighting for a scene.** This happens once at development time using the render system of a game engine or 3D modeling software. This system calculates how the surfaces of objects in the scene should appear based on their position and size, as well as the position and direction of the lights, and according to the models of direct and indirect illumination. These calculations can take a long time in practice, especially for larger scenes with many models—perhaps several hours or even as long as several days on slower hardware.

2. **Storing the result of the lighting calculations.** The result is stored in the form of color pixel-based textures, which are packaged and shipped with all the other textures of the game when it is completed. The light-mapping process generates these textures using the UV-mapping of models in the scene. It calculates how light should fall across the surface of a model and renders that information to a flat texture. It does this by "unprojecting" the 3D model according to its UV-mapping so that the light-map texture can be projected back onto the model when the game is running, as though it were a regular texture.

3. **Projecting the light-map textures onto each model when the game is running.** These are blended with the regular textures and materials to make the model appear illuminated. In this way, the cost of light-mapping is reduced from real-time lighting calculations to a texture memory footprint and texture blending. (See Figure 7.10.)

Material   Light Map   Baked Lighting

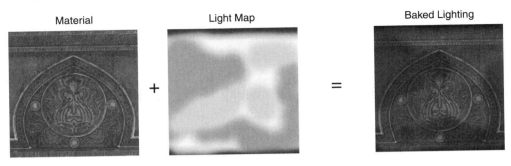

Figure 7.10
Light-map mechanics. Texture with light map added.
Source: *Autodesk Maya*

In short, the potential of light-mapping as a technique for producing global illumination should not be underestimated. It can, and frequently does, produce strikingly realistic results for games. But it has an important drawback that should be highlighted here—not to discourage developers from using light-mapping, but to demonstrate its limitations. Specifically, light-mapping cannot be used for illuminating dynamic meshes—that is, meshes that animate, change, or move over time during the game. Why? Because light-map textures, which are produced as a result of light-mapping, are produced at development time, not at run time. They are generated by developers while making the game (development time) so they may be applied as textures when the game is running (run time). This means the lighting calculations are valid for the scene and game generally only as long as the level and its objects do not change from their state at the time the light maps were produced. If objects move or change, then the lighting would also have to change in response, because light rays would follow a different path and will bounce differently. But light-mapping can never allow for changes to be made to the light maps because the fundamental purpose of light-mapping is to produce light maps ahead of time to improve run-time performance.

All this is to say that light-mapping cannot allow for change, and thus cannot be used to illuminate dynamic objects. It is used for illuminating static objects: walls, floors, tables, chairs, houses, mountains, hills, and all kinds of structural and prop objects that will not move or change at run time. In other words, light-mapping can save you in the case of objects that do not move, but what can be done to illuminate those that do?

REAL-TIME LIGHTING: VERTEX-BASED VERSUS PIXEL-BASED

A game engine's render system is responsible for drawing the lighting for a scene in real time. Therefore, the work of drawing the lighting for dynamic objects is the work of the render system (or renderer). To achieve this end, the renderer relies on a shading technique that is a systematic method, formula, or algorithm for shading the surfaces of objects on a per-frame basis—meaning, many times per second. It is referred to as a "shading technique" because the task of drawing lighting involves shading the surfaces of objects in the scene, brightening them or darkening them.

During the late 1990s, one of the most notable shading techniques for illuminating objects in real time was Gouraud shading, named after its originator, Henri Gouraud. This method is a form of vertex-based lighting. (See Figure 7.11.) It works by considering every vertex of a model currently in view of the camera, determining whether a vertex is directly exposed to a light source, and if so, determining the extent of brightness. When every vertex of a polygon is given a weight or brightness value, the polygon surface is then shaded continuously as a smooth gradient between the vertices, the brightness of the gradient being controlled by the brightness of the vertices.

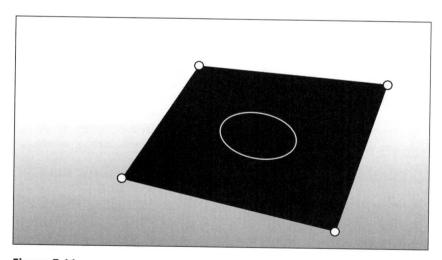

Figure 7.11
Vertex-based lighting at work. Although the ring of light is shining at the center of the surface, it still appears black because it is not intersecting any of the corner vertices.
Source: *Autodesk Maya*

This method is frequently used for its speed rather than its accuracy. The complexity of the method is determined mainly by the number of light sources in the scene and the number of vertices of the mesh that are currently in view and exposed to a light source. Notice that, as with most rendering methods, this method does not take into consideration objects that are not visible—those not in view of the camera. This is because unseen objects do not need to be rendered.

The benefit of Gouraud shading and vertex-based lighting methods generally is performance. They typically work well with older hardware and can produce results quickly. But the performance here is typically at the expense of realism. Surfaces shaded in this way tend to look smooth and artificial because of the linear gradient interpolated between vertices. In addition, a further problem emerges: The shading method is tied directly to the geometry of the scene—namely, to their vertices. The result is that meshes must be densely tessellated with polygons to produce believable lighting. If a flashlight object is shone onto the center of a square wall mesh (say, a large wall that has only four vertices, one at each corner), then the wall will still appear completely black if the flashlight fails to directly illuminate any of the corner vertices.

Problems like these have resulted in a reduction in the use of vertex-based lighting on almost all gaming platforms except for games targeted at legacy hardware or mobile platforms. Instead, most games now use pixel-based lighting solutions, primarily because most hardware allows it and greater realism can be achieved.

Note

Objects not visible to the game camera on any specific frame are said to be outside the view frustum, at least for that frame. The view frustum essentially corresponds to a hypothetical three-dimensional volume in front of the camera lens that mathematically describes what the camera can see: the camera's field of view (FOV) and focal length. Objects that are ignored by the rendering calculations because they are outside the volume of the frustum are said to have been "culled." Culling is a performance optimization for ensuring renderers work only with objects that can be seen. This is consistent with the RAMS principle of simplicity and with Occam's razor: working with the minimum number of entities necessary.

Pixel-based lighting, (also known as per-pixel lighting) is an alternative to vertex-based lighting that shades the surfaces of meshes in the scene on the basis of pixels rather than vertices. With pixel-based lighting, meshes visible to the camera are rendered to the screen. For each pixel, the render system decides how much it should be brightened or darkened according to the lighting in the scene. Pixels that are unlit are rendered black and light sources are typically rendered at full intensity, with every other kind of pixel at some value between these extremes.

In many respects, pixel-based lighting is computationally more expensive than vertex-based lighting, but it typically produces more realistic looking results. This is because the intensity of lighting across a surface is calculated on a pixel-by-pixel basis, meaning that lighting intensity can vary non-linearly as it does in the real world. Pixel-based lighting is a technique often used in conjunction with normal mapping to further enhance the realism of renderings.

NORMAL MAPPING

When a per-pixel shading technique is selected for lighting in a render system, a whole new world of possibilities and realism becomes available to the game developer. Specifically, a range of other pixel-based tricks can be used and combined with per-pixel lighting to increase the realism of the scene and to open up new possibilities for optimizing the run-time performance of the game.

One of these tricks or techniques is normal mapping. (See Figure 7.12 and Figure 7.13.) This technique is used primarily to simulate the appearance of roughness, bumpiness, dents, marks, and other finer details to meshes and their surfaces. All these affect the lighting of a mesh, as dents and cracks tend to darken a surface while protrusions and extrusions tend to brighten it.

Figure 7.12
Surface before normal mapping is applied.
Source: *Autodesk Maya*

Figure 7.13
Surface after normal mapping is applied.
Source: *Autodesk Maya*

Consider, for example, the rocky and craterous surface of the moon, with its bumps, hollows, and irregularities. All these details could be modeled directly into the geometry itself with vertices, edges, and polygons. Indeed, there is nothing wrong doing that, per se. But doing so would increase mesh complexity, raising the polygon count and increasing its computational expense. In contrast, much of this expense can be alleviated with normal mapping—without losing the realism and details. The purpose of normal mapping is to enable developers to use a map to define the details of a mesh surface—its roughness, jaggedness, dents, notches, etc.—without having to actually model that detail with polygons.

Normal mapping works by using a specialized RGB texture that is mapped onto the model. Its pixels encode not graphical data that is intended to be shown on the surface of the model like a regular texture, but normal data. That is, each pixel of the texture encodes a normal vector—a directional arrow that points out from the model at the specified pixel and tells the renderer which way the pixel is facing in relation to the lights of the scene. Pixels that point toward a light (those whose normal vector points toward a light) receive more illumination than those pointing away. Indeed, the brightness of a pixel (its RGB value) is to some extent an expression of how far its normal is orientated toward an incident ray of light. In short, normal maps offer developers per-pixel control over the way light appears to react to a surface and its details. Specifically, developers can set some pixels (*X*) in the normal map to point in one direction, and others (*Y*) to point in a different direction. This difference in direction in normals between set *X* and *Y* means that set *X* will receive a different degree of illumination from set *Y*.

This power to set normals and to thereby change levels of illumination on a per-pixel basis can be harnessed to create the appearance of details and depth on a flat polygonal surface where none, in fact, exist. This is because much of the lighting detail on a surface arises from the contrast in luminance between pixels—the contrast between lights and darks (lights and darks being something created by lighting, with dark areas being those areas less accessible to light and light areas being those areas more accessible to light).

The technique of per-pixel lighting in combination with normal mapping goes a long way toward achieving realism in the real-time lighting of scenes, even though there are still further technical hurdles for the developer to overcome. Normal mapping takes advantage of per-pixel control by varying the brightness of pixels according to values in a normal map to create the illusion of depth and bumpiness on a surface, even in cases where the surface is completely flat in terms of its mesh topology. The appearance of roughness that normal mapping produces is simply an appearance.

RENDERING METHODS: FORWARD VERSUS DEFERRED

Renderers using per-pixel lighting, in combination with normal-mapping techniques, can produce impressive and highly realistic results in real time. However, despite the benefits to be had, additional performance problems can still arise, primarily because of the render method being used for the render system. The "render method" is the exact order and the sequence in which visible objects in the camera frustum are chosen and sent to the graphics hardware for processing to be drawn to the screen.

Different render methods differ in their performance and efficiency because they differ in the way they order and render objects. The traditional or default rendering method used by many games is known as "forward rendering"; it was the most common rendering method in AAA games prior to 2007. This method often raises performance problems for scenes that feature many objects and many lights, as you shall see. These problems arise because of how forward rendering works, and relate specifically to the features of overdraw and render redundancy. In response to these problems, a more recent rendering method has been developed: deferred rendering. To see more clearly the problems posed by forward rendering and how deferred rendering can solve them, as well as the implications it can have for your games, consider the following scenario.

Imagine a 3D daylight scene in a video game with many lights and meshes, including a verdant terrain with buildings, picket fences, hills, people, animated water, and more—an idyllic rural village. The camera object is positioned close to the center of that environment, facing just a small selection of the many objects that exist in the environment. For the sake of the example, say the camera is viewing several buildings (some in the foreground and some in the distance) as well as some other nearby objects including fences and shrubbery and some trees. These are the objects within the camera's viewing frustum, and thus these are the ones that factor into the rendering calculations for that frame. Now, the question arises: How should this scene be rendered optimally with real-time lighting on a per-pixel basis? If the screen is thought of as a canvas on which pixels can be drawn, the question is: How should the renderer draw pixels to the screen on the basis of the scene? Specifically, given a complete list of all objects in the camera frustum in no particular order—including a list of all the scene lights that affect the objects—what is the optimal way or order to process those objects to produce a final rendered frame on screen? This question is one of the recurring questions facing almost every game-engine developer. The answer is far from a settled matter. The "traditional" rendering method, insofar as any method can be considered traditional, is forward rendering.

Forward Rendering

So how does forward rendering answer this question? Given a list of all objects in the camera frustum, including the light sources affecting those objects, how does forward rendering render them to the display? In short, forward rendering starts by sorting all objects in the list based on their nearness to the camera, so nearer objects are rendered after more distant objects. It might do this using a sorting algorithm (painter's algorithm) or it might use other methods such as a depth buffer. The specifics of sorting are beyond the scope of this book. The important issue here is that, whatever means is used, the objects to be rendered are in some way sorted on the basis of their depth in the scene from the perspective of the camera. Its purpose is to sort objects so that nearer objects are drawn over the pixels of more distant ones. This makes sense because closer objects should appear in front of more distant objects. For example, buildings in the distance are drawn first, and then nearer buildings are drawn after.

So far so good. But the problem with forward rendering and per-pixel lighting is that for each pixel of every object drawn, it calculates its lighting data without regard for pixel overlap. This is a problem because some objects will overlap others, because nearer objects appear in front of distant objects. Thus, a lot of pixel data is overdrawn, meaning that many lighting calculations are wasted. That is, many pixels are shaded and illuminated on distant objects, only to be overdrawn later by pixels for nearer objects. This creates render redundancy, or wasted processing, because time is spent calculating lighting for regions of objects that will not be seen due to over-lapping and occlusion. (See Figure 7.14.)

Figure 7.14
Forward rendering leads to redundancy due to overdraw. Pixels for foreground objects are drawn over those for background objects. In this image, many objects overlap: Foreground buildings appear in front of distant buildings, as well as in front of the terrain, road, background hills, and more. All overlap leads to redundant lighting calculations in forward rendering.
Source: *Autodesk Maya*

The computational complexity of forward rendering for any scene can, in fact, be measured. The complexity of forward rendering can be seen as:

number of pixels drawn for all objects in frustum × number of lights in scene

The rendering performance of forward rendering, then, is intimately connected to the number of lights in the scene, the number of objects to render, and the size of each object (because object size relates to number of pixels on screen). Thus, final performance is strongly geometry dependent—hence the reason performance suffers, especially in larger scenes with many lights and objects.

Deferred Rendering

Deferred rendering, or variations of it, have now become the default rendering method for most contemporary games on high-powered devices such as consoles and gaming PCs. Deferred rendering is a largely alternative rendering method that attempts to solve many of the performance problems resulting from forward rendering as well as to introduce a range of additional benefits that can further increase the realism of scenes.

Deferred rendering begins, much like forward rendering, with a sorted list of all objects in the viewing frustum. It renders those objects, but not with scene lighting applied. Instead, it renders them unlit, with their materials applied to a temporary, off-screen pixel surface called the geometry buffer (G-buffer). It does this in a similar fashion to the forward renderer, overdrawing pixels where appropriate—but it does not calculate lighting for each object. Instead, objects are drawn in light-neutral conditions. After the G-buffer has been rendered and all pixels composited there, featuring all objects at their correct depths in the image, the deferred renderer then proceeds to a new render pass. In this pass, lighting is calculated on the basis of the G-buffer. The lighting pass is thus said to be "deferred." (See Figure 7.15.) Here, the lighting is calculated on the basis of each final pixel in the G-buffer rather than on each pixel for each object as it is rendered, as is the case with forward rendering. In other words, lighting is calculated only for the pixels that will actually be seen and not for the pixels that will be overdrawn. This makes deferred rendering less complex than forward rendering in a fundamental sense.

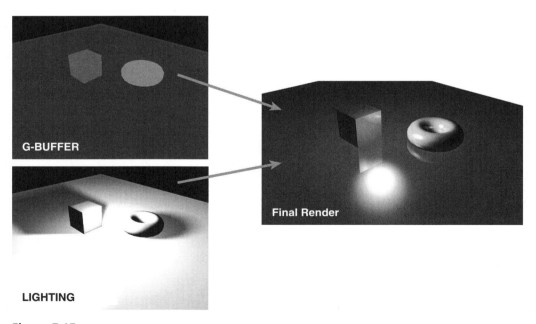

Figure 7.15
Deferred rendering solves many problems found in forward rendering. Lighting is calculated on the basis of the G-buffer.

Source: *Autodesk Maya*

The complexity of deferred rendering for calculating lighting might be expressed as follows:

$$\text{number of pixels in G-buffer} \times \text{number of lights in scene}$$

Each pixel in the G-buffer is iteratively brightened or darkened according to the intensity of each light in the scene that reaches the surface at that pixel. One of the main advantages of deferred rendering is that it decouples or disconnects scene geometry from scene lighting. It does so in the sense that the complexity of lighting calculations depend only on the number of screen pixels and the number of lights, but not on the size or number of meshes in the scene. For this reason, small and simple scenes (in terms of meshes) theoretically render just as fast (or slow!) as larger and more populated scenes if the number of lights and screen pixels are held constant.

Deferred rendering offers benefits to the developer apart from those that address the complexity of forward rendering. With lighting and geometry decoupled, developers have independent access to and control over both the final geometry of the scene and the final effects of lighting. That means pixels for both the geometry and lighting can be tweaked, edited, and changed independently at run time, on a per-frame basis, to produce all kinds of real-time special effects. The blurring of lighting and highlights, for example, can produce bloom effects, rim glows, or halos to add a fantastical, dream-like feel to objects in your environments.

Note

Deferred rendering is not without its technical limitations, which require workarounds of their own. One of the most notable flaws is its inability to successfully render transparent or even semi-transparent objects such as glass, crystal, magical barriers, and others. This limitation arises primarily because deferred rendering does not illuminate or refine the shading of surfaces until after the scene geometry is rendered opaquely to the G-buffer. Thus, overdrawn pixels in the G-buffer are overwritten entirely, and only the pixels for the nearest foreground objects are stored.

LEARNING FROM LIGHTING AND RENDERING

So what practical insight and advice can be gleaned from the issues considered here surrounding both direct and indirect lighting in real-time render systems? See the following list to find the answer to this question.

- **Use directional lights and point lights.** Avoid spot lights whenever possible. Typically, spot lights are the most computationally expensive lights in real time. Thus, the general recommendation is to avoid using them for real-time lighting whenever possible, and to instead use directional lights and point lights. Note that this advice does not apply in the case of static lighting (light-mapping) because light maps are generated at development time and not at run time. It applies only in cases of real-time lighting—lighting that must be calculated for moving objects at run time.

- **Use light-mapping over real-time lighting when possible.** If one point has been made time and again throughout this chapter, it is this: Real-time lighting calculations are computationally expensive. This expense should not be underestimated. If real-time lighting is not strictly limited and carefully regulated throughout a scene or game, it can, and likely will, bring the game to a crashing halt, leaving it unplayable for most users. In short, use real-time lighting only when and where it must be used and no cheaper alternative is available—typically for moving objects such as the player and enemies. In most cases, static lighting through light-mapping should suffice.

- **Use vertex-based lighting for older hardware and pixel-based for newer.** Vertex-based lighting offers a cheaper method for shading surfaces in a scene. It's comparatively fast and can produce reasonable results, especially for synthetic and retro looks, but it comes at the price of realism. Pixel-based lighting opens up a whole new world of realism for those who choose it for their games. Nevertheless, performance is a consideration for older hardware and mobile platforms. For this reason, vertex-based lighting is frequently chosen for older hardware, and pixel-based for newer. This rule also applies generally in the case of choosing between the forward and deferred render systems: forward for older hardware, and deferred for newer.

- **Minimize transparency and shadow effects.** Both transparency and real-time shadows are among the most computationally expensive effects. Consequently, you should use them sparingly. As with all other points, this advice applies only to real-time lighting and not static lighting, such as light-mapping.

CONCLUSION

Real-time lighting, and the effects created by lighting, remain among the most studied and researched areas of computer graphics. It is an area where developments are continually being made to simplify lighting calculations, increase lighting realism, and improve lighting performance in real-time graphics. At present, hardware limitations place strict and rigorous guidelines on developers as to how scenes should be illuminated if they are to perform well for most users. Some of those guidelines were outlined in the previous section.

Overall, this chapter introduced the basics of lighting by considering direct and indirect illumination, as well as the difference between the two. Then it considered the most notable light types used in video games, including the directional light, the point light, and the spot light. Subsequently, it delved into the specifics on issues such as vertex-based lighting, pixel-based lighting, normal mapping, and render methods. The two most notable render methods for contemporary video games are forward rendering and deferred rendering, the latter having spawned a number of variations and enhanced systems, which can be found in many famous game engines such as the Unreal Engine and the CryEngine.

Still, there is much more to be said on the issue of lighting and rendering, and this chapter—like most in this book—should be considered only an introduction to a subject that is much deeper. Nonetheless, this discussion of lighting must close here. Fortunately, it should leave you with some firm conclusions and advice for creating games with lighting. The central theme running through the advice for working with lighting makes reference to the RAMS principle of simplicity. More details on how to find out more about lighting in video games can be found in the appendix.

The next chapter leaves the world of graphics, which has occupied you over the last three chapters, and enters the world of audio.

CHAPTER 8

SOUND AND MUSIC

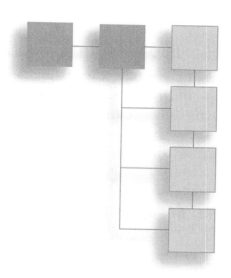

"Music is the strongest form of magic."

—Marilyn Manson

By the end of this chapter you should:

- Understand sound, music, and audio as assets.
- Appreciate the difference between 2D and 3D sound.
- Understand attenuation and distance.
- Understand volume and reverb.
- Appreciate the importance of audio file formats: WAV, MP3, and OGG.

In video-game development, audio is generally an umbrella term that refers loosely to sound and music in all their various forms, as well as to voice, vocals, and everything audible. Audio, like graphics, refers not to specific intrinsic features of a game or game engine, such as path-finding or interfaces, but specifically to assets. That is, it refers to independent digital data that must be created by an artist outside of a game engine and then later imported into the game by way of specific file formats, where they can be used and played.

This chapter focuses on audio assets—on their importance for games generally, and on some of the tips and techniques used by game developers for working with audio in an optimized way. As you shall see, audio is a powerful asset at a game developer's disposal—not simply for the obvious benefits it has for adding atmosphere and dramatic mood, but also for its potential to save the developer both money and work when creating graphical assets. This is because sometimes—perhaps more often than is generally accepted—what is heard need not always be seen.

Sound, Music, and Audio

To prepare to work with audio, music, and sound data, it is helpful to get an idea and an understanding of what exactly is meant when those terms are used, as well as some other terms. The three main terms—sound, music, and audio—are frequently used interchangeably in general conversation, especially sound and audio. Although their definitions are imprecise in many respects, I still think it is reasonable to draw careful distinctions between them in the field of game development—at least, it is when talking about these terms and concepts as I am here. The distinctions in audio might be given broadly as described next (the distinctions being made based on how the audio is used in the game).

Sound

Sound refers to any audible data—anything that can be heard—that is used to increase the realism of a scene, to punctuate or complement events occurring in the scene, or to provide some kind of feedback to the gamer based on his or her input in the game. The recorded sound of rain, for example, can be played on a loop to increase the realism of a rainy scene. The recorded sound of a gunshot can be played each time a gun is fired during gameplay to complement the activity and action of the scene. And finally, the synthetic sound of a beep or blip can be played whenever a GUI button is pressed or when an error occurs to provide the user with important sensory feedback about what is happening in the game—that is, it tells the user what he or she has done or achieved.

As can be seen from these examples, there are no main acoustic or intrinsic properties in the audio itself that unites them or makes them all belong squarely to the conceptual group of sound. Instead, it is in their function for the game that their commonalities can be found. Sounds for gunshots, explosions, wind, rain, beeps, bangs, howls, whirls, and more share the fundamental aim of acting as a kind of audible punctuation to games and scenes. The explosions might be an exclamation point, the beeps perhaps a kind of full stop or period. Audible data that has this main punctuating aim are typically classified as sound. In practice, sounds typically are audio-file assets that are less than one minute in length.

Music

If sounds are punctuation, then music essentially represents the content or narrative that is punctuated. Each musical score in a game is commonly called a *track*. Tracks themselves come in various forms, all differing subtly in their purpose. Two of them are discussed here:

- **Musical tracks.** Musical tracks are full-blown scores and compositions. These are usually played seamlessly on a loop as a background piece during gameplay to convey an overarching mood, feel, or emotional impression of the scene. Fast-paced techno tracks, for example, often permeate racing and driving games involving expensive sports cars or motorcycles to emphasize an adrenaline rush. Mechanical and militaristic scores underpin war and strategy games to remind players of regimentation, order and force. And somber or whimsical tracks accompany magical and mystery games to conjure up images of wonder, amazement, and poetic sensibility.

- **Incidental tracks.** These are typically shorter musical tracks that can be introduced and blended on demand with existing tracks to create a sudden transition or change in mood. For example, the peaceful serenity of a garden scene, complete with its whimsical music from flutes and pipes, can be suddenly and dramatically interrupted by the invasion of a well-armed horde of orcs and goblins, complete with a sudden change in musical track to drums, fast-paced beats, and suspenseful cymbal clashes. Such a sudden change as this would represent a significant incident in the scene, and hence its appropriate musical accompaniment would be the introduction of an incidental track: the drums and beats.

Voice

Many video games feature voice acting in some form or other. Some of the voice acting will be to give voice to specific characters in the game, while other voice work will be of the kind that breaks the fourth wall. That is, it will be voice work directed at the player, offering some kind of guidance or instruction to the player about how to play the game.

Voice is distinct from both music and sound in its purpose. It also introduces a number of additional technical problems and considerations for a game. Unlike sound and music, voice is typically included because of the content of what is being said rather than because of the emotion that is generated from its acoustical properties. Further, voice introduces a localization issue because the spoken word is typically in a specific natural language such as English or French or Dutch, as opposed to Simlish, the gibberish language that originated in *The Sims*. Because of this, most of the spoken word must be adapted and substituted in the game for each specific language version, assuming multiple versions of the game will be made in different languages. This has important implications for how the game is developed, not to mention the cost of development. More on the issue of voice later in this chapter.

FILE FORMATS AND AUDIO WORKFLOWS

Because audio data differs in the form of sound, music, and voice, and because these differences influence how the audio is used and the length of the audio, there are often differences in the way developers work with such data when making games. That being said, there are similarities, too.

One of the most notable similarities is the general choice of file format that developers make when saving audio data. Generally, only one or two file formats are used in games today. There are, nonetheless, a wide range of file formats available from which to choose for saving audio data assets. These include WAV, MP3, AAC, OGG, and more. But, as with image formats, these files differ in terms of lossless and lossy compression, and in terms of software patenting issues. These considerations tend to narrow the feasible choices for developers who are after the best quality free of charge and free of legal concerns.

The lossless and lossy compression methods determine how much, if any, quality is lost from the original data when the audio is saved to a file. (Lossy versus lossless compression was discussed in Chapter 5, "Graphics, Pixels, and Color," in the section "Image Formats: Lossless Versus Lossy.") In short, lossless formats, such as WAV, lose no quality when data is saved. In contrast, lossy formats, such as MP3, *do* lose data because they save only an approximation of the original.

The patenting issues surrounding audio file formats determine whether you can even legally use a particular file format for your own projects and how much you might have to pay in license fees for doing so. Even if you are technically capable enough to use and work with a specific format to encode and save your audio data, it does not necessarily mean that you can legally do so in practice—especially if you plan to sell your game. A whole range of legal caveats could apply. As a result, only two formats are commonly used for audio in games nowadays: WAV and OGG. The former is lossless and the latter is lossy, and both can be used free of charge.

Both WAV and OGG are used commonly, and are suited for different stages of development. Developers, musicians, and sound engineers involved directly in the recording and editing stages of audio data will typically work in their software of choice using the WAV format or some similar lossless format to ensure that no audio data is lost along the development cycle. However, when the audio asset is finalized and ready for import into a game engine, the audio is often converted or baked down from the lossless WAV to the lossy OGG, which is in many respects similar to the MP3 format. This is primarily in the interest of run-time performance and for keeping data size small, as WAV files are usually a lot larger in terms of megabytes than their OGG counterparts.

Some established game engines, such as Unity or the Unreal Engine, typically expect imported audio to be in WAV format and not OGG, but this is only because the engine automatically and internally compresses the WAV into OGG or some equivalent compressed format. When making your own custom engines, it is likely you will use the OGG Vorbis framework or a compliant technology to implement audio.

LOADING AND STREAMING

After audio is imported into an engine in OGG or an equivalent format, the developer faces an important technical choice about how the engine should load and play that sound asset when the time comes during gameplay. This choice is no trivial matter because it can significantly affect the run-time performance of a game in the long term. Any framework for audio playback will inevitably cause an overhead or performance burden on an engine. There are two main options available:

- The engine can load the sound file in its entirety into system memory and then play it once loaded using any audio library.

- The engine can load only a subset of data from the file and then play that subset, while continually shifting the horizon as playback progresses, unloading and loading in new sections to maintain a single, fixed-size segment of audio in memory at any one time. This method is known as *streaming*.

Both methods (loading and streaming) are used in games, for different reasons.

Loading

The loading method is used typically for sounds. These are usually audio samples that are small in file size, short in duration (less than one minute), and played frequently during the game. Such sounds include gunshots, footsteps, punch and kick sounds, bleeps, lasers, branch snaps, bird songs, door bangs, floorboard creaks, and more. These sounds, when loaded, do not leave a large memory footprint due to their smallness. In addition, being entirely loaded in memory, they can be played back optimally without the additional computational overhead involved with file streaming. This generally makes loading the preferred method for all small audio files, but not for files such as music, voice tracks, and longer sound samples.

Streaming

Audio streaming is the practice of making large files and extensive data digestible to a computer. It's particularly helpful when running a game, a situation in which every inch of performance should be treated as precious. Streaming attempts to make a large audio file bite-sized. It does this by playing and loading the file in parallel—specifically, by considering the audio track as a linear sequence of data. A fragment of the file is loaded, and then played in sequence. As playback commences, more and more data is removed from memory to make room for loading data further along the sequence that has yet to be played.

The practice of streaming incurs a performance overhead that has no comparison to the loading method. This is because streaming must always be loading and unloading data on the fly, as well as keeping track of playback progress. But, streaming does mean that potentially enormous files—such as music and voice tracks—can be played back without substantially affecting memory usage. This is because the file itself is never loaded entirely into memory. Streaming is generally the recommended—or sometimes the only—playback method feasible for larger files, including music and voice.

The advice given in both this section and the previous regarding audio can be summarized in the following points:

- Record, edit, and change audio using a lossless format such as WAV to ensure maximum quality.

- Import finalized audio into a game engine in either a lossless format (if the engine performs an automatic conversion to OGG) or a lossy format such as OGG (if no automatic conversion occurs). If using a pre-made engine, be sure to check out its documentation to see which case applies to you.

- Use audio file loading to play back sound files that are short in duration, are small in file size, and must be played back frequently during gameplay.

- Use streaming to play back all other audio files.

2D VERSUS 3D AUDIO

Audio that is played during gameplay, whether fully loaded or streamed from a file, can be classified even further as being one of two different major types: 2D or 3D. Before the advent of 3D engines and games in the early 1990s, all audio was 2D. Back then, the term "2D audio" didn't even exist because it could not have been used to legitimately mean anything beyond simply "audio." 3D audio was born from 3D games. But what does the distinction mean in practice?

In practice, 3D audio aims to increase the realism of a video-game scene by imitating how audio is heard in the real world. In the real world, of three dimensions, audio is not simply heard like audio on a set of speakers. Rather, things in the world—like birds and people and brass bands—make noises, and those things have a genuine position in 3D space. Further, people are also standing at a particular position in 3D space when they hear these noises—a certain distance away from the sound, and at a certain angle and orientation. These spatial properties found in both audio emitters and audio listeners—those who make and hear audio, respectively—have a significant impact on how the audio is actually heard, along with other factors, such as the acoustics of the environment. For example, audio travels differently in a music hall than in an open-air stadium. All these properties of audio as heard in the real world are those that 3D sound seeks to emulate.

These properties are not something that a sound designer builds into an audio asset. They are not effects that are intrinsic to the audio file or audio data itself. Rather, 3D sound effects are added programmatically by the engine to the sound in real time as a post-processing effect. This makes sense because, prior to running the game, the engine cannot possibly know in advance from where the audio will be emitted, nor can it know the position of the player when the audio is heard. Thus, these effects must be calculated and applied while the game is running. More details follow.

2D Sound

Given what has been said so far about 2D and 3D audio, it might initially seem that 2D audio is part of a bygone area, long superseded by the more "advanced" 3D sound, which can achieve "greater realism." However, this is not the case. Both 2D and 3D audio are used in both 2D and 3D games, and for different reasons.

Remember: The fundamental difference between 2D and 3D audio relates to their ability to convey a certain real-world 3D-ness to a scene. But, some audio elements do not benefit from 3D-ness. Music is one notable example. Typically, music that is played as an emotional accompaniment to a scene does not have a 3D position because the music is not really supposed to be in the world itself. The music is there for its emotional, psychological, and phenomenological qualities, not because it is more realistic for it to be there. (Sadly, most of us do not really live our lives to musical accompaniment!) This kind of audio is not subjected to 3D positional effects because such effects would damage the impact and purpose of the music itself. Music played as an emotional piece should not change in volume as the player moves around the level because the player's position is irrelevant to the musical score. The music should just play in this case. The same principle applies to feedback sounds used for menus and other game options, such as bleep and bloop sounds. These, too, are not typically situated anywhere in the game environment, nor are they heard by any particular person or listener.

Thus, 2D sounds—that is, sounds that have no 3D effects applied—are important for games. They typically include music, menu sound effects, and even some voiceover elements (such as when a voice addresses the gamer specifically, or when the voice is supposed to be an internal monologue). In short, be on the lookout for 2D versus 3D sound in your own projects, and use each appropriately.

3D Sound

To determine whether an audio sample should act as 3D audio, ask yourself: Does this audio exist in the game world? Does it, for example, come from a gun, a tree falling in the forest, or a person talking on the other side of the room? If the audio is supposed to be in the game world, then it is eligible to be 3D audio.

Being a 3D sound means it should have 3D effects applied. The implementation specifics of 3D audio differ, as always, from game engine to game engine and developer to developer, but the same fundamental and recurring development principles underpin 3D audio in all its various guises. These are the subjects of this section.

The implementation of 3D audio begins from two basic concepts:

■ There is something that *makes* a sound in 3D space (the audio source).

■ There is something that *hears* that sound in the same 3D space (the audio listener).

To this a third ingredient can be added: the 3D environment itself, in which both the source and listener are located. This environment might have all kinds of acoustic properties.

In this system, it is important to recognize that there are things that can be both audio sources and audio listeners, just as some things can be neither. Fog and mist seem to make no noise and hear no noise. People, in contrast, can both hear and make sounds. But these specifics should not trouble you unduly, as most engines can and do allow entities in the game to be both or neither at the same time. That is, a source can make sounds, and a listener can hear sounds that are made—and that's all you need know. On this basis however, some properties and features of 3D audio emerge:

- Volume and attenuation
- Panning and direction
- Reverberation and acoustics

Volume and Attenuation

The properties of 3D space influence the volume and attenuation of the audio sources in relation to the listener. In short, the further away a listener is from an audio source, the weaker and lower the source will sound from the perspective of the listener. An explosion, for example, will always sound louder to a listener who is closer to it than to a listener who is further away.

The volume at which an audio source is heard by a listener is related to the distance the listener is from the source. An imaginary sphere could be drawn around the source to graphically represent how the volume of that source falls off with distance for any listener, from full volume at the sphere center to silence along the sphere circumference and beyond. This graphical representation of volume to distance represents the attenuation of audio. (It could also be plotted on a graph using a quadratic equation.) In short, 3D audio means that the volume of audio sources will change based on the relative position of audio listeners, such as the player character.

Panning and Direction

Most gamers today play on computers with many speakers to create 5.1 and 7.1 surround sound, so named because the sound seems to surround you. In these kinds of configurations, provided the speakers are positioned correctly, 3D sound can further enhance the realism and 3D-ness of video games. It does so by adjusting the volume of audio sources non-uniformly across speakers, making specific sounds louder in different speakers at different times depending on the position and orientation of the player in the scene.

This effect can be used to simulate orientation. If you were to travel along a road in a car and hear the rumble of a distant factory on your right side, it would be heard loudest in your right ear because that ear would be nearest to the source. But if you were to turn around and travel in the opposite direction, the factory would be heard loudest in your left ear because that ear would be closer to the source than your right. 3D sound in games can enhance the depth of a scene by independently controlling the volume of each sound, in each speaker, depending on the orientation of the player's head in relation to surrounding audio sources.

Reverberation and Acoustics

Most 3D sound systems feature support for environment effects and acoustics. For example, imagine standing inside a music hall and listening to the orchestra play. Then imagine stepping outside while they are still playing and closing the door behind you. Consider the difference in the audio quality. The orchestra, when heard from outside the hall with the door closed, would not only sound weaker in terms of volume, but would sound more muffled and blurred than it did from inside the hall.

This effect happens because of the obstacles and the environment in which the sound must travel and reverberate before it enters the ear. Effects such as these, as well as echo effects, are usually part of the 3D sound arsenal—although the extent of support for such effects and their variety and realism vary from engine to engine and system to system.

AUDIO TIPS AND TRICKS

The use of audio in games is extensive, and its importance for creating realism and atmosphere is difficult to understate. Indeed, it is sometimes said that sound can make or break a game. If that is true, then it is important to ensure audio is used to gain maximum effect. Following are some general tips and tricks for audio. These are not exactly hard-and-fast rules used throughout the industry, but they have nonetheless proved valuable to me in the game projects I have pursued, and I know from conversations with many other game developers that they, too, follow similar principles when working with audio.

Beware of Over-Mixing

So you have created a really splendid game. Everything is working just as it should, and now is the time to start adding sound and music to make it even better. You have a sound library full of sound effects, and you have access to all the music you need. The question is, which sounds and music do you include in the game?

There is a strong temptation for some to include as much sound as possible. Surely, they reason, it's a shame to waste perfectly good sound effects! If they have it (and they do), and it can fit somewhere in the game (and it does), then they should include it! The result of this unfortunate strategy is usually a confusing mess of noise that might sound reasonable to the uncritical developer on first hearing, but usually leaves the player reaching for the mute button on their speakers or TV.

Only later does the developer finally come around to the player's view point after hearing his or her own game several weeks later, without his or her uncritical hat on.

The strategy that I pursue is, less is more. If a game must feature too few or too many sound effects, then it is usually better to have too few—though ideally it should be somewhere between. Start by adding only a few sound effects to a scene. Stop, and then check the scene. Continue to add more effects only if the scene seems bland, hollow, and empty. This might also mean returning to the game several weeks later to check how it sounds with your "critical hat" firmly on.

Graphical Substitutes

There are times during development when sounds can successfully replace graphics to produce the required sense of motion, animation, and life in a scene. This is significant because it represents a window of opportunity for developers to reduce the cost and time of their work. Consider, for example, a famous technique used in movies and games, often for comedic effect, with crashes and explosions. A man is standing on his driveway, cheerily waving goodbye to some relatives or friends departing in their car. The camera remains focused on the man and his waving, and you know about the departure of his relatives based only on what you hear through sound. You hear their car reverse, and then accelerate. Then continues the sequence of sounds that charts the events well enough for you to construct a picture in the theater of your mind: the sound of skids and of crashes into a lamp post, the rumble of garbage cans, the screeching of a cat, the screaming of a woman, the gushing of water from a fire hydrant, and finally the sound of sirens and commotion in the distance. Presumably, if this were a comedy, the man would still be there on his driving waving cheerily!

This example demonstrates the awesome power of audio and its impressive ability to create comprehensive action and motion in a scene, even when the main events are not themselves visible. For this reason, always be on the watch for time-saving opportunities like this, where audio can provide a more economical if not more powerful alternative to creating direct visual stimuli.

Intrusive Music

Most games, like most movies, do not feature musical scores with extensive and prominent vocals, and those that do, do so only sparingly. There is a reason for this, and it applies especially in the case of video games. It was mentioned at the start of this book the extent to which games have become firmly ingrained in our culture. Indeed, most gamers now spend hours in succession playing the games of their choice. That means many music tracks are played on a loop and are repeated during gameplay. Further, gamers also make mistakes. They get things wrong and play specific sections of a game over and over again to get things right and to reach the next level. That means much of a game is repeated and involves repetition. The problem with vocal music tracks (especially vocals the player can hear and understand) is that they tend to emphasize rather than detract from the repetitious nature of gameplay. The same notable phrases repeated over and over in vocals can draw attention to repetition, which can be irritating, removing the gamer from the experience. For this reason, I recommend avoiding the use of musical tracks with vocals unless there is an overriding reason to use them or an exceptional scenario that requires it.

Voice and Localization

Try wherever possible to isolate voice audio into separate files, distinct from the music and sound effects of the game. The aim here is to make the voice data easily substitutable as an asset, without affecting other assets such as music and sound effects.

Voice is typically spoken in a natural language, such as English or French, and thus is language and region specific. Releasing your game into other regions and markets will often require localization, the process of translating the game from one language to another, including subtitles and voice. Those markets will thus expect to hear voices and to read subtitles in their local languages. For the developers, localization can involve a substantial amount of work, but much of the work can be minimized if the assets are planned and created with care. Making the voice audio assets isolated and substitutable files means the files themselves can be replaced for localization purposes with other languages alternatives.

Tip

Keep localization in mind from the very beginning of development. Don't leave it as an afterthought.

CONCLUSION

This chapter detailed some of the key game-development principles surrounding audio, music, sound, and voice in video games. Audio, as with other aspects of game development, has specific implementation details that vary from platform to platform and engine to engine. But underneath, there remains a fundamental core of underlying principles. These concern the file formats used for encoding and storing audio in optimized ways for video games, as well as the methods for audio playback, including file loading and file streaming.

In addition, this chapter considered 2D versus 3D sound, highlighting the fact that there is no inherent antagonism between the two models. 2D sound is used for music and non–world specific sound effects, while 3D sound is typically used to embed or locate sounds within their environment. The mechanics of 3D audio involve the concepts of an audio source and an audio listener. They bring several key properties: volume to distance, speaker alignment to orientation, and environment type to special effect.

Finally, the chapter considered a range of tips and advice for creating and using audio in your own projects. The next chapter focuses on the subjects of special effects and post-processing, which encompass a whole range of popular and pervasive topics including particles systems, render effects, and animated textures.

CHAPTER 9

SPECIAL EFFECTS AND POST-PROCESSING

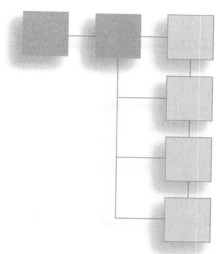

"Don't wake me for the end of the world unless it has very good special effects."

—Unknown

By the end of this chapter you should:

- Understand performance issues relating to special effects.
- Understand particle systems and texture effects.
- Appreciate the importance of post-processing.
- Understand how effects such as blur, depth of field, bloom, vignetting, chromatic effects, cel shading, and lens flare work.

This chapter focuses on special effects and post-processing for computer games. Stated in this context, both of these terms are broad and vague, and thus require further definition and clarification.

In short, game developers typically like to add further graphical realism or surrealism to their games by including features such as rain, fog, water, magical sparkles, explosions, laser beams, gooey alien slime, pillars of smoke and fire, blurs, sun flares, and all kinds of other effects. These are examples of special effects and post-processing effects. Although there is perhaps no single characteristic intrinsic to these examples that unites them in any way, there are nonetheless good reasons why all of them are classified as special effects or post-processing effects, as you will see shortly. Regardless of the reasoning behind the names, however, special effects and post-processing raise a number of important developmental issues for games, which have an important influence on how games are made. This chapter considers these issues in detail, drawing special attention to the general principles, concepts, and ideas that underpin them.

CREATING SPECIAL EFFECTS IN GAMES

There is, as far as I am aware, no general consensus about what exactly a "special effect" is in a video game. Rather, there is only an intuitive or vague understanding that it is some feature that adds glamour or realism, and that requires special effort on the part of the developer to produce. Of course, given this vagueness, there is a sense in which almost anything and everything in a game could be considered a special effect—and perhaps everything is! However, the term "special effect" is usually applied to a more narrow group of effects that attempt to simulate natural or supernatural phenomena that are otherwise difficult to create using the standard tools and features available to developers. Hence it requires special effort to make. For example, consider the effect of the common natural phenomenon of rain. Considering what you know about meshes, and textures, and graphics, as discussed in previous chapters, how should such an effect as this be created in a 3D video game? How would you do it? Think about it for a moment....

If you go about making this effect in the same, traditional, tried-and-tested way that you go about making most other objects for a game, such as tables, chairs, and characters, then you would start, as with all objects, by sculpting and modeling it—that is, by building a water droplet model using the standard mesh ingredients of vertices, edges, and polygons. Then, after having carefully modeled a highly detailed and impressive-looking droplet, you would continue by texturing the object with a water-like image to make it actually look like a water droplet. Then finally, once modeled, you would import it into an engine, duplicating it perhaps thousands of times in the scene, animating all of the duplicate droplets downward from the sky to the ground to create a successful rain effect: droplets pouring down from the sky to the ground.

This traditional method could, of course, be used in this way to create rain. But it poses significant developmental problems, which can be seen by simply examining how this method works more closely—problems in terms of both game performance and time and budget. First, the traditional method, when applied to rain like this, will take you a lot of time—time to model and texture the droplet, and then *more* time to define the animation of the droplets in which they fall to the ground under the effects of gravity.

Second, and perhaps most importantly, the presence of so many thousands of highly detailed droplet meshes in the scene, complete with water-texture effects such as gleams and shines and transparency (see Figure 9.1), could *on its own*—without the presence of other effects or graphics—overburden the system with computations so intensive that it could bring down even the most powerful consumer hardware available today. So clearly, this traditional three-step method of model, texture, and import that works so well for most tangible objects is not the way to approach the problem of creating rain. By extension, neither can it be the way to create any similar kind of effect involving many little pieces—snow, sparkles, dust, flocks of birds, swarms of bees, among others.

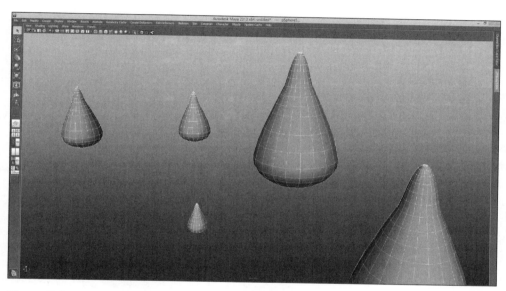

Figure 9.1
High-res raindrop meshes, modeled and prepared to create a rain effect using the "traditional method."
Source: *AutoDesk Maya*

All these effects involve the same basic problem: The traditional workflow simply is not designed for creating these kinds of effects. So how should you respond to this problem? One way would be to simply avoid creating games with rain and other such effects! Indeed, some games can and do take this road. Usually, this is because they do not really require such effects. But what about games for which these effects would really enhance the atmosphere and mood? Can anything be done in these cases? The answer is a resounding *yes*.

Adding rain, sparkles, or other kinds of effects to a game without killing performance requires the development of a new and special technique. Thus, the measures you take to achieve this are known as "special effects." In general, each special effect requires its own specific technique or clever workaround, and each developer has his or her own ideas about the "best" way to do it. Whenever I play games by other developers, I find myself studying the screen intently, trying to reverse-engineer their work in my mind to figure out how they approached creating some of the effects that I see and like. I never cease to be amazed by the different and ingenious ways in which different developers have tried to simulate similar kinds of effects, each method giving the game its own distinctive style and flavor. Despite this ad-hoc and developer-specific approach to creating special effects, however, a number of general systems, ideas, and techniques have been established for creating some of the most notable effects that you observe around you, including rain. The most prominent of these techniques is the particle system, and it is considered in depth in the next section.

PARTICLE SYSTEMS

You can solve the problem that arises when using the traditional modeling method for creating rain, as described in the previous section, by using a particle system. In fact, the particle system solves the problem for almost all cases in which the effect to be created involves lots of small pieces moving in a predictable and horde-like way, including rain, snow, fog, sparkles, dust, birds, bees, ants, waterfalls, bullets, fire, and more. Nowadays, particle systems are so common and pervasive in game development that almost every game engine available—both free and commercial—features some degree of support for them. In fact, most engines feature extensive support for them, such as the Unity engine, the UDK, and the CryEngine. Figure 9.2 shows a particle system at work.

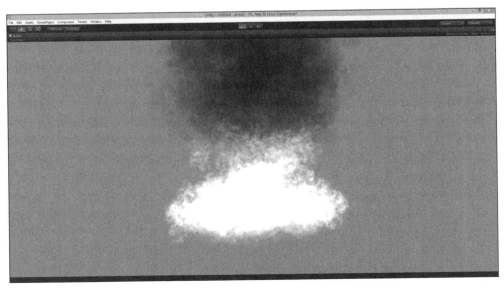

Figure 9.2
A fire particle system at work in the Unity 4 engine.
Source: *Unity*

It should be mentioned here that the particle system is not a discrete and tangible object or thing such as a mesh, an image file, or a sound file. Rather, it refers to a package of general ideas and concepts, which can be applied when making games to achieve all kinds of particle-like effects. Conceiving of these effects in terms of a particle system can help you to see the phenomenon differently and provides you with guidance on how best to implement it in a game.

The particle system depends on three main ideas working together:

- The particle
- The emitter
- The behavior

The Particle

Perhaps the central-most concept of the particle system is the particle itself. A rain droplet, for example, can be considered a particle. In other systems, a single sparkle, a single bee, a single bird—each of these is a unique and separate particle that is part of a larger and more complex system. When these particles come together and behave in unison, they form a particle system.

Earlier, when I talked about how a rain system might be made using the traditional method, I constructed a particle using a rain droplet mesh. The problem with that idea was that the high-resolution droplet mesh, along with its texture data, would prove performance prohibitive when multiplied many times. The game could simply not run with particles that were so detailed. Typically, therefore, a particle system features less-detailed particles. It achieves this by using *billboards*.

Rather than model a complex mesh for each particle, as I did earlier in the case of the water droplet, a particle is instead represented using a plane mesh—that is, a rectangle mesh with only four corner points. This mesh is constantly aligned to face the camera so that the camera always sees the particle from a direct, face-on view. This kind of simpler mesh is called a *billboard*; each particle corresponds to a billboard. The billboard is then mapped with an appropriate texture—a droplet texture for raindrops, a fire texture for sparkles, a bee texture for bees, etc. Together, the billboard and its texture constitute the particle. (See Figure 9.3.)

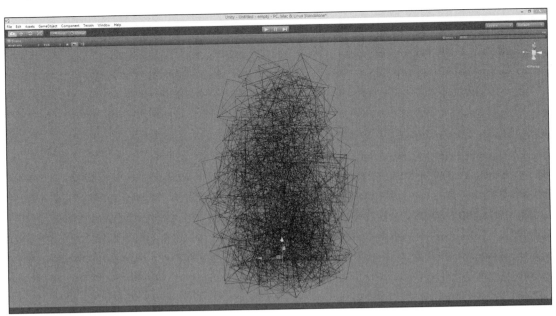

Figure 9.3
The fire particle system featured in Figure 9.2 is generated from a mass of billboard quad meshes, with textured applied, moving in unison.
Source: *Unity*

This simpler method for representing particles has proved both effective and performance friendly, despite the drawback that the particles themselves turn out to be 2D planes and not really 3D objects at all (even though they can exist and move in 3D space). If you can imagine flat sheets of textured paper flying through the air, aligned to your eyes, moving like raindrops or bees or birds, then you have imagined the particle system.

The Emitter

A garden hose is used to spray water—typically on the garden rather than, say, on your best friend. The water leaves the hose and enters the atmosphere, where it falls upon its target. The tip or nozzle of the hose might be identified as the point where the water enters the atmosphere. It is the source, or origin, point of the water. In a particle system, this point is referred to as the *emitter* (see Figure 9.4). The emitter is the place or thing that gives birth to particles. All particles start their life at the emitter.

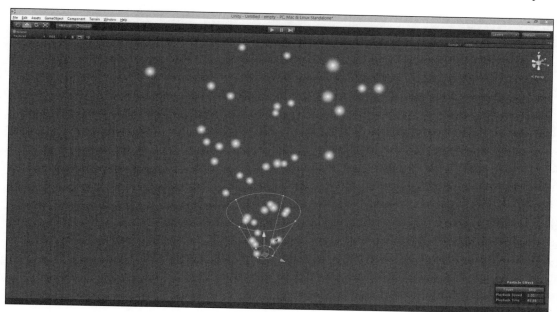

Figure 9.4
The particles in this system are generated upward from a cone emitter aligned to the ground.
Source: *Unity*

Emitters come in different shapes and sizes. For example, for the rain particle system, the emitter can be imagined as a giant plane or flat surface suspended far above the clouds that is facing downward. The raindrop particles are emitted *en masse* from random points on the emitter surface and travel downward at varying speeds under the effects of gravity before reaching the ground and terminating. Thus, the emitter is the birthplace for all particles in the system. All particles must begin at the emitter, though they rarely end, or terminate, there.

Depending on the effect you need to create, particles will be emitted from different shaped emitters, from different points on the emitter, and at different rates. While rain systems can be created from plane-shaped emitters that throw out particles at a steady and monotonous rate, a burst of sparkles from the tip of a magic wand requires a different configuration. In such a system, the particles will typically emit from a single point—the tip of the wand—and in a short and explosive burst that terminates almost as quickly as it begins. The shapes, sizes, and rates of emitters differ between particle systems, but all particle systems rely on the concept of an emitter regardless of its specifics.

The Behavior

The emitter injects particles into the system at a specified rate. However, once the particles have been emitted, they are little more than lifeless, free-floating particles. Something else—some overarching and governing law or force—needs to make them move, change, and otherwise behave as intended in unison to achieve the effect required. In short, after a particle is born, something needs to give it its stage directions.

The component responsible for this is the behavior component. The duty of this component is to manage how every particle changes over the course of its life until it terminates or dies. (All particles must terminate at some point.) Typically, the behavior component relies on a lot of mathematics and physics work under the hood to animate the positions of particles to resemble real-world behaviors or features, such as gravity, micro-gravity, inertia, wind, flight trajectories, and others. Different behaviors will require widely different implementations, but beneath the implementation it is still the behavior component itself that governs the movement and changing of particles over time.

PARTICLE PROPERTIES

Even a cursory glance of the natural world around you reveals phenomena in which small pieces or fragments move together: Ants march in rank and file, the many leaves on a tree wave and sway in the wind, crowds of people move in armies to attack or retreat. With some imagination, you can probably think of other cases, too: a dark, *Blade Runner*–style cyberpunk future in which the sewers have become infested with hordes of bloodthirsty mutant rats, or a steampunk world featuring a squadron of approaching air ships and balloons. The possibilities are endless. All these cases appeal to the concept of the particle system because they involve horde like behavior. This section considers the particle in more detail and how some of its features, in the context of the particle system, can be used or adjusted to create specific types of particle effects.

Particle Scale

Like images and meshes in a game, which all have a default size, a particle in a particle system can be stretched and shrunk dynamically at run time. Particles can be drawn at their standard width and height, shrunk to imperceptibly small proportions, or expanded to incredibly large proportions. Scaling the particle is simply a case of scaling a quad mesh, extending the position of the corner vertices.

The scale of a particle and the way it changes over time is important for the kinds of effects that it can create, and thus it is a property that is typically animated by the behavior component. Some particle systems will almost never need to change the scale of particles because their particles retain their size over time. Consider a flock of birds, for example. The birds move and fly around, but the birds themselves do not stretch or shrink. Rather, they retain their form and hold their size. In contrast, there are many natural phenomena in which particles are not so tangible, rigid, and fixed as a bird or other living organism. Consider the case of smoke particles rising from a house chimney or pouring out of the locomotive on a steam train. The smoke initially rises from the chimney in a pillar, initially matching the tubular shape of the chimney. But as it rises further, the pillar seems to expand outward, and the smoke itself seems to widen as it seeks to fill a less-confined space. Here, the scales of the smoke particles enlarge. Each particle of smoke widens and grows larger as its height increases. Contrast this case to a flame on a candle, in which the flame seems to thin out the higher it reaches, suggesting that the scale of the particle decreases with its height and lifetime. In short, be on the lookout in natural phenomena for the scale of particles, because imitating scale correctly in a particle system is important for creating believability in many kinds of effects.

Particle Transparency

If a particle in a video game really is a textured billboard mesh—and indeed, it often is—then it follows that almost all particles will require some form of transparency because hardly any real-life particle looks like a rectangular billboard. It will be necessary to hide regions of the particle texture to create believable-looking particles. The leaves on a tree, for example, are not square in shape. Instead, the organic curvature and development of a leaf ensures not only that no two leaves are the same, but also that all leaves are very far from a rectangle shape. Thus, particle textures will likely feature alpha transparency to mask out areas of the image, like the background, which should be hidden when shown on a particle in the game.

This is not the only use for transparency with particles, however. Besides the transparency features of a texture to mask out regions in an image, particles also possess a more pervasive and overall transparency. This transparency determines the particles' general visibility and conveys information about the kind of material from which they are made—whether they are a solid and opaque object like a bird or a leaf, or a wispy, partially transparent, and intangible thing like fog, smoke, or a ghost. In short, the transparency properties of a particle send out strong messages to the eye about the particle's composition, and changes in transparency over time can lend credence to certain kinds of effects. For example, by successively strengthening and then weakening the transparency of particles back and forth on a loop, you can add extra believability to pulsating lasers, aberrant holograms, force fields, futuristic computer consoles, fairy dust, and more.

Particle Color

Particles in games tend to have an overall color blended onto their texture to tint or shade the texture with a specific hue. Like most other particle properties, color can be animated over time by the behavior component to simulate all kinds of real-world effects. It does this, as it animates most particle properties, by bringing them into relationship with the particle life.

The particle life can be represented mathematically on a scale of 0 to 1, where 0 marks the time at which the particle is born from the emitter and 1 marks the time at which the particle is terminated and removed from the system. Decimal values between 0 and 1 mark points during the particle lifetime. Given this, particle color—and almost any other mathematical property of a particle—can be charted into a relationship with lifetime and changed over that lifetime. This is especially useful in the case of color because there are many effects in the real world in which particles change their color based on their age. Consider a campfire effect: The flame at its bottom-most point is bright, white, and hot, transitioning upward from yellow to red, and eventually tapering into blackish smoke.

PARTICLE SYSTEMS IN SUMMARY

The details of the particle system have already been given. Here it is worthwhile to distill that information into some general and practical advice for working with particle systems, regardless of whether you choose to use your own engine or a pre-made one. This list of tips and tricks is by no means exhaustive, but it nonetheless captures many of the tips that are useful for particle systems.

Minimize Particle Systems

In keeping with the ever-popular principle of simplicity, do not make more particle systems than you really need in your game. This might at first glance seem shallow, trivial, or obvious advice, but it is not always easy during development, when working with many complex entities, to spot all opportunities for reducing the number of entities that you actually work with. There are multiple routes to the same destination, but some routes are simpler than others. Although particle systems are optimized for performance, they are still comparatively expensive and should not be taken lightly. Do not use two of them where one will suffice. The volume of particles as well as the behavior computations for particles do place a burden and overhead on valuable processing power.

What You See Is Not Always What You Get (WYSINAWYG)

It is easy to believe that if you are creating an environment in which it is raining, then your rain particle system will need to span the entirety of the game world. After all, the game world is the place where it is raining. This is not always the case, however. Remember, if the player cannot see something, then an opportunity for optimization may exist. In other words, if the player cannot see into the distance, then it does not need to be raining there. You could, in fact, engineer your raining particle system to be like a little raincloud that follows the player wherever he or she moves in the level, emitting rain only on the player and his or her immediate surroundings. As long as the particle system hovers over the player and emits rain particles as far as that player's eye can see, then the player cannot tell the difference between a moving raincloud and a world in which it really is raining everywhere. In short, keep a particle system as simple as possible and confine it only to regions where it will be seen.

Disable Particles That Are Out of View

The philosopher René Descartes wondered whether objects such as tables and chairs continued to exist when there was nobody around to observe them existing. Most people today believe that such things do continue to exist, even though we cannot prove it beyond all doubt. But in the world of video games, this belief need not be applied by game developers. If a particle system moves out of view and can no longer affect the player, then you should disable or deactivate it to spare the processor the behavioral computations of particles. Just ensure that the system is activated again if it comes back into view. The accumulative performance benefits to be had from optimizations like these can be phenomenal.

FLIP-BOOK TEXTURES

Developers frequently desire another kind of special effect in games, but it cannot be achieved successfully by any of the conventional methods or by particle systems. Imagine walking through an urban cityscape. You turn into a long, narrow alley with a brick wall on one side. The wall features interesting and colorful graffiti, including a giant image of a zombie creature—the kind seen on skateboards or heavy metal album covers. Suddenly, the creature moves, walks about on the surface of the wall, and takes on a life of its own, living in the flat world of graffiti on the wall. In a video game, this wall might be a flat, planar mesh, and its texture would be the graffitized surface. But here, the texture must be animated. It cannot simply be a static image like a JPG or PNG. Specifically, it must move and change like the frames of a motion picture. Similar situations seem to arise in many other cases: animated computer console screens, flashing buttons and lights, traffic lights, movie screens, and more. In short, there are many cases in which a flat surface needs a texture that animates. It is not the mesh or its vertices that change or move, but the texture itself.

These kinds of effects are created in one of two ways, both of which involve a specialization of textures: movie textures and flip-book textures. Movie textures are where standard movie files (such as MPG, MOV, AVI or OGV files) are applied to a mesh surface as a texture instead of a still image file like a PNG, JPG, or TGA file. These kinds of textures are not considered further here. The second kind, however—called flip-book textures—are more common and are considered throughout this section.

A flip-book texture works much like the old flip-book animations, often shown to children at playschool or nursery. These are books where each right-hand page shows a single frame of animation and each subsequent page shows the next frame. That means the complete animation can be played back from start to finish by flipping through all the pages of the book in sequence, from beginning to end. The speed at which the pages are flipped, showing each frame, creates the appearance of motion and movement.

The concept of the flip-book texture requires the artist to pack all the frames of a complete animation onto a single texture, stacking the frames in rows and columns. After the frames are packed into a single texture, the texture can be applied to an object in a scene, such as a wall. The flip-book texture then works by animating the UV coordinates of the mesh. It starts by configuring the UV-mapping so that the surface can show only one frame from the texture at any one time, whichever frame is required. But because the frames are packed neatly into predictable rows and columns, the flip-book texture can show the complete animation by animating the UV coordinates, frame by frame in sequence. In this way, flip-book textures provide a fast and convenient method for showing texture animations, without the overhead of using memory-intensive movie files. Further, flip-book textures can even be combined with particle systems to create animated particle textures! Although the implementation details and performance metrics of flip-book textures differ from engine to engine, the basic concepts underpinning them remain the same. I recommend you consider flip-book textures whenever you need texture animation. (See Figure 9.5.)

Figure 9.5
A flip-book texture a work. Assigned as a texture to a plane, the texture animates between frames.
Source: *Unity*

Note

You can view more information on how to work with flip-book textures—specifically in the UDK engine—on my YouTube Channel at http://www.youtube.com/user/alanthorngames.

PROCEDURAL GEOMETRY

The term *geometry* is used in video games to mean mesh data, which in turn refers to vertices, edges, and polygons. Mesh data is typically created by artists making models using their modeling software of choice, such as 3DS Max, Maya, or Blender. This kind of mesh data—that is, mesh data made in advance by artists—is sometimes referred to as *static mesh data*, *baked mesh data*, or even *hard mesh data*. The main feature of such mesh data is that it has been made in advance of the game being run.

In contrast, *procedural geometry* refers to mesh data that has been generated on the fly from code while the game is running. That means the vertices, edges, and polygons of the mesh are generated at run time according to a specific formula, specific parameters, and perhaps specific inputs from the gamer (hence the term procedural geometry). Thus, procedural geometry is essentially a dynamic rather than a static way of making meshes—the process of making meshes from code or script.

This description goes quite some way to stating what procedural geometry is, but the question remains why anybody would want to use such a feature and what it could possibly achieve in terms of creating special effects.

Perhaps the most obvious use of procedural geometry is to offer the player specific customization over the game world. For example, games like *Sim City* and *Cities XL* enable gamers to design and construct cities, offering them extensive control not only over the city's tax plans and economic policies, but also over town planning—where roads run and where buildings are placed. To create roads, players can plot points using the mouse; the road can then be generated between the points in response to their input. Typically, what is happening in these cases is procedural mesh generation: The vertices, edges, and polygons of a road mesh are being generated in the scene, in real time, according to a set of player-defined parameters (the points for the road), the purpose being to generate a road that matches the player's design. This kind of behavior and effect, however, is not the limit of procedural geometry. In fact, the powerful and versatile technique of generating meshes at run time can produce a potentially limitless list of effects—so many that a whole book could be dedicated to the usage of such a technique. One notable effect resulting from procedural geometry is called *fog of war* (see Figure 9.6).

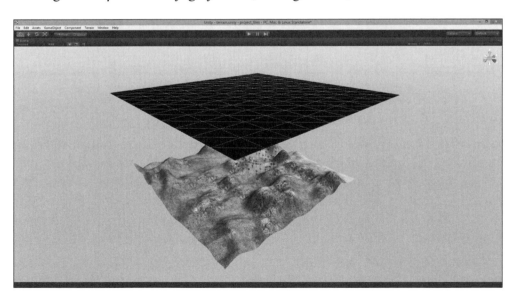

Figure 9.6
A plane created from procedural geometry, configured for a fog-of-war effect. The plane is suspended above the terrain, and regions of the plane will become transparent to reveal the terrain beneath in areas where the player is supposed to be able to see. Fog of war is commonly used in real-time strategy games.
Source: *Unity*

The fog-of-war effect, though old (in that it was invented at some unknown and highly debated point during the 1980s), can still be found alive and well in most strategy games today, including such games and game series as *Warcraft, Starcraft,* and *The Battle for Wesnoth.* The basic idea of the fog of war is to act as a cover or dark veil over the landscape for regions of the battlefield that your units or troops have not visited or have left unattended. The purpose is to create balance, tension, and fairness in a game—to make sure you, as a military commander, cannot see what is happening in the world where you have no military presence. It is there especially to make sure you cannot observe enemy movements and tactics without making an effort at reconnaissance.

The question remains for the game developer as to how such an effect as this can be created. There are differing solutions, but almost all of them involve procedural geometry of some kind.

One popular method is to procedurally generate a tessellated plane or rectangle surface—that is, a plane mesh with many vertices. This surface is then assigned a black, opaque texture for the fog of war, and is suspended in the air between the units on the ground and the camera in the sky from where the player views the world and its events. By default, the plane is opaque and obscures the ground beneath entirely, preventing the player from witnessing what is happening. Each game unit on the ground belonging to the player, however—such as a tank or a soldier—is given an invisible arrow or ray that sticks out of the top of its head and continues to shoot upward in a straight and vertical line until it intersects the fog-of-war plane above. When this intersection with the plane is detected, mathematically speaking, the engine can then know implicitly that the player has a friendly unit directly beneath that should be visible to the gamer. In response, the surrounding vertices of the fog-of-war plane above the intersection can be made transparent, turning the corresponding part of the texture invisible. This enables the player to see through the plane to the ground and events below. If, in contrast, no intersection occurs, then the player must have no friendly units beneath, and so the plane should remain black and non-transparent in that area, concealing the events beneath.

Here, then, is a simple but effective special effect technique that makes use of procedural geometry and is commonly found in games. Solutions like these, and others, can result in some stunning and memorable effects. In short, never underestimate the power of procedural geometry. Whether you are using a pre-made engine or making your own, I recommend coming to grips with procedural geometry at your earliest opportunity.

RIBBON TRAILS

Ribbon trails are an especially notable and common application of procedural geometry in games. In racing games, cars and bikes often zoom around the track, leaving behind them a blurry trail of colors or ghosted impressions of themselves to convey a sense of speed. In fantasy games, as warriors aggressively swing enchanted swords and axes, the weapons leave behind a ghosted trail of colors, giving a faint impression of the trajectory. In pinball games, the ball often leaves behind itself, as it moves, a ghosted trail of color to signify motion and travel. All these common effects are the result of ribbon trails, an effect used to emphasize movement. (See Figure 9.7.)

Figure 9.7
A ribbon trail of light behind a ball lends the ball a comet or meteorite appearance.
Source: *Unity*

So how do ribbon trails typically work, and how do they make use of procedural geometry? Effectively, the moving object—whether a sword, a car, or a ball—generates behind it a connected chain of temporary billboard objects, all of which are textured to produce the appearance of existing in one long and continuous chain. Once generated, each billboard in the caterpillar-like chain acts as a separate and independent link, which accounts for the chain being able to bend and twist. Further, over time, all the billboards in the chain fade out into destruction in the order in which they were generated to produce the appearance of fizzling out, or dilution. In short, the famous effect of ribbon trails offers a classic example of the power of procedural geometry.

POST-PROCESSING

The word *post* is often prefixed to terms to mean after, later, or posterior. It is designed to draw your attention to the fact that it comes after something. In the case of video games and post-processing, *post* refers to all the things a game does on each frame after the render has been produced.

It should be remembered here that the game render system is responsible for drawing pixels to the two-dimensional space of the screen—a snapshot of the 3D world, complete with its lights and objects, from the perspective of a camera. Specifically, it uses the graphics card hardware (hardware acceleration) to convert a 3D scene from a camera viewpoint and draw it onto the screen as pixels, and it does this on each and every frame. Rendering the scene in this way on each and every frame means that the game-render system is a real-time renderer. Thus, the scene is rendered possibly as many as 100 times per second (100 frames per second). Regardless of the frame rate, however, each separate frame constitutes a unique render and snapshot of the scene at that time. Post-processing effects, then, refer to all those effects, adjustments, and processes that are applied to the pixels of a completed render on each frame.

If you have used Adobe Photoshop or GIMP, you will likely be familiar with post-processing, because almost all of Photoshop's work is a form of post-processing. Adding blur filters, creating new layers, and adding twist effects and color adjustments are all forms of post-processing because they are all applied to an existing image that was created at some earlier time—perhaps by a render system, digital camera, or scanner. The difference in video games is that such effects are applied not simply once or twice, but typically on each and every frame. This happens through the use of a *vertex shader* or *pixel shader*—a special kind of low-level program that runs on the graphics hardware itself and is written in a shader language such as Cg or HLSL. Programs in these languages contain instructions on the kinds of effects to be applied to the pixels of a render.

Again, as in the case of special effects more generally, post-processing effects are diverse and potentially infinite in number. They are limited only by the creativity of the developers, the computing power of the target hardware, and—alas—the budget. Nonetheless, various general and commonly used post-processing effects have established themselves, and are often provided out of the box with many well-known game engines. Some of these post-processing effects have become fashionable; others have since moved out of fashion; and still others are simply old favorites that have been used, tried, and tested for as long as post-processing has been in games. This section considers some of the most common post-processing effects.

Blur

Perhaps the most well-known post-process effect is blur and its many variations, such as motion blur and radial blur. Under the hood, blur effects essentially duplicate pixels in the render and then stagger them nearby in such a way as to create a blurring or smearing effect that approximates an out-of-focus look, sometimes termed *unsharpness*. The default, standard blur effect applies blurring indiscriminately to all pixels in a render. In contrast, a specialized blur, like motion blur, is selective in its application, blurring only objects that were known to be moving in the scene at the time of the render. Blurring effects are as old as the hills, informally speaking; they have been around in some form since the earliest arcade games in the '70s and '80s, and are still used today to emphasize motion and movement, and to simulate drunkenness, drug effects, sleepiness, myopia, and more notably depth of field, as you shall see soon. Most established engines today support blurring and many of its derivative effects, and it is likely that you will use it frequently in your own projects. (See Figure 9.8.)

Figure 9.8
A blurred landscape created using the Blur Image effect in Unity 4.
Source: *Unity*

Depth of Field

Depth of field as a post-process effect is a specialization of the blur effect. Its purpose is to increase and strengthen the 3D-ness or depth of a render. It does this by imitating a camera lens or the human eye. In essence, depth of field (DOF) breaks down a render of the scene into two main areas or regions—foreground and background—based on their significance to the observer according to the intentions of the artist. The foreground features the subject and things that the eye should be focused on, and the background features everything else behind—the negative space of the image. DOF blurs and softens the background while leaving the foreground sharp and in focus. In this way, it emphasizes the foreground, thereby helping to guide your eye unconsciously toward the foreground of the image while still leaving you intuitively aware of a background out there somewhere in the scene (even if that background does not grab your attention or scream out to you).

Overall, depth of field is an understated and powerful effect that is used commonly in movies, games, and photography, as well as in comic books, where backgrounds are drawn in less detail. Despite its prevalence, however, most people are entirely unaware of its presence and potency. The absence of DOF can entirely change the feel or character of an image, causing it to look flat and to feel directionless. A common response of people who see an image lacking depth of field is to say, "I'm not really sure what I should be looking at." It is statements like this that hint at the power of blurring to guide your eye and to make the subject obvious to you. (See Figure 9.9.)

Figure 9.9
Depth of field in Unity 4. Notice how the foreground terrain appears sharper and more focused than the background, and it captures your attention more easily.
Source: *Unity*

Bloom

One of the more recent and fashionable specializations of blur is bloom. If you have ever played a game and thought it looked kind of dreamy, whimsical, or enchanting, it was likely due in part to the use of bloom. Indeed, bloom has been used in many games—especially RPGs with a fantasy medieval setting, such as *Oblivion* and *Skyrim*. In short, bloom identifies all highlights (the brightest pixels) in the scene, and subtly blurs those areas to intensify their brightness. The result is that blurry and subtle halos of illumination appear to surround objects in the brightest areas. The glow follows their contours, as though the world were being viewed through sleepy or half-open eyes. Bloom has been used extensively of late, and it can arguably lend a lot of mystical character to a game. It is, however, computationally expensive, and should thus be used with caution. (See Figure 9.10.)

Figure 9.10
Bloom can create a dream-like feel to an environment.
Source: *Unity*

Vignettes and Vignetting

The concepts of *vignette* and *vignetting* are, like most video-game terms, borrowed from other disciplines—in this case, optics and photography. There, as well as in games, *vignetting* refers to the process of darkening or reducing the saturation of an image at its edges. This darkened or desaturated region is termed the *vignette*.

Imagine an image surrounded by a black oval frame, which is blurred at the edges to merge with the image. This is a vignette. In some ways, a vignette is reminiscent of the world as you see it when your eyes are squinted or half open. In these cases, a softened dark border, created by your eyelids and lashes, appears to surround what you see, obscuring the image at its fringes. Vignettes are typically used to convey the emotions of fear, uncertainty, confusion, panic, tension, action, and anticipation— and sometimes they can be used also to create a melancholy. Nowadays, this effect is extensively used, especially in horror movies, thrillers, or whenever suspense and dramatic tension is required. (See Figure 9.11.)

Figure 9.11
Vignetting adds a darkened frame around a scene, creating dramatic and stormy undertones.
Source: *Unity*

Chromatic Effects

Chromatic effects are the first post-processing effects discussed here that do not rely primarily on blurring. Instead, chromatic effects dramatically change or invert the colors of the rendered image, transforming them into colors wholly different from their original values. Generally speaking, chromatic effects are used sparingly in games. When they are used, they are typically designed to simulate the effects of intoxication, other-worldliness, nightmarish visions, or the psychoactive effects of poisons (see Figure 9.12). Strong contrasting mixtures of greens and blues are common with chromatic effects, which can also be used to simulate night vision.

Figure 9.12
Chromatic effects are useful for representing intoxication, poisons, illusions, and nightmarish dreamscapes.
Source: *Unity*

Cel Shading

If you have played *XIII*, *The Legend of Zelda: The WindWaker*, or *Borderlands 2*, then you will have seen the famous cel-shading, or toon-shading, technique in action. Cel shading is a special shading algorithm and post-processing effect that can transform a regular-looking 3D scene into a cartoon-looking scene, complete with a reduced color palette, low-contrast lighting, and bold inked outlines around objects. The results, being created by an algorithm, tend to look more synthetic than hand-drawn cartoons and graphics. Nonetheless cel shading can and does produce an authentic cartoon feel to a game. In practice, cel shading changes the way the render system lights, shades, and colors the models of the scene, without resorting to blurring or chromatic changes. In short, if you want your 3D game to have a cartoon feel and you don't want to change the geometry of your models, then cel shading might well be what you are looking for. Further, cel shading is often a comparatively cheap effect compared to blurring effects such as bloom and motion blur.

Lens Flare

Lens flare refers to the bright, star-like halo that appears typically when a camera is facing toward the sun and the light has scattered and bounced around the camera's lens mechanism. The effect itself was originally an unintentional byproduct of how bright and pervasive light interacts with the camera. But many thought the effect pretty, pensive, and enchanting, and thus have made efforts to re-create it artificially in video games.

The lens-flare effect has received much criticism and scorn among game developers, described by some as "silly" and "overused" and as making no sense because lens flare is a phenomenon that applies only to camera lenses and not to the human eye. Despite this criticism, however, the effect continues to appear again and again in games. The use of lens flare is in many respects a judgment call on the part of the developer. Some avoid this effect entirely, while others think there is a time and a place for them, just as there is a time and place for most effects. Lens flares can be used to emphasize tranquility, natural wonder, romanticism, sunny days, and verdant and beautiful landscapes.

Note

Technically, the lens flare effect is not always implemented as a post-process effect. Sometimes it is a texture-based effect added to the scene before it is even rendered. However, it can be implemented in post-processing too.

CONCLUSION

The focus of this chapter has been on the general principles governing special effects and post-processing in video games. Each and every special effect can be seen first and foremost as a logistical problem—something that can be implemented in a game only by resorting to techniques and measures that are not made available implicitly by the traditional workflow of creating assets, importing assets, and putting the assets into a scene. Each special effect requires special effort on the part of the developer to solve the problem to create the effect required—hence the reason such effects might reasonably be termed *special*.

In this chapter, you looked at the concepts of particle systems, flip-book textures, and procedural geometry for creating a range of common effects found in games. The particle system is ideal for creating hordes of moving pieces acting in unison as part of a single system such as a flock of birds, a swarm of bees, and even magical sparkles. Flip-book textures, in contrast, are useful for facilitating movement and animation at the level of textures themselves, as opposed to on the level of objects.

Procedural geometry has a wide application of uses for fog of war, ribbon trails, and more. After considering the concept of special effects, the chapter moved on to cover a more narrow range of effects under the umbrella of post-processing. These effects apply to the rendered image of a game and include blur, motion blur, lens flares, bloom, depth of field, cel shading, and thousands of others that are not named here.

Overall, special effects are pervasive in games. The details of their implementation are of critical importance because this influences how well or badly the effect will perform on the target hardware. It is not enough for a developer to simply create the desired effect. The implementation must be optimal with regard to performance if the effect is truly going to be usable.

The next chapter takes a completely new course. Rather than considering the lower-level technicalities of game development, it takes a higher-level look at the business practices surrounding games: marketing, selling, and distributing games to end users. This might sound like an exercise in soulless corporate/marketing rhetoric, but there is indeed much of interest to be said regarding marketing, and much of importance, too—at least for the game developer who intends to make money from his or her hard work in making games.

CHAPTER 10

DISTRIBUTION, PUBLISHING, AND MARKETING

"Many a small thing has been made large by the right kind of advertising."

—Mark Twain

By the end of this chapter you should:

- Understand the basics of distribution, publishing and marketing.
- Be able to make an informed decision as to the distribution model for your game.
- Appreciate the challenges of marketing.
- Understand how to use social media for marketing.
- Understand the relationship between publishing, distribution, and marketing.

If you have absolutely no intention of selling your game, or if you really don't care whether anybody ever knows about or plays your game, then you can safely ignore this chapter. This, however, probably applies to only a few, if any, developers, most of whom typically create games with the hope that others will play them, even when their games are made available free of charge. This motivation—the desire for others to play your game—seems common to almost all developers, despite the other differences that may exist among them.

Some have suggested that a desire to make lots of money from games is the overriding motivation of all game developers, if there is one. Indeed, they say, without the prospect of earning money, there would be no games at all. This line of thinking is generally based on a simplification of human motivations, even if most games really *are* made for money. After all, as with many creative works such as movies, books, paintings, sculptures, and others, there are always people for whom the creative urge is so deep-rooted that they create primarily for its own sake—for the enjoyment it brings them and for the pleasure of giving to others—regardless of the costs involved. Although some developers will be further motivated by making money from their games, some will not.

It is on that basis that this chapter has been written. It has much to say about the core motivation: how you can tell others about your game through marketing and the ways in which you can deliver your game into the hands of an audience through publishing and distribution. However, it has little to say about all the different ways in which you can monetize your games or maximize profits, although it does touch on this issue. Such a shallow treatment of monetization is not a reflection of its lack of importance or of a careless disregard on my part. It's merely because there is so much to say on the subject that a single chapter is just not enough to do it justice, especially when much has been said about it elsewhere.

From here onward, I will assume that you have a completed game in "gold master" state, real or imaginary, free or commercial. This game will have been designed, implemented, and tested. I assume further that your game is completely unknown to the wider gaming masses, is *not* a highly anticipated blockbuster sequel to an established series, and so has not marketed or "sold itself." At this point, you are now faced with the task of how to put your game into the hands of gamers who are willing to play. That task is the focus of this chapter.

Marketing

Before people can even want to play your game, they must be aware that your game exists. After all, they cannot genuinely want what they don't know about. In this context, then, the term marketing can be used to refer to two main activities:

- Making gamers aware of your game's existence
- Making your game an attractive proposition—that is, not just something that exists, but something that engages people emotionally and psychologically enough to see and feel its benefits and qualities

The aim of marketing, stated in this way, can make it seem a simple process, but this is an illusion.

Before the advent of the Internet and widespread digital communications, developers faced many tangible barriers and more restricted options to reaching an audience with advertising. The question that faced them then was typically whether to advertise on television (if it was within their budget), in magazines or brochures, in video-game shops, or on radio. In most cases, developers could and often did advertise their games by creating small-sized demo or shareware versions that were tasters for the full product. These were typically delivered to gamers on magazine cover discs.

Now that the Internet has arrived, however, the face of advertising is much changed for video games, as it is in many other fields. Despite that, it is no less difficult for developers in many respects. The Internet offers so many varied cheap and even free channels for advertising, not to mention press opportunities. But the result of this democratization is that gamers are constantly assaulted with special offers, free gifts, press announcements, screen shots, viral videos, YouTube trailers, and even subscription-based services promising a steady supply of games throughout the year. Due to this constant bombardment, gamers must separate the foreground from the noise. This can sometimes inspire inertia and cynicism toward advertisements generally, making it difficult to engage gamers because there are none so resilient to your message as those who don't want to see it.

The primary challenge, then, facing today's game developer is not so much about whether your target audience can be physically reached by mail, TV, or high-street store, because they can be reached easily online. Rather, it's whether your game and advertising can stand out in the digital space from among the multitude of other games. Can your ads truly shine among the relentless saturation of other, competing ads that seem to appear practically anywhere where gamers are known to frequent—even inside some other games during game play? This section considers various online platforms where game developers often find success in advertising and reaching audiences. It also considers some general tips and techniques for improving the effectiveness of your game marketing campaign on those platforms.

Press Releases

In the video-game world, a press release is typically a one- or two-page written document addressed to members of the gaming press, such as magazines and news sites, and not directly to gamers. The purpose of the document is to announce the development or the release of a game, the general idea being to inform members of the gaming press so that they will in turn produce related news items or articles, addressed to gamers, about your game. If you are making or releasing a game and want the gaming press to mention it, then a press release may be one way to achieve this end.

Press releases are generally, but not always, created by the developer or publisher. They are then submitted by email either directly to gaming press sites, such as to magazines, news sites, and review portals, or indirectly to services such as gamespress.com, which is read by many in the gaming press for news on new releases and other articles.

The press release may be an effective means of getting a mention for your game and of attracting attention, but it can only be effective if the release is acknowledged and acted upon by members of the press, who are under no obligation to do so. It's up to you to write a press release that is compelling enough to attract their attention. Your spelling, punctuation and grammar should be consistent and correct. In addition, it is helpful to include links to a website or page for your game, as well as to game screen shots and other media. Try searching the Internet for "Bounders and Cads press release" to see an example of a press release composed for one of my games, *Bounders and Cads*.

Websites and Development Blogs

Developers will typically create a website for their game, which interested parties can visit to see in-game screen shots and more information about the game. This site does not have to be hosted on your own domain, if you have one. It could be a Web page hosted anywhere using practically any service, such as WordPress or Tumblr, provided the page is publicly accessible. Wherever you host your site, be aware that gamers respond favorably to sites that feature in-game screen shots, video trailers or footage of the game being played, and short but concise textual descriptions of the game and its core features using clear and unassuming language.

In addition to websites advertising a game, developers often keep development blogs or developer diaries, which are diaries written by the developers addressed to a general audience of gamers and other developers. These diaries discuss aspects of the game as its development unfolds, as well as aspects of the developer's personal life and their experiences. They are frequently personal and are always a work in progress; developers typically make entries into the log each day, week, or month, depending on progress. Development blogs are especially useful for staggering the release of tantalizing tidbits of information about the game over time to generate anticipation. They are also useful for receiving ongoing feedback from gamers and other developers through their comments, which can sometimes be integrated into the game, if feasible.

Very few reliable studies have been performed on development blogs, partly because the phenomenon is so difficult to quantify due to confounding variables. For example, how can you measure the influence of development blogs in isolation, when so many other influences exist to confuse the results? That means that any conclusions about the development blog's effectiveness in marketing cannot be easily reached, at least statistically speaking. Anecdotally, I have received mixed reports from other developers about whether they believe their developer blog was successful. Some developers, especially RPG developers, found them to be an impressively effective and enjoyable means of boosting their game's exposure as well as connecting with their gamers. In contrast, others, especially casual game developers, felt their blog had made little appreciable difference in increasing their game's profile. Generally, it seems from this analysis at least, the worst-case scenario for a developer is that the development blog will make little difference. If that is the worst that can happen, it still means the developer blog is a positive rather than a negative step for marketing games in terms of its effects. Developer blogs are typically hosted on the developer's site using a content management system (CMS) like Joomla! (www.joomla.org/), Drupal (drupal.org/), or WordPress.org (wordpress.org/). Sometimes, they are also hosted on dedicated blogging sites such as Blogger (www.blogger.com), WordPress.com (wordpress.com/), and TypePad (www.typepad.com/).

Demos

There are, perhaps, few marketing tools for games as controversial as the demo, short for demonstration version. It seems almost every developer and game commentator has a strong view on the subject. Some think the demo is a worthwhile marketing effort, and others think it is a waste of time at best, or a damaging and potentially disastrous effort at worst.

A demo is a free sample or taster of the full game. It is made available to gamers to allow them to see what the game is like through a try-before-you-buy strategy. Some demos are a cut-down version of the full game, while others include the full game but are time-limited. Their main purpose in marketing is to convince gamers who are already aware of your game through its marketing to purchase it. The demo is supposed to be that enticing "something more."

The question debated among developers is whether the demo is really what it purports to be, and some significant concerns have been raised. Some claim demos frustrate gamers because of their brevity and their abrupt ending, and so really exist only to help gamers find faults and complaints—all of which lead them into justifying both to themselves and to others why they have chosen *not* to purchase. Further, some have claimed that demos generate ill feeling or animosity among gamers toward the developer because the restricted nature of the demo constantly reminds them that the developer is "in it for the money." In other words, the gamer's enjoyment must be cut short just because he or she hasn't "coughed up the cash yet."

Some developers respond that it is both unreasonable and unfair that gamers should take exception to developers wanting pay for their time, hard work, and creativity. Regardless, the question here is not whether gamers are justified in their resentment, but whether their resentment does, in fact, turn them away from purchasing on the basis of the demo. It is true that an increasing number of games are being released without a demo version, but it is also true that an increasing number of smaller, casual games are being released for which a demo would not in any case be suitable because they are intended to be short-lived, quick-play games, even in their fullest form. Overall, then, it seems the jury is still out on the ultimate effects of the demo. Despite the reasonable criticisms leveled against it, the demo is still commonplace, and can still be found to accompany commercially successful and popular games. That means you will need to make a judgment call for whatever you think is best for your game.

Videos and "Going Viral"

Video is undoubtedly a powerful medium for inspiring and motivating audiences. This applies, too, for video games and their marketing. In 2011, the now-famous homemade video of Fenton the black Labrador relentlessly chasing deer across a field managed to claim over 7 million YouTube views in just a few months. As far as I am aware, this was not initially on the backing of any focused or sponsored advertising campaign, but simply because, largely through word-of-mouth, users developed an interest in the humorous video. This spontaneous and uncoordinated spreading around of news about a video is termed "going viral."

Viral video is, in a sense, a powerful form of self-perpetuated advertising because the original content creator effectively leaves it to the audience to distribute among themselves. Viral videos of Fenton fame are not common in video games. Nonetheless, much smaller-scale virals are possible and could be used to increase a game's exposure.

The exact mechanics and process for creating successful viral videos, if any guaranteed formula exists at all, is beyond the scope of this book. In general, adding videos of trailers and game play for a game to YouTube or similar video site is a free and easy way to give exposure to your game to a potentially enormous worldwide audience. For developers seeking free and powerful exposure for their game, there are almost no powerful reasons why a video trailer or video demonstration should not be created.

Twitter, Facebook, and Micro-blogging

The term blog, a contraction of the fuller term Web log, refers to the practice of keeping a public and online diary or article database, to which one frequently contributes. The term micro-blogging specifies an even narrower type of blogging in which articles are quite short, perhaps limited to just a few lines of text. Twitter, Facebook, Google+, and Pinterest are famous examples of social media that support micro-blogging, whether through words, pictures, or both. This medium can be useful for posting quick, bite-sized updates, thoughts, ideas, quotes, and other snippets of information.

Micro-blogging is used today by practically all game developers, both large studios and small independent developers. It can be used to post notifications of important dates related to your games such as release dates and beta-test dates, as well as information about the release of patches, updates, add-ons. Further, it can be used to connect and interact with other developers as well as those who play your games. Specifically, micro-blogging has been used to provide technical and sales support, to answer queries about games and features, and to post screen shots and updates of a game during its development. As with YouTube, most social media networks enable users to join and post content for free, and almost all of them offer you access to a large audience of friends and users. As such, there are almost no strong reasons why these media should not be used to increase the exposure for your games.

Targeted Banner Advertising

Like many people who share a common interest, gamers tend to hang out at specific meeting places online. Within the gaming community as a whole, many subgroups can be identified along genre lines, meaning there are smaller communities of FPS fans, RPG fans, sports fans, indie fans, adventure fans, and more. Each of these groups tends to congregate at different places, preferring some sites over others because of their focus on the genre they favor. Some famous video-gaming communities include GameSpot (www.gamespot.com), MCV (www.mcvuk.com), IGN (www.ign.com), VideoGamer (www.videogamer.com), Steam (store.steampowered.com/), Desura (www.desura.com/), and others.

Whether small or large, most gaming sites offer both developers and publishers advertising opportunities, typically in the form of banner advertisements—that is, animated or static images of a game that appear in a pop-up window or in the margins of the Web page. These images are clickable, allowing users to link directly to a page where the advertised game can be purchased or pre-ordered, sometimes at discounted prices.

Despite its general unpopularity because of its perceived intrusiveness or because of its power to interrupt your browsing experiencing, this form of advertising has proven surprisingly effective, primarily in securing impulse purchases—that is, purchases resulting from spur-of-the-moment decisions made on the basis of whim, excitement, fascination, or interest aroused by the advertising and imagery. Banner advertising, however, is almost never free, and is often beyond the budget of smaller, indie developers (unless those developers have the commercial backing of a larger publisher). The exact mechanics, expenses, and cost programs involved with banner advertising vary dramatically from site to site and developer to developer—so much so that no single model can sensibly be described as standard. In short, if your budget allows, then banner advertising can be a profitable marketing tool.

Sequels and Series

Sequels are games that follow up on ones that have come out previously. They typically involve the same characters and settings and similar gameplay to their predecessors. A series is two or more sequels, taken together with the original, which overall form a whole or collection—for example, the *Harry Potter* series or the *Lord of the Rings* series, which include all the movies or books bearing that name. In the world of video games there are *Super Mario Brothers*, *Sonic the Hedgehog*, *Ultima*, *Civilization*, *Elder Scrolls*, and lots more.

It might seem strange to list sequels and series as forms of marketing, but in some genuine senses, that's just what they are. Audiences develop strong psychological and emotional attachments to people, places, and things, whether real or imagined. The academic journals of psychology and sociology are replete with references to studies that confirm that this is case. Such ideas are also found in the world of post-modern literature, too, from Italo Calvino to William Golding. But most of us really don't need these "expert" opinions to be convinced of this; our personal experiences are enough in themselves. It is not difficult to think of cases in which we find ourselves identifying or sympathizing with fictional characters from movies or books simply because we happen to connect deeply with something they say, do, think, or feel. Nor is it difficult to think of cases in which children, playing with each other, take on the role of fictional characters they like and connect with, acting out how they believe those characters would be in different situations. The specific characters we identify with will, of course, vary from person to person and across media, including movies, books, and video games. For games, many famous characters include John Shepard from the *Mass Effect* series, Lara Croft from *Tomb Raider*, Gordon Freeman from *Half Life*, and more. But the fame or notability of a character is not the central issue here, because we can identify with people and characters regardless of their fame.

These attachments can grow to be strong in some of us, establishing loyalties that lead gamers to collect and anticipate sequels with excitement and glee simply because of the emotional investment they have already made in its characters and setting. It is as though they are eager for the sequel in order to be reunited with old friends. Not only can such attachments develop and expand with time, but people actively seek to develop new attachments, consciously or not. For this reason, not only do existing gamers purchase sequels and later installments, but those who are latecomers to an already established series will also go back to purchase previous installments.

In my view, the sequel and series model is one of the most powerful and potent forms of marketing for video games available today. This is in many respects confirmed statistically by the increasing number of successful games adopting the series-based model, in which a set of characters and their adventures (or misadventures) persist across multiple installments. Some series-based games include *Sam and Max*, *Tales of Monkey Island*, *Agon*, *Half Life 2*, and *Penumbra*.

MARKETING IN SUMMARY

The previous sections highlight a range of online options for informing others about your games and their benefits. These opportunities might be described as "marketing opportunities," with different media holding different potentials depending on your game, circumstances, and budget. Regardless of which option you choose, a number of general marketing principles apply. These can be framed, albeit a little simplistically, in terms of general dos and don'ts.

- *Do* **identify your target audience or market at the design phase.** Before you make your game, be sure to know who your game is for—not in terms of specific individuals (such as this person Jack or that person Jill), but in the abstract sense, in terms of demographics such as age groups, gender, and interests. After you identify the target market, use it as the basis for developing a **marketing strategy.** Use what you know about your target audience—their habits and routine—to help focus your decisions about where to advertise and about what is and is not a suitable medium.

- *Do* **develop a marketing strategy before doing marketing.** All marketing follows a marketing strategy of some kind, even if that strategy is "just do what feels right." The point here is to emphasize that the most successful marketing campaigns are those that are not simply left to chance, but that are carefully planned and coordinated. Just as the first three chapters of this book stressed the importance of planning in the development of video games, so too must the importance of planning be stressed for the work of marketing. Plan ahead and decide how the marketing is to happen. Where will you market? When will you market? Will the marketing be synchronized to key stages in the development of your game so that when the game is released, marketing will be at its peak to ensure gamers know it is available for purchase? Will there be a pre-release marketing campaign to secure pre-orders? No single method is right or wrong, but answers to such questions must, at some point, be settled if the marketing plan is to be effective.

- **Do use free social media wherever possible.** Some doubt the effectiveness of social media advertising, primarily because there is so much of it. But regardless of whether you are a social media enthusiast or skeptic, content such as videos, images, and short, bite-sized comments can undeniably have a powerful effect when seen by the right people, in the right circumstances, and at the right time. You can choose to use social media or not to use social media, but it is generally only by its use—by engaging socially with gamers and other developers—that your messages, ideas, and games can be received so widely (unless you have access to other, often more expensive, outlets).

- **Do create lots of screen shots and videos for your game.** It is often said that a picture is worth a thousand words. This is particularly true in the case of marketing games. Create lots of screen shots and videos for your game. Make sure it is really easy for gamers to see images and videos of your game in action. Minimize text where possible (except in the cases of blogs), and keep what text you have concise, to the point, and accessible in style. In the case of text, less is usually more.

- **Don't think of marketing as something that comes after game development.** Although it may appear to be a general theme of this chapter to think marketing only after a game is complete (a theme further reinforced by this chapter's placement at the end of the book), this is not my intention. Throughout the development process, you should take advantage of developer blogs to discuss the game, sharing screen shots and other materials. Encourage gamer interaction, allowing them to comment on your game's progress and to establish an emotional attachment to the work as it unfolds. Be aware, however, that this process of allowing user interaction can be a double-edged sword, as there will sometimes be gamers who are especially critical. Some will have a genuine desire to help, but others may be careless with their words or simply take great pleasure in vicious and sometimes personal criticism. This can damage the morale of sensitive developers during development and have an overall damaging effect on the outcome of the project. Indeed, I have seen developers come to a crashing halt in their work because of insecurities born from insensitive comments made by others in developer blogs. Sometimes the criticisms are not justified, but sometimes they are. In any event, it can be helpful as well as humbling to see that everyone makes mistakes; it is part of the human condition. Fortunately, each mistake represents an opportunity for learning and improvement.

Note

In theory, you could solve this problem by blocking all user comments on the blog. Instead, however, I recommend you make inward efforts to deal with your sensitivity (remember, the customer is not always right) and to separate the constructive criticism from the rest.

- **Don't lose sight of marketing as an investment.** When planning a marketing campaign, it is easy to take an all-or-nothing attitude, thinking your game and message must be heard by everybody at all costs, with no mountain too high and no distance too far to spread that message. This strategy of over-stretching has led many a developer into reckless and ruinous publicity campaigns that succeeded in being heard but failed to recoup the costs involved. There are some messages that can be "overheard"—some voices, images, and ideas that can be seen and experienced too much, becoming tiresome. Take care when planning your marketing to keep your material fresh and inspiring without over-stretching your resources and without becoming intrusive. Settle on a marketing budget before the campaign begins and don't allow yourself to exceed it despite the temptations. Of course, sometimes the temptations prove too much; we take the risk in the face of danger anyway. Although this can sometimes pay off, it usually involves putting our faith in chance—and chance is not reliable. (Otherwise, it would not be called "chance.")

- **Don't lie or over-hype.** There is, I think, a genuine distinction to be made between the two, although both can have dangerous effects on your business. In its most blatant form, lying involves mis-selling a game—knowingly announcing features the game does not (and will not) have, promising content that is not really included, and pledging future content that will not be delivered. In contrast, over-hyping involves over-selling a game. Hopefully, you possess enough common decency and honesty to see the problems with blatant dishonesty. Even apart from these, there are still more utilitarian and business-minded reasons to avoid lying—namely, it generates resentment and a justified feeling of having been cheated. For consumers, this feeling dies hard, leaking into all future decisions when it comes to purchasing games. In contrast, over-hyping is typically born not from the intent to deceive, but from an excitement or enthusiasm about the game being developed. Excited developers promote their games by speaking of the thrilling features they have planned; in the end, however, these features are never actually realized. For consumers, the result of over-hyping is often disappointment and annoyance—the feeling that, despite the benefits of the game, it did not deliver on what it promised.

Regardless of whether marketers lie or over-hype, both incline the gamer toward incredulity and apathy to future marketing campaigns—a feeling of having heard it all before. In short, it makes gamers prejudicial toward marketing campaigns from their outset. This creates for the developer an uphill struggle that can be overcome only with the greatest of difficulty. Given that marketing is difficult enough as it is, it can never be rational to make it more so!

DISTRIBUTION AND PUBLISHING

The terms distribution and publishing are not clearly defined in the games industry, and are sometimes used interchangeably. Here I use the term distribution to mean the process of providing gamers with access to your game. If you send gamers a copy of your game by mail on a CD, then you have distributed your game via mail distribution. Similarly you have distributed your game if you have made it available for download online, called digital distribution (DD) or electronic download (ED).

The term publishing has taken on different meanings in the industry. Sometimes a game is classified as published as soon as it is released on any medium and in any place. Sometimes, published means that the game is available at specific sites, stores, or portals online. And sometimes, in its more traditional sense, it means that the game has been signed to a larger publishing company who markets, distributes, and sells the game on the developer's behalf at retail outlets and online, and who pays the developer an advance and a share of profits from sales. In this section, I use the term publishing to mean this third and more traditional sense, with all other meanings falling under the heading distribution or DIY distribution. Both distribution and publishing have the aim of delivering the game into the hands of gamers.

If distribution is about giving gamers access to a game, the question arises as to the best or most suitable method of distribution. This question, as it turns out, reveals one of the most heated disagreements in the games industry (as well as in almost all other digital media industries). How a game should be distributed, who should be allowed to distribute it, who should be able to play it, and who can make copies are all issues involving political wrangling as well as power struggles that are far from settled and are far from pretty, touching on controversial issues such as digital rights management (DRM).

This chapter cannot possibly hope to cover this subject with anything like the completeness it deserves, but I shall nevertheless offer an introduction to the subject as far as it has practical relevance for someone looking for methods of distributing their game. I shall also evaluate some of those methods, at least in summary. In doing so, I cannot entirely maintain a position of impartiality as I have tried to do, as far as humanly possible, throughout this book. Because this subject is not like that of mathematics, physics, or logic, I must take a position somewhere to begin discussion. The result is that some of my conclusions are skewed in favor of my own view. I do, of course, think my own view is the correct one; you might, however, take a different view from mine. In any event, I hope the information included here gives you some guidance and food for thought.

Retail Versus Digital

The term marketplace refers to any space, physical or non-physical, where a commercial exchange can occur—in this case, between developers and gamers. In short, a marketplace is where developers can sell games and where gamers can buy games on offer.

There are two main marketplaces in the games industry: the retail market and the digital market. Although the distinctions between these two markets are not as hard and fast as some have claimed, the digital market typically refers to the Internet or, more accurately, to any site at which games can be purchased digitally and downloaded immediately. The defining feature of this market is that the gamer never receives a tangible copy of the product and the developer never receives tangible money in the form of notes and coins. In contrast, the retail or traditional marketplace for games refers to the high-street stores where boxed copies of games are sold from store shelves and to the mail-order market, where games are purchased online or from catalogs and delivered in a tangible form to the customer's mailing address.

There is a great interest at present among developers, economists, and others about the supposed decline of the retail market in favor of the digital market, and indeed many retail outlets have closed under economic pressures. But although it is difficult to deny that with video games, the more common trend now is to sell games online via digital means, I think if most developers were asked, "Where would you like to sell your game?" their answer would be, "In as many places as possible." For this reason, the retail outlet still remains an attractive option to many.

These markets need not be antagonist for the game developer. Access to these markets, however, varies, from developer to developer and across territories. As you shall see, most developers have access to digital markets in some form, but retail markets can pose greater obstacles for smaller developers who don't already have established relationships with stores, as well as packaging and printing companies for preparing the tangible materials. For this reason, most developers contract with established publishers to access retail markets.

DIY Versus Publishers

There comes a point when most developers face the question as to whether to distribute their game solely from their own resources or to contract with a publisher to distribute the game on their behalf. The question is essentially whether to choose the publishing route or the self-publishing route. The preceding section discussed some of the motivations a developer might have to choose a publisher for retail markets. But what can be said in the digital case, where it is possible for developers to distribute their games directly to customers via downloads from their own website?

Developers disagree fundamentally on this issue. Some—in fact, many—contend that there is *no* motivation to seek a publisher for any game in the digital case because developers already have direct access to the marketplace. Thus, the publisher, if there is to be one, can exist only to reduce the sales really due to the developer. Others, in contrast, think this contention a simplification, observing that it ignores other legitimate benefits that a publisher can offer a developer, even in digital markets—specifically, advertising, promotion, funding, and support for creating localized versions of the game; front-line and ongoing technical support to customers; and even advance payments to support development or future development. In the end, developers must make careful judgments about what they think best for their game and their gamers, and about what they stand to gain and lose. Different circumstances will inevitably lead to different conclusions. But for the reasons stated here, there seems no strong case for dismissing a publisher for digital distribution simply because developers have direct access to the marketplace. That reason, on its own, does not seem sufficient to always weigh the balance of the argument against publishers.

DIY Digital Distribution

One of the most beautiful qualities of the Internet, as well as of the games industry more widely, is its openness—or at least its potential for openness. (I say potential because there are questions and disagreements about the true openness of the games industry, and also about how open it ought to be.) Here, openness is intended to signify how easy it is for people anywhere to become a member of the game-development community and to sell their games to interested gamers.

In theory, with the relevant skills, training, and experience, as well as a computer and an Internet connection, almost anybody can become a game developer and sell their games online to a multitude of people across the globe. That means millions of determined and hard-working Internet denizens, regardless of their physical location, age, or gender, can in principle turn their dream of making games for a living into a reality. Using the Internet, developers can market their games and upload them to public Web spaces to which they can provide access to users for a fee or for free. With this method, developers can sell directly to customers from their own websites or through intermediate services that accept payment via credit cards and other systems such as PayPal. E-commerce and hosting services, such as BMT Micro (www.bmtmicro.com), Share-It (www.shareit.com), and BlueSnap (www.bluesnap.com) exist alongside many similar services. These sites enable developers to open accounts and upload files to the service, often for free, with a commission charged only on sales of the software made through the system. These services typically accept payments from customers and are responsible for delivering the purchased files. The developer has access to online accounts, where they can view sales statistics and receive regular payments.

These systems make it easy for developers to provide gamers with convenient access to their software. Indeed, using this kind of DIY digital distribution, many developers have established highly profitable businesses, and they continue to do so. However, as with all media, not all developers have reported success here. The general contention is that although DIY digital distribution can lead to success, especially for developers with an established following or public profile, it makes business sense to expand and find additional outlets and marketplaces within the digital space, especially if large and established markets for games exist elsewhere.

Gaming Portals

The term gaming portal is commonly used to mean an online supermarket that sells games to its members. It is in essence the digital equivalent of a mall or shopping precinct—a place where gamers can congregate to search for, purchase, and play games. Some portals offer their users additional features such as social networking capabilities and the ability to interact with other users via community forums, chat rooms, profile pages, and so on. Some even offer services that are integrated with the games themselves that enable gamers to automatically share their gaming achievements with other users of the site.

Famous gaming portal sites include (in no particular order):

- Steam (store.steampowered.com/)

- Desura (www.desura.com/)

- Big Fish Games (www.bigfishgames.com)

- GameHouse (www.gamehouse.com/)

- GOG (www.gog.com/)

- Kongregate (www.kongregate.com/)

- Spil (www.spilgames.com/)

- IndieVania (www.indievania.com/)

- Indie City (store.indiecity.com/)

- GamersGate (www.gamersgate.com)

- GetGames (www.getgamesgo.com/)

- Amazon (www.amazon.com)

- Google Play (play.google.com/store)

- Ubuntu Software Center (https://apps.ubuntu.com/cat/)

- The Apple App Store (www.apple.com/osx/apps/app-store.html)

Each offers different sets of features, ways to purchase games, and ways to interact with other gamers. The characteristic common to them all is that they represent large and established digital marketplaces where gamers can actively search and shop for games. That means many gamers, when hungry for more games, log on to these sites rather than Google or the Internet more widely to find new games.

These sites depend for their success largely on game developers for a constant supply of new games to offer their users, and there seems to be no shortage of supply. The result is that many new game developers actively seek to enter these marketplaces to sell their product, and some developers have made great commercial successes here. For this reason, it often makes business sense for developers to connect with these markets to access a large and established user base. However, entry and access to these markets differ from portal to portal and from developer to developer. This differential access has led some to strongly contest the openness of the games industry.

Walled Gardens

Gaming portals raise the issue of walled gardens because almost every portal operates under this framework. Walled gardens are about enclosure and regulation. The concept of the walled garden is not new. Throughout most of its history, the games industry has been torn by opposite tendencies—toward openness on one side and closure on the other.

Ever since people began selling games, people have questioned how open the industry should be. Different companies have taken different stances, depending on their aims and strategies. The most radical demand for openness is that anybody, anyplace should be allowed to make and sell games about anything to anybody. That stance, however, is not the one taken by most gaming portals. For this reason, the issue of walled gardens is important for the games developer, regardless of whether they like or believe in them.

The walled garden refers conceptually to an idyllic landscape (a marketplace) of beauties and benefits surrounded and protected by fortified walls from the dangers outside, real or imagined. It is a metaphor for a closed marketplace to which access for both buyers and sellers is closely guarded, made available only on specific terms set by a central authority, or gatekeeper. whose job it is to tend and improve the garden. Such a selective marketplace as this means that some sellers and some buyers must necessarily be excluded because they don't satisfy the entry requirements, whatever the authority has decided they should be. These issues and requirements are important for developers because different gaming portals operate using different policies and requirements, or different hoops that must be jumped through. These govern which developers will be allowed access to the market.

Portals differ in the extensiveness and height of their garden walls, as well as in the justifications or rationales for those limits. Specifically, three main kinds of walled garden can be identified in terms of extremity and closure:

- The most relaxed kind requires only that developers be the true and original authors of their work, that their game is a complete and full product, and that it does not contain malicious or dangerous code such as viruses. In this garden, provided they meet these conditions and offer their assurances subject to testing and proof, developers are allowed entry to the marketplace. That is, they are permitted to offer and sell their product to the user base within the garden.

- The second kind of garden builds on the former but goes further, requiring developers to adjust or restrict the content and features of their games in specific ways. Such a garden might require developers to allow advertisements in their games from selected sponsors; to censor (or add) objectionable content such as gore, violence, or drug references; to include subtitles or localization features to support specific languages; to work on specific hardware and platforms; to include specific logos or branding; as well as potentially many other requirements. This kind of garden is usually preoccupied with ensuring all games in the market have a consistent look and feel and are suitable for a specific kind of audience or demographic such as a family audience, a teenage audience, or a hardcore gamer audience.

■ The third and most elitist walled garden builds on the former two, going further still by adding metaphorical turrets and fortifications to its walls. Specifically, it requires developers to prove the commercial potential of the game, to take active steps in marketing and generating both publicity and anticipation for the product, to have a renowned or established reputation as a developer, to be innovative and to produce quality content (where innovation and quality are ultimately judged by the authority), to accept an established pricing system, and to add and integrate community features into the game that work with the existing features of the portal website. One of the aims of this kind of garden is a special preoccupation to be, or be seen as, a center of excellence—as a hive of cutting-edge creativity, and as a supplier of the best in video games.

Walled gardens are controversial, making them a topic of many a heated debate among developers, publishers, and gamers. Some object wholesale to walled gardens in every form, considering them pernicious in principle to the industry, to developers, and to gamers. Some are more moderate, objecting to them practically in only some forms, such as their most extreme kind. Others, in contrast, think walled gardens don't go far enough—that even further control and regulation is required in the games industry for its improvement.

Despite the different forms disagreements take on the issue, I think it is possible to identify a root cause of the passionate antagonism and resentment felt by the most fervent critics of walled gardens. It rests, I believe, in the implied judgments that such gardens seem to make about developers and their games by way of the entry procedures. It is similar to the kind of resentment felt when someone believes himself or herself to be the victim of discrimination because of unfounded judgments made by others, regardless of whether those judgments are stated explicitly. The question of whether the discrimination is ever justified, or whether walled gardens make the industry a better or worse place for everybody, is a contested matter about which I shall draw no conclusions here.

Regardless of these specifics, most game developers today choose to work with walled gardens to sell and distribute their games. Thus, developers who make this decision should carefully study the entry requirements of such portals on a case-by-case basis according to their plans to ensure their games are likely to fit and be welcomed in their intended walled garden.

Piracy and DRM

Sociologists often describe the Internet as a "time-space compression" because, with its famous ability to transfer information across the world in only seconds, it seems to give us a certain mastery over space and distance. Messages that would once have taken days or even weeks to send by pigeon, car, boat, or airplane can now be transferred across the same distance in seconds.

This ability has been used by different people in different ways. One way is to make copies of games and to send them to others. The laws of different countries typically have something to say on the issue about who has the right to make copies of games; these laws fall under the name of copyright. The explicit intention of these laws, as they relate to games, is to legally protect developers and their work by denying others the right to copy their games without their consent, which is an act termed piracy. Thus, copyright exists to protect developers from piracy, and piracy is traditionally regarded as a bad thing because, when others copy a developer's games for free, that developer is inevitably deprived of income for his or her time, dedication, creativity and hard work.

Whether this argument against piracy is sound or even makes sense is perhaps one of the most hotly debated issues in software development and digital media today, where piracy and copyright have become household words, particularly in the context of illegal music and movie downloads through file-sharing services. However, regardless of what the answer might be, if there is an answer, many developers think it largely irrelevant. This is because although copyright laws exist to protect software, it is still easy to make copies and to distribute them illegally via the Internet. It is also expensive and difficult for developers to identify and pursue possible infringements, especially when infringement occurs across national borders as is often the case with digital infringement. As a result, many developers and publishers have moved away from seeking protection for their software through legal processes and have instead actively developed systems that ship with their games to try to prevent them from being copied and distributed by the end user. These systems are termed digital rights management (DRM)—or, as they are sometimes called by their more vociferous critics, digital restrictions management.

DRM takes many different forms, and with the advent of cloud computing, those forms have widened further still. Some common forms are software activation and connection-based DRM. Software activation limits the number of times a game can be installed on a user's system. On each installation, a connection is made to a remote server across the Internet where an installation counter is incremented. When the counter exceeds the maximum number of installs, further installations are prohibited. Connection-based DRM, in contrast, requires the gamer to be permanently connected to the Internet while playing. During this time, it actively prohibits any other instances of the same software with the same serial identification from being run, limiting the number of running instances to only one.

Regardless of the specifics, DRM exists in many different forms, some more explicit than others. All forms, however, share the same general intention to prevent unauthorized copying of the software. Some DRM systems are purchased by developers from third parties, some are created directly by the developers themselves, and some gaming portals have tightly integrated a single DRM solution into their system for all games they offer.

There is widespread disagreement over the issue of DRM among both developers and gamers. These disagreements focus largely on the ethics of DRM as well as on its effectiveness—on how closely it really achieves its stated aim. Some contend DRM is both an ethically justified and practically necessary means for protecting software, and is in principle no different from an act of self-defense—the defense of livelihood against theft. In fact, some gamers even go so far as to demand DRM from their games, taking it as a sure sign that the developer values and respects their purchase by making efforts to prevent pirates from freely downloading what they have worked hard to pay for. But mostly, DRM has proven unpopular with the gaming community in almost all of its easily recognizable forms—so much so that DRM has become a stigma rather than a passionless designation. This unpopularity arises for a multitude of reasons. These are too numerous to list in full here, but I do note some of the most common reasons:

- Some argue that DRM oversteps what is ethical by denying the gamer certain crucial freedoms that the law does not deny them, such as (perhaps) the ability to make personal backup copies.

- Some argue that DRM is instrumentally monopolistic because it often leads to vendor lock-in. This refers to a situation in which gamers find themselves after having invested heavily in a sizable library of games through a single vendor or site. They feel psychologically and financially trapped with the vendor because, due to DRM, they cannot resell their purchases to other users, and (in some cases) they cannot continue to play their games without an active subscription.

- Perhaps the most powerful reason against DRM is that it generates strong resentment among most gamers, many of whom frequently voice their anger through forums and community sites. Their frustration lies in the implicit distrust that DRM shows toward them. Some gamers have gone so far as to launch boycotts, petitions, and protests against specific companies and games to demonstrate their intolerance of DRM.

Overall, in the face of these reasons, it seems difficult to strongly recommend DRM for video games, even if it is effective, which is open to doubt. This is because DRM exists, but the issue of piracy has not gone away. DRM raises an uneasy dilemma that is far from resolved. It repeats itself in almost all digital media industries where creative professionals seek to earn a living from their work. The dilemma might be stated in this way: The mere existence of copyright laws is demonstrably not enough to prevent the widespread copying of games through the Internet. Given this, developers can choose to integrate DRM into their games or not. But the reasons against DRM integration are truly compelling and powerful. Moreover, for some developers, worthwhile DRM is not an economically feasible solution, even if they wanted to implement it. However, the alternatives to DRM are not entirely clear. Perhaps developers should simply do nothing and trust that in charging reasonable prices, the gaming public will honestly support their work. Indeed, this is the stance some developers take. But it is not a stance to which everybody can or is willing to reconcile themselves.

CONCLUSION

This chapter covers much troublesome material. It is fraught with politics, power-struggles, and controversy, from individuals to mega-corporations and government institutions. There seems to be no aspect of it on which strong opinions and interests are not held, and these opinions differ dramatically. Moreover, the controversies show no sign of fading because for every argument for one side there is seemingly a negating counter-position.

In such a climate it easy for wealthy and powerful interests to rationalize and implement their solutions regardless of where ethical argument might lead. These solutions have a defining influence over the gaming landscape that developers must work with every day, whether they like it or not. Beneath these disagreements, however, I have tried to extract some general and fundamental concepts and details that underpin the backdrop for these controversies. In so doing, I hope to have offered some useful advice and guidance as to ways to market and distribute your game to the masses.

There are no hard and fast answers when it comes to finding the correct marketing solution or the right way to distribute. Each developer must make judgment calls as to what is best in his or her circumstances. It is the aim of this chapter to help you make more informed decisions on these matters.

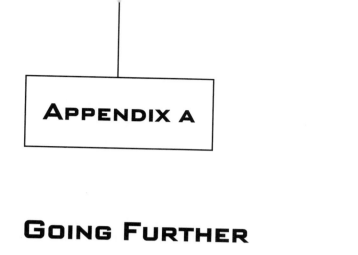

Appendix A

Going Further

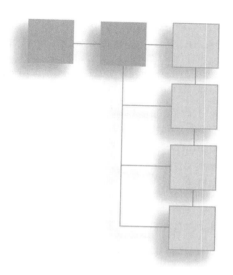

"If you have an apple and I have an apple and we exchange these apples then you and I will still each have one apple. But if you have an idea and I have an idea and we exchange these ideas, then each of us will have two ideas."

—George Bernard Shaw

The primary purpose of this book is to describe the fundamental principles underlying game development generally, regardless of whether you are developing for the PC, consoles, mobile platforms, or the Web. However, understanding that theory is all very well and important, the main motivation and reason for its learning is to apply it in practice when making games. The reason we look to the principles is to have them guide us in our practical game-making decisions so that we can make better and more informed choices and perform our work more productively and skillfully.

Inevitably, though, there will come a point at which our learning of theory must stop, albeit temporarily, for the purpose of making a game in practice. When that time arrives, our questions turn away from what things are or how things can be understood toward how things can be done and what tools there are to achieve our designs. Largely, that point is where this book ends—hence the reason this appendix appears at the end as it does.

The purpose of this appendix is to focus on the practical, not on the theoretical. Its aim is to act as a summary guide about how to approach making a game in practice. It looks at the tools and technologies available for specific tasks and where to find them online.

This appendix begins by assuming you have read and understood the chapters in this book entirely. It then asks, "What next?" The rest of this appendix is a possible answer to that question, given in general terms. It is intended to be read from start to finish, section by section. It assumes your aim is to actually make a real game, and it sees that aim as a problem to be solved or an obstacle to be overcome.

The specifics of the solution to that problem will necessarily differ from developer to developer, depending on their requirements and needs, because no two developers plan on making the same game in the same way. The answer given here is simply a boilerplate answer. It offers a structured guide about the tools and technologies you might select along the way for making your game and applying the principles learned here.

Designing

Games are in essence manifestations of ideas and imagination. They are an externalized consciousness encoded in digital form. Game development begins as soon as a game designer has an idea with potential that he or she wants to pursue. The game designer's ultimate aim is to translate that raw idea in his or her head into a digital world on the computer and have nothing lost in the process of translation. The purpose is so that people who play the game can experience in their own minds the same kind of vision and imagination the designer had in his or hers when he or she first conceived the idea.

Chapter 1, "Games and Game Design," focused on the design process. It explained how the designer typically builds a design document to express his or her vision for the game and for the work that is to come in making it. When you set out to make your own game, the first step will be design. This is not a curious recommendation; design is where every game has to begin. But how do we actually design? Are there tools and software to help that process?

The first and perhaps greatest tool for design—for all stages of game development, for that matter—is your own mind. When design begins, do not worry about tools or software. Instead, sit down and just *think*. Think about the game—not in simplistic terms, but as though you were really playing it. Think about what it would be like to play—what it looks like, what it sounds like, and what it feels like. Perhaps even link your idea to media around you. Think about movies, songs, or other games that somehow connect with your idea.

After you have established an idea, software and tools gain importance. The aim of software for the designer should be to facilitate the expression of ideas in written and image form. For this, a wide range of tools are on offer, from word-processing applications for writing the game-design document to spreadsheet applications and chart-drawing software for representing ideas in pictorial form. One of the most famous and widely used suite of applications for creating documents and spreadsheets is Microsoft Office (office.microsoft.com), but there are many increasingly popular alternatives also on offer such as the freely available LibreOffice (www.libreoffice.org/), OpenOffice.org (www.openoffice.org/), and the cloud-based Google Docs (docs.google.com). Most of these applications have the ability to export documents in the commonly supported PDF format.

Do not be afraid to take out a pen or pencil, or to use a graphics tablet such as a Wacom Bamboo or a Wacom Intuos, to create drawings, sketches, and concepts. If you have an idea for characters, locations, items, sketch them. Alternatively, if you see places in the world around you that are inspirational, photograph them, even if you use the camera on your phone or an old disposable camera that has been locked away in your desk drawer for years. If you hear sounds that are useful for your game or for developing ideas, record them, even if it is using the microphone attached to your webcam. Avoid thinking any technology is crude or substandard if you think it could be helpful. Embrace all the means you have and make the best use of them.

SOFTWARE DEVELOPMENT AND PROJECT MANAGEMENT

After you have created a design, it is necessary to formulate a plan of action for realizing that design. This plan should chart how the design, as described in the design document, can be turned into a reality through the organization of work. This work includes coding, graphics, sound engineering, testing, and more. This process determines who will be working on the game, where they will be, what they will do, and when they will do it. It specifies this work in terms of a schedule and deadline, and it manages the work over time by dividing people into departments with responsibilities.

This process is referred to as project management, and was discussed in Chapter 2, "Game Software Development." Different teams manage their work differently, but one especially significant factor influencing the division and arrangement of work will be how spatially distributed team members are. In some teams, all members are located in the same office space—the same physical proximity—during the same hours of the day. In others, some members are distributed across the world in different offices or spaces. And in others still, all members are located in different parts of the world and across different time zones. The issues of spatial and temporal differences are significant for a project because they influence when and how members of the team are available to each other. The latter kinds of working arrangements are becoming more and more common. This rise has had an impact on the kinds of project-management tools on offer and on their features. Here are some useful project-management tools for running software projects:

- **BaseCamp (basecamp.com/).** This Web-based project-management tool can be used to isolate tasks into tickets that are assigned to specific users. Members of the team, wherever they are, can log in at any time to see what their responsibilities are, as well as their deadlines and any comments or conversations that might have been submitted by other users. Other software and systems that are similar to BaseCamp include Unfuddle (https://unfuddle.com/) and LibrePlan (www.libreplan.co).

- **ActiveCollab (https://www.activecollab.com).** This is similar to BaseCamp and other project-management systems. However, it allows developers to self-host the project-management system. That means developers can download the ActiveCollab source files and manage the project from their own server. ActiveCollab is the project-management software I use for my own projects.

- **Microsoft Project (office.microsoft.com/en-us/project/).** This software was originally a desktop-based project-management application, meaning that the software ran on a local system. Now, however, it offers a range of features for connecting with other systems and for managing projects across space and time.

- **Git (git-scm.com/).** Git is fundamentally distinct from the other management tools listed here. It should not be considered a replacement or competitor for them, but a tool that can be used alongside them. Unlike the others, its purpose is not to manage projects specifically, but to manage the source code of projects that is used by programmers. In short, Git is a version control system. It enables different programmers at different locations and at different times to download and work on a common set of source files, and to then upload their changes back into the system. This happens in such a way that their work is integrated with the work of others, without destroying others' changes and allowing all programmers to work with the latest set of source files. Git could be an important tool for you if your project requires a lot of source code and changes.

PROGRAMMING AND DEVELOPMENT

Chapter 3, "Games Programming," and Chapter 4, "Game Math," focused on programming and on its importance for game development. It is when thinking about these issues specifically that important decisions about programming tools and development pathways are made.

One of the main questions that arises is whether the team will be using an existing game engine for development, or whether it will make its own game engine. This decision is perhaps one of the most important technical decisions that can be made. Its answer will have dramatic consequences for the way subsequent development unfolds. If this decision could be plotted on a graph or drawn on a diagram, it would look like a branch or a forking pathway. This section talks a little about both of these pathways and the tools and software available for each of them.

Option 1: Using an Existing Game Engine

Using an existing game engine typically means the team will select a third-party engine, which contains a set of ready-made features for game development, and use this as a tool to produce their game. There is a wide range of engines available, some free and others commercial, and some which are free for non-commercial use but non-free for commercial use. Some engines are listed here:

■ **UDK (www.unrealengine.com/udk/).** An acronym for Unreal Development Kit, UDK features a suite of tools as well as the Unreal Engine itself. Together, these tools form the UDK. This software can and is used to produce video games for desktop platforms, consoles, and even mobile games. The Unreal Engine is perhaps one of the renowned engines in the games industry, and has been used to develop games such as *BioShock, Duke Nukem Forever, Borderlands 2, Gears of War: Judgment*, and others. The UDK is typically associated with big-budget blockbuster titles, often termed AAA titles. However, it has also been used for indie games and student projects. The UDK is available for free to download, and can be used for free in non-commercial projects. For commercial projects, a license is required.

■ **Unity (unity3d.com/unity/).** Unity is a general-purpose game engine, complete with a world editor, scripting editor, and other tools for making both 2D and 3D games. It has seen rapid growth and increasing popularity in the games industry and is used by many studios. Some games made with Unity include *Endless Space, Dungeon Land, Undead Slayer, Flee Symphony*, and also my most recent game, *Bounders and Cads*. Unity is available in two versions: the feature-limited free version and the commercial professional version, for which an advanced royalty-free license must be paid.

■ **CryEngine (mycryengine.com).** Like the UDK, CryEngine is frequently associated with AAA games and big-budget titles. And like the UDK, it is available to developers free of charge for non-commercial games, and on various license terms for commercial games. CryEngine features a suite of tools for making games, and has been used to create games such as *Crysis 3*, *Far Cry*, *MechWarrior Online*, and *Sniper: Ghost Warrior 2*.

- **Shiva 3D (www.stonetrip.com/).** This shares with Unity an aim of being a complete all-in-one game-development solution for programmers and level designers making both 2D and 3D games. It is a complete engine with world editor, scripting editor, and other development features. Furthermore, it supports a wide range of platforms, including Windows, Mac, Linux, iOS, Android, Nintendo Wii, PalmOS, Blackberry Playbook, and others. Games developed with Shiva 3D include *Babel Rising*, *PinBallYeah*, and *Non Flying Soldiers*.

- **GameMaker Studio (www.yoyogames.com/gamemaker/studio).** This is a complete engine dedicated to creating 2D games for desktop platforms and mobile devices. It supports a range of platforms, including Windows, Mac, HTML5, iOS, Android, and Windows Phone, as well as the Windows 8 Metro Interface. Games developed with GameMaker Studio include *Grave Maker*, *Rick O'Shea*, *Reflexions*, and *They Need to be Fed*.

- **Blender Game Engine (www.blender.org/).** This open-source game engine can be used for free to create both non-commercial and commercial games. It features world-editing, shader-coding, and other scripting tools for building 2D and 3D games. Some games created with the Blender Engine include *Yo Frankie!*, *Dead Cyborg*, and *Sintel the Game*.

Note

There are many other engines too numerous to list in this book. Some others worth checking out include Panda3D, Leadwerks, Irrlicht, DX Studio, Linderdaum, Torque 3D, C4 Engine, BigWorld, Construct2, Stencyl, RPG Maker, FPS Creator, NeoAxis, Wintermute, Multimedia Fusion, Cocos2D, and Gamebryo.

Option 2: Using a DIY Engine

Developers can choose to avoid using a pre-made engine altogether and instead opt to create their own. The advantages and disadvantages for doing this are discussed in Chapter 3. Some of the tools, libraries, and packages available for creating custom engines include the following:

- **Integrated development environments (IDEs).** This refers to a range of different applications that can be downloaded and used for creating and compiling source code. Chances are high—almost 100%—that if you are going to create your own game engine, you will need an IDE to write your code and build your software. IDE applications include Microsoft Visual Studio (www.microsoft.com/visualstudio/), Apple Xcode (https://developer.apple.com/xcode/), MonoDevelop (monodevelop.com/), Eclipse (www.eclipse.org/), and C++ Builder (www.embarcadero.com/products/cbuilder).

- **Graphics libraries.** These are the libraries and packages that enable you to render graphics to the screen for games. Examples include OpenGL (www.opengl.org/), SDL (www.libsdl.org/), OGRE 3D (www.ogre3d.org/), Android SDK (developer.android.com), and Quartz2D (goo.gl/P8uQ8).

- **Audio libraries.** These are the libraries and packages that enable you to play audio and music for games. Examples include OpenAL (connect.creativelabs.com/openal/), SDL Mixer (www.libsdl.org/projects/SDL_mixer/), BASS Audio (www.un4seen.com/), FMOD (www.fmod.org/), and libpd (libpd.cc/).

GRAPHICS AND ART

The world of graphics-creation software is vast. There are so many options. This section lists many common as well as not-so-common tools for creating 2D and 3D graphics for video games. Software is categorized here in four main groups:

- **Vector graphics.** Vector graphics can be upscaled without quality loss. Chapter 5, "Graphics, Pixels, and Color," discussed pixel-based and vector-based 2D-based graphics in more depth. There are two main vector-based graphic editors used in the games industry today: Adobe Illustrator (www.adobe.com/products/illustrator.html), a commercial application from Adobe that is a part of the Adobe Creative Suite, and the open-source, freely available InkScape (inkscape.org/). Both of these applications work with vector-based images as their raw material and can produce impressive results.

- **2D graphics.** The term 2D graphics is used here to mean any rectangular, pixel-based image. These are often used in video games for backgrounds, GUI elements, sprites in 2D games, and textures in 3D games. There is a multitude of software available for working with these graphics in the context of games. For general-purpose image editing, two applications dominate: Adobe Photoshop (www.adobe.com/uk/products/photoshop.html) and GIMP (www.gimp.org/), both of which were mentioned previously in this book. Additional image tools are also on offer that provide specialized functionality for games. These include NDo2 (quixel.se/) for creating normal maps and texture effects, BMFont (www.angelcode.com/products/bmfont/) for creating pixel-based images from system fonts, and a handy little tool called TexturePacker Pro (www.codeandweb.com/texturepacker), which automates the task of combining individual image files into larger texture images. This is often useful for optimizing graphics performance in games. I recommend checking out all these applications to see how they can be of use for your games.

■ **3D graphics.** 3D graphics are common in video games and typically refer to models composed from vertices, edges, and faces. More information on 3D models can be found in Chapter 6, "Meshes, Rigging, and Animation." There is a wide range of software from which to choose when creating 3D graphics, some free and some commercial. These applications include Autodesk Maya (usa.autodesk.com/maya/), Autodesk 3DS Max (usa.autodesk.com/3ds-max/), Autodesk SoftImage (www.autodesk.co.uk/softimage), Lightwave (www.lightwave3d.com/), Cinema4D (www.maxon.net/), Autodesk Mudbox (www.autodesk.com/mudbox), PixoLogic Zbrush (pixologic.com/), Luxology Modo (www.luxology.com/modo/), and the freely available Blender (www.blender.org/).

■ **Animation.** Many of the 3D applications discussed here can also achieve 3D animation—that is, animation for 3D models. This software includes Adobe Affects (www.adobe.com/products/aftereffects.html), Adobe Premiere (www.adobe.com/PremierePro), Adobe Flash (www.adobe.com/uk/products/flash.html), and Toon Boom Animate (https://www.toonboom.com/).

AUDIO, SOUND, AND MUSIC

When it comes to music and sound effects, game developers either create their own or buy stock music and sounds under specific licenses, such as royalty-free licenses. A range of software is available for creating and editing music and sound effects. Again, some of these are commercial and some free.

■ For sound-effect editing, software includes Adobe Audition (www.adobe.com/products/audition.html) and Audacity (audacity.sourceforge.net/).

■ For music composition and editing, software includes FL Studio (www.image-line.com/documents/flstudio.html), Steinberg Cubase (www.steinberg.net/en/products/cubase/), Reaper (cockos.com/reaper/), and Ardour (ardour.org/).

■ Websites where pre-made music and sound effects can be purchased under various terms include Sound Rangers (www.soundrangers.com), Shockwave Sound (www.shockwave-sound.com/), SoundJay (www.soundjay.com/), and SoundSnap (www.soundsnap.com/).

Caution

When obtaining files for music and sound effects, always be sure to check through the license terms to know the legal conditions under which you can use and include the music in your game.

FURTHER READING

Having come this far, you may be hungry to get started creating games for yourself. But you might also have more questions about technical and theoretical matters—questions that were perhaps raised by discussions in this book. These questions might relate to game design, graphics, color, lighting, game mathematics, physics, and other topics. Here, I provide a list of additional reading materials for more detailed and focused treatment of specific subjects:

- **Game design:** *The Art of Game Design: A Book of Lenses* by Jesse Schell, ISBN: 978-0123694966.

- **Game mathematics:** *Essential Mathematics for Games and Interactive Applications: A Programmer's Guide* by James M. Van Verth and Lars M. Bishop, ISBN: 978-0123742971.

- **Color concepts and image-processing techniques:** *Principles of Digital Image Processing: Core Algorithms* by Wilhelm Burger and Mark Burge, ISBN: 978-1848001947.

- **Lighting and rendering:** *Real-Time Rendering* by Tomas Akenine-Moller, Eric Haines, and Naty Hoffman, ISBN: 978-1568814247.

INDEX

Q–R